THINKING WITH HISTORY

CARL E. SCHORSKE

Thinking with History

*Explorations in the
Passage to
Modernism*

PRINCETON UNIVERSITY PRESS

Copyright © 1998 by Princeton University Press
Published by Princeton University Press, 41 William Street,
Princeton, New Jersey 08540
In the United Kingdom: Princeton University Press,
Chichester, West Sussex

Library of Congress Cataloging-in-Publication Data
Schorske, Carl E.
Thinking with history : explorations in the passage
to modernism / Carl E. Schorske.
p.   cm.
Includes bibliographical references and index.
ISBN 0-691-05977-2 (cloth : alk. paper)
1. Europe—Civilization—19th century.   2. Europe—
Intellectual life—19th century.   3. Modernism (Aesthetics)
4. Historicism.   I. Title.
CB204.S37   1998
940.2'8—dc21   97-44484

This book has been composed in Janson
Designed by Jan Lilly

Princeton University Press books are printed on
acid-free paper and meet the guidelines for permanence
and durability of the Committee on Production
Guidelines for Book Longevity of the
Council on Library Resources

http://pup.princeton.edu

Printed in the United States of America

1   3   5   7   9   10   8   6   4   2

To Eppie

CONTENTS

plorations in Culture" in *New York Review of Books*, May 27, 1993. The latter paper was presented at a conference on Psychoanalysis and Culture, Stanford University, 1991.

"History and the Study of Culture" was presented at a conference at Scripps College, March 2–5, 1988, and published in Ralph Cohen and Michael S. Roth, eds., *History and . . . Histories within the Human Sciences* (Charlottesville and London, 1995). Reprinted with permission of the University Press of Virginia.

≈⊚ *ACKNOWLEDGMENTS* ⊚⩫

THE ISSUES and intellectual substance of the essays on the nineteenth century in this volume arose in the context of teaching. Two of my partners in team-teaching in Princeton's European Cultural Studies Program, Anthony Vidler and Lionel Gossman contributed fundamentally to defining the subjects of the essays on England's Medieval Revival and Burckhardt's Basel, and to my approach to them. John Rockwell, as my teaching assistant at Berkeley, helped me to grasp Richard Wagner's development as musician-in-history.

Through Norman O. Brown I first became engaged with Freud when in the context of the Cold War that thinker was becoming a focus of new intellectual interest. Forty years later, Brown introduced me to the poet H.D., and our lifelong intellectual engagement reached a new intensity in discussions about the meaning of Egypt for Freud. From two generous scholars of H.D., Rachael Blau Duplessis and Susan Stanford Friedman, I received more enlightenment on that wonderful poet than, alas, I could put to use in the Freud essay in this book.

Arno J. Mayer, another lifelong friend, urged me to organize the essays into a book. He both helped to define its structure and offered valuable criticisms of the Introduction. I owe heartfelt thanks too to three other sharp, constructive critics of the Introduction: Katherine Hughes for her insistence on clarity; Michael Roth and my son Richard for their conceptual suggestions.

To William J. McGrath I owe a special debt of gratitude. He contributed to the book at every level: the organization, the substantive articulation of the Introduction, and the fusion of two essays on Freud into one. For many years we have worked on Viennese culture together. Hence, even in much of its substance, this book is his as well as mine.

Walter Lippincott and his enthusiastic staff at the Princeton University Press have been a joy to work with—despite setting a pace of production that would be daunting to a mind and body more vigorous than mine. Particular thanks go to Margaret Case. She has assumed with energy, tact, and generosity burdens far beyond those assigned to her as copy editor.

For her valiant services in typing these and many other papers, my warmest thanks go to Chris McKinley. Finally, I should like to nominate my wife Elizabeth as unofficial member of the production team. She has served not only as stylistic critic but as organizer of illustrations and the other chores that attend the making of even a modest book.

INTRODUCTIONS

ONE

The Book: Theme and Content

"THINKING WITH HISTORY": it is not the same as thinking *about* history as a general form of meaning-making. That is what philosophers or theorists of history do. Thinking *with* history implies the employment of the materials of the past and the configurations in which we organize and comprehend them to orient ourselves in the living present. In one mode, we think with the substantive yield of historical inquiry, with the images we form of the past, in order to define ourselves by difference or by resemblance to it. Here history is an object for us, and appears as static, a picture or *tableau vivant* of a bygone culture. We can also "think with history" in another mode, when we conceive of history as a process. Then history is dynamic, linking or dissolving static elements in a narrative pattern of change. We can still treat this process an an object, but it is difficult to divorce it from our existence as thinking subjects. If we locate ourselves in history's stream, we can begin to look at ourselves and our mental life, whether personal or collective, as conditioned by the historical present as it defines itself out of—or against—the past. "Thinking with history" in the first sense, then, implies the utilization of elements of the past in the cultural construction of the present and future. "Thinking with history" in the second sense relativizes the subject, whether personal or collective, self-reflexively to the flow of social time.

The essays in this volume were not conceived with the purpose of explaining systematically what it means to think with history. Rather than explicating it as theory, they show it as cultural practice—a practice by no means confined to those who call themselves historians. In nineteenth-century Europe, history became a privileged mode of meaning-making for the educated classes. Some examples of that cultural practice and the turn away from it in favor of an ahistorical modernism as the century ended provide the theme of this book.

In most fields of intellectual and artistic culture, twentieth-century Europe and America learned to think without history. The very word "modernism" has come to distinguish our lives and times from what had gone before, from history as a whole, as such. Modern architecture, modern music, modern science—all these have defined themselves not so much *out* of the past, indeed scarcely *against* the past, but detached from it in a new, autonomous cultural space. The modern mind grew indifferent to history, for history, conceived as a continuous nourishing tradition, became useless to its projects. Postmodernism, to be sure, has found uses for elements of the past in its own constructions and deconstructions. But even as it consigns modernism to the past, it reaffirms as its own modernism's rupture from history as continuous process, as the platform of its own intellectual identity.

If we turn our gaze from the high culture of the mid-nineteenth to the mid-twentieth century, we realize how drastic has been the break from the historical consciousness. The backdrop of our modernism was historicism rampant, pervasive. Never in the history of European culture had Clio enjoyed such preeminence—not to say hegemony—as in the mid-nineteenth century. If in the eighteenth century philosophy had been queen in the realm of intellect, with history as her modest handmaiden in "teaching philosophy by example," in the nineteenth, history inherited philosophy's dominion. History's mode of thought and its temporal perspective penetrated most fields of learning, while the models of the past inspired the nineteenth century's arts. Even as science developed its own autonomy from natural philosophy, natural history claimed a large portion of the legacy. Historical painting and the historical novel acquired new salience in artistic practice, while the study and criticism of the arts were reconceived as the *history* of art, of literature, etc. The very process of modernization in the economy and society of the nineteenth century, with the unprecedented effects of industrial technology on land and people, paradoxically evoked this quickened quest for ties to the past. In an era of growing nationalism, collective identities were redefined as a summa of the convergent cultures of the past. The architecture of cities appropriated the styles of bygone times to lend symbolic weight and pedigree to modern building types from railway stations and banks to houses of parliament and city halls. The cultures of the past provided the decent drapery to clothe the nakedness of modern utility. Historicism in culture arose as a way of coming to grips with modernization by marshaling the resources of the past. Conversely, at a later stage, modernism in culture arose in reaction to this effort as intellectuals attempted to confront modernity in its own terms, free from the manacles of mind that history and historicism were now thought to impose.

To master modernity by thinking *with* history, to master modernity by thinking *without* history: these then are not simply antitheses, but rather successive phases in the same effort to give shape and meaning to European civilization in the era of industrial capitalism and the rise of democratic politics. The essays in this collection, whatever the particular issues they embody, should help us think with history about the passage from the nineteenth century's culture to that of our own time.

"ENCOUNTERING History," the second essay of this Introduction, is a professional self-portrait. The American Council of Learned Societies originally commissioned it as part of its Haskins lecture series, "The Life of Learning," in which scholars of various disciplines are invited "to reflect and to reminisce on a lifetime of work. . . ." It suits well, however, the purpose of this collection.

All autobiography is personal history, a narrative construction that involves both remembering and forgetting, evoking some parts of one's past and repressing others. Yet most autobiographers define their past on a narrow band of personal experience, with little reference to the wider world. In writing of my own life, I became aware that I could hardly think of it except as it had been implicated in larger historical developments. To account for my self, my values, and professional commitments, I *had* to think with history: the confrontation of German and American cultures in World War I in my childhood; the power of American progressivist culture in my home and in my college education; its displacement by a new, formalist academic culture formed in the political freeze of the 1950s that stimulated a rethinking of my scholarly mission; the political and university crises of the sixties that compelled a redefinition of my teaching role. These are but a few of the changing historical contexts in which my personal and vocational identity were, for good or for ill, formed, redirected, transformed. I had always found challenging Nietzsche's exhortation, "Become what you are." As I worked on this essay, however, I came to feel the need to attend to its inverse: "You are what you become." Through ever-renewed encounters with the shifting elements in the stream of history one can come to know oneself in the present, and also acquire an altered understanding of what one has been in the past. In autobiography, to think with history helps to establish a

certain distance from one's self by seeing it as both shaped by the structures and conflicts of society and as responding creatively to their pressures. Thus if I reflect in my life story the larger development of the
society, I also reflect (as knowing subject) on that particular historical
consciousness, its formation and changes, that my personal encounters
with my time elicited as modes of coming to terms with it, whether by
resistance or adaptation.

THE essays in Part One, grouped under the title, "Clio Ascendant," are
probes into some ways in which intellectuals in different parts of nineteenth-century Europe confronted the promises and perils of modernity.
The tremendous awareness that continuous transformation had become
endemic to the world they lived in stimulated historical reflection.
Spurred by the need to account for change, Clio's ascendancy drew
power from the variety of national and local responses to modernization
as it spread across Europe from west to east. The city, the social entity
most visibly affected by the processes of change, became a favored focus
of critical reflection on the condition and prospects of modern man.
Three of the essays are directly concerned with it. I wrote them to illuminate in comparative perspective the importance of the city as a symbolic condenser of socio-cultural values in different parts of Europe. Yet
as I read them now, a second theme surfaces: that of the variety of forms
of historical discourse in which the ideas about the city were constructed.
I ask the reader to read them with both themes in mind.

"The Idea of the City in European Thought" (Essay Three) offers a
broad sampler of evaluations of the city made by intellectuals from the
Enlightenment to Nazism. The passage of cultural criticism from historical to ahistorical discourse can be seen behind the succession of social
and moral ideas. Different forms of historical outlook are evident even
among the thinkers who saw in the city an agency of human progress.
Voltaire and Adam Smith shared a progressivist view of history as a dynamic process in which economic activity fueled the amelioration of the
human condition. Despite some differences in their goals, both saw the
city as the scene of society's productive transformation. The past for
them was a condition to be overcome, but contained within itself forces
which, once released by human desire and reason, propelled mankind, via
the city, into a gratifying future. On a more complex level, Marx and
Engels similarly stressed the processual and dialectical aspect of historical
thinking with their orientation toward a pre-visioned future.

Johann Gottlieb Fichte, who valued the city's contribution to civilization no less than Smith and Voltaire, thought with history in a different way. He focused not on temporal development but on the synchronic coherence of the city in an exemplary moment of the past. Troubled by the chaos of his unfree and divided nation, Fichte found in the late medieval and early modern city-state a German paradise lost that could serve as a moral-political model for constructing a modern national community. The concern with process, through which one synchronic complex is transformed into another, so important to progressivist thinkers such as Smith, Voltaire, and Marx, had little centrality for Fichte. In his stress on a past to be recuperated, Fichte engaged in an archaistic form of historical thinking that would find even stronger articulation in England's medieval revival, considered in Essay Four.

Beyond the processual thinkers such as Voltaire and Smith who placed the city and modernity in a future-oriented trajectory and the archaists such as Fichte who recovered from the past historical forms to renew modern society, there emerged in the mid-century another class of intellectuals who had neither the need nor the inclination to think with history about the condition of man. Confronting the modern city as their existential reality, whatever their different senses of its pleasures and pains, its virtues and vices, they were presentists, pioneers of an ahistorical modernism. French artists such as Baudelaire and the Impressionists were decisive in developing this new mode of thought and feeling. They changed the city's relation to the ordinance of time. For them the modern city had no temporal locus, but rather a temporal quality. The city offered only its present—an eternal here and now, whose content was transcience, but whose transcience was permanent. Past and future lost their orienting function here; history lost its usefulness.

A specific city provides the setting for "History as Vocation in Burckhardt's Basel" (Essay Five). There Jacob Burckhardt and Johann Jakob Bachofen harnesed historical understanding to preserve their threatened city-state culture against the forces of modern change. Their native Basel had adroitly preserved into modern times many of the social and institutional forms of Fichte's German idealized free city-state. Now threatened by democracy and industrial capitalism from within and without, the patriciate to which our two historians belonged constructed their defenses against modernity with a revitalization of their inherited humanistic culture. Conservative Basel thus generated a new kind of historical thinking, lacking either archaistic sentimentality or futuristic illusion. As academic professional and as civic educator, Burckhardt sought to cultivate in Basel's citizens a traditionalist sensibility of a kind that would yet prepare them to live in a world of the unexpectedly emergent and to adapt with cosmopolitan cultural flexibility to the forces of change. The essay sketches Burckhardt's particular contribution to twentieth-century historical consciousness: a richly associative synchronicity in structure that is at the same time processual and undeterministic in its recognition of a diachronic trajectory. Bachofen's special kind of archaism celebrated the civilizing power of women in preclassical culture without attempting to restore the vanished past. His work complemented Burckhardt's humanistic realism in combatting their contemporaries' use of ancient history to glorify the modern state.

In "Medieval Revival and Its Modern Content" (Essay Five), the scene shifts to England and a different form of conservative historical thinking. Three intellectuals, Coleridge, Pugin, and Disraeli—none historians by vocation—are examined as they seek in a specific past culture the conceptions and practices to criticize and hopefully to remedy England's problems. All three shared a conviction that the abuse of power, particularly that of property, had brought moral ruin and social division to modern England. All extolled the religion-centered Middle Ages as representing a social and cultural wholeness that had been sacrificed to greed and excessive individualism. In so doing they shared a widespread Tory outlook to which each thinker gave the color of his individual concerns. For all three the Tudor and Whig destruction of the autonomy of the Church as a moral force through the confiscation of its property became an historical turning point for the destruction of England's ideal past. Despite their shared conservatism, all three were in some degree futurists in their archaism. They reached backward to move forward. Each incorporated in his particular exploitation of the presumed medieval legacy an element utterly foreign to it in which we can recognize modern traits. Coleridge aspired to create a base of economic independence for a modern moral intelligentsia. Pugin advanced the idea of volumetric functionalism in architecture against the Victorian preoccupation with a symbolic façade. Disraeli projected a new Christian social ideology of paternalistic industrialism for his era of labor conflict and mass politics.

Essay Six, "The Quest for the Grail: Wagner and Morris," examines two thinkers whose discourse lies in the borderland between history and myth, nurtured by materials from a common cultural heritage. Both found themselves in constant critical engagement with the problems of their respective countries. While Germany was still struggling through much of the century to work out the political problem of liberalism and the construction of a unified national state, England in the time of Morris faced the social dislocations of advanced industrialization. In view of the differences in the problems they confronted, it is all the more remarkable that the two artists drew so extensively on the same repertory of mythic materials. To the extent that they can be said to exemplify thinking with history, this is manifested not only in their idealization of Nordic and medieval cultures, but in the way they drew on nineteenth-century historicism's enlargement of the mythological inheritance beyond the traditional focus on classical culture. Their use of this heritage of myth increasingly undermined the historical components in their thinking as the modern problems they confronted drove them in different directions. While Morris passed from the religious and aesthetic medieval revivalism of his youth to active engagement with the political world that led him to socialism, Wagner early embraced political and social radicalism and moved—in the disappointment of his political hopes—into a reactionary communitarian nationalism. Wagner ended with a pseudo-religious aestheticism not unlike the starting point of Morris. The interweaving of these inverse trajectories and their historical meaning are the focus of the essay.

With "Museum in Contested Space" (Essay Seven), we return to the city as a locus of nineteenth-century historical thinking. The first essay of Part One surveyed panoramically the intellectuals' ideas about urbanism and the role of historical thinking in their formulations. The second examined the specific case of Basel as a civic community whose endangered elite pressed historical education into the task of equipping the citizenry with a cultural armamentarium for survival in the modern world. Turning now to Vienna, Essay Seven explores the narrower use of historicism in a concrete task: constructing a modern capital for an ancient empire.

Like the rest of Europe, Vienna conceived its monumental public architecture as historical style architecture, with the choice of style related sometimes to the function of the building and always to show forth the values of its patrons. In the construction of the Ringstrasse, Vienna's new capital space after the revolution of 1848, stylistic issues permeated the substance of political conflict. The contests over the location of buildings were struggles of political priority and prestige. The restored, newly entrenched court, aristocratic, ecclesiastical, and military forces on the one hand and the still aspiring liberal bourgeoisie on the other jock-eyed for capital space as for political power, with a new bureaucratic element playing an often independent, sometimes mediating, formative role between them. The historical cultures of the past—Classical, Medi-eval, Renaissance, and Baroque—supplied the symbolic architectural vo-cabulary in which the contest for representation in space was expressed. As the contending parties achieved some compromise, they concretized it in the arrangement of buildings executed in previously conflicting histor-ical styles as parts of the larger, unifying capital space. The final design of the Ringstrasse thus represented both the contending elements through their respective historical symbols and the overcoming of conflict among them through their eclectic presence in the same space. In that sense the new "modern" Vienna of the mid-century was the summa of Austria's historical components. Here historicism becomes modern, in the sense that it achieves mastery of the past by the present: what the Germans call *Vergangenheitsbewältigung*. It is modern by virtue of absorbing history and its elements eclectically, not yet modernist by breaking from them.

The Kunsthistorisches Museum, one of the last buildings to be erected on the Ringstrasse, serves in this essay to clarify the place of historicist culture in the liberal-aristocratic compromise of the later nineteenth cen-tury. Designed to contain the already accumulated imperial collections, both the historistic program of the Museum's architecture and ornament and the organization of its contents celebrated the creators and collectors of past art. The personal collection of the imperial house, however, was opened to the people whose patrimony it was to be. Yet the very name signifies closure: It is an "art-*historical*" museum. Not intended to expand to include new art, it is both a monument to past art and a mausoleum for it.

CENTERING on the culture of a single city, Vienna, the essays of Part Two, "Clio Eclipsed," approach from different perspectives the ways in which certain intellectuals of that city struggled to find and speak directly the truth of the modern condition as they conceived it. Not for nothing is the subtitle of Part Two, "*Toward* Modernism." There was no sudden leap out of history into modernism here. Rather the cultural innovators were in continuous dialogue with a present that was still tradition-laden. They were themselves engaged in transforming their cultural legacies as much as rejecting them. Indeed, some of the most self-consciously radi-cal creators of the "New" culture—such as Adolf Loos in architecture or

Arnold Schoenberg in music—would temper their break from the past with claims of attachment to some aspect of tradition even as they shook its systemic foundations.

The two dominant cultural traditions of early modern Austrian history were those of the Baroque and the Enlightenment. We encountered both in the last essay—first in conflict, then in relative integration—in the construction of the capital at the height of the liberal aristocratic compromise. "Grace and the Word" (Essay Eight), aims to characterize briefly their respective religious and philosophical roots. It then exemplifies their tension and interaction through brief probes into two vital Austrian institutions: the theater, queen of Austria's arts and citadel of Baroque secular culture; and the university, stronghold of rationalism and the Enlightenment. Toward the end of the nineteenth century, the fragile liberal synthesis of the two cultures broke down. Both traditions, however, survived in transmuted form as vehicles for the articulation of two radically different kinds of modernism. The Baroque tradition of Grace, exalting the life of feeling and beauty, fed the sensitivity and sensuosity of fin-de-siècle aestheticism. The Enlightenment tradition of the Word nurtured the rigorous pursuit of ethics and truth.

In three theater pieces, three major artists, carriers of the cultures of Grace, of the Word, and of their synthesis, dramatized the modern fate of their respective heritages and the language systems that sustained them. Each confronted in theatrical form an element of the early twentieth century's apocalyptic reality: revolution (Hugo von Hofmannsthal), war (Karl Kraus), and the incommunicability of truth to humanity (Arnold Schoenberg). There is no thinking with history here, in the nineteenth-century senses encountered in Part One. The thought is of an end in history, out of a consciousness at once deeply traditional yet in its drastic sense of rupture profoundly modern.

Where Essay Eight exemplifies diachronically the transformation of Austria's traditional high cultures from their eighteenth-century relations to their modern fate, Essay Nine, "Generational Tension and Cultural Change," explores synchronically the rupture that marked Austrian modernism's first major intellectual breakthrough.

Die Jungen (the Young Ones)! Such was the term used by those who saw themselves in the 1880s and 1890s as pioneers of modernism, establishing their collective identity as a generation with new, shared values. Their sphere of action included politics, literature, and the visual arts. Over time their initial search for community and for a reordering of society gave place to a preoccupation with the psychological. This concern found creative expression not only in psychoanalysis but also in a new intellectual cohort of visual and literary artists. For them social pessimism and existential anguish fueled the quest for a new art beyond generational or historical concerns. This psychological tendency gave its special stamp to Viennese modernism.

Architecture and its criticism, the subject of Essay Ten, provided an arena in which Viennese culture's path from historicism to modernism came to be clearly defined. Even while the Ringstrasse complex was still under construction there were those who criticized it for an inherent contradiction. While its buildings expressed fidelity to a variety of historical traditions, its street layout and spatial design were conceived in the spirit of rationalistic modernism. But the critics divided over which of the terms of the contradiction should have primacy over the other: historical stylistic representation or functional utility. The terms of this debate were civic. How should the society collectively present itself to itself in urban form: as the proud product of historical culture or as the city of a new man?

In the 1890s Die Jungen, with their cult of renewal, altered the terms of this architectural discussion, redirecting it from historical and social to psychological discourse. Essay Ten, "From Public Scene to Private Space," examines the redefinition of architecture's function as it came to focus on the individual person. United in their rejection of the historical, the architects of the turn of the century divided broadly into two groups. One, identified with the Secession movement in art, pursued an aesthetic and sensuous psychologism that was essentially aristocratic in its wish to cultivate and manifest in style the individual's personality and grace in the world. The second, led by Adolf Loos, developed a more democratic and rationalistic ethical functionalism, championing public unobtrusiveness and modesty for the private man. He should seek neither to cultivate his exceptionalism narcissistically nor to project his image into the public sphere. Against the pursuit and public display of beauty by the aesthete, Loos and his allies posited in and through the unadorned house the puritan virtues of plainness in façade and functional truth in spatial form. In its very facelessness, the house itself becomes a criticism of the culture of representation and of style itself, whether historical or modernistic. Thus the traditional conflict between Grace and the Word, between Art and Truth, was projected into the heart of twentieth-century architectural culture in two types of modernism. Even in eclipse, Clio lived on, metamorphosed in new forms.

In music more than any other field of high culture, Austria set the pace and tone for the modernizing European world. The first Viennese School of Haydn, Mozart, and Beethoven defined the classical canon for the nineteenth century; the second Viennese School of Schoenberg, liberating dissonance, charted the high road for the musical innovators of the twentieth century. After the turn of the century, the gulf between the two schools opened swift and deep. Gustav Mahler, the subject of Essay Eleven, was among the few musicians respected, even idolized, on both shores of the gulf. Lowly born at the moment of Jewish emancipation, Mahler was acculturated into a welcoming world of ascendant liberalism in his provincial city, absorbing in his childhood and youth its Enlightenment intellectual values and its musical heritage. As a Vienna University student, however, he participated in the generational cultural rebellion. The populist sentiments and the Nietzschean existentialist vision that Mahler drew from the counterculture went into the very substance of his musical work. In his Third and Fourth Symphonies Mahler constructed a modern *teatrum mundi* with its multiplicity of nonhomogenous components and its rapid, whipsaw-like succession of psychological states.

If as a composer Mahler affirmed in music a nonhomogeneous, contradiction-ridden modern world no longer easily contained in historically given forms, in his career as a conductor, he devoted himself to the preservation of the musical tradition. As director of the Court Opera, Mahler served as guardian of the most official—and most Baroque—of all of Austria's arts. Reared in the culture of the Word, both as Jew and as liberal, he thus became, through his conducting career, identified also with the culture of Grace. Yet in addition, he projected into his symphonies many of the ideas he had acquired from Die Jungen in their revolt against both those cultures of the fathers. Mahler embraced all three cultures in his capacious consciousness. When the two modernist inheritors of the sensuous Catholic and rationalist Enlightenment sensibilities, the aesthetes and the ethicists, fell into conflict, Mahler collaborated well with both. He drew the modernizing aesthete-artists of the Secession into the Court Opera to modernize its productions. At the same time he championed the ethicist-musicians by defending their revolutionary music with his prestige and by promoting its performance with his personal influence.

In our exploration of Austria's passage to modernism, Mahler stands forth as a creative and powerful composer (in the literal sense) of contradictory and fragmented forces. He comprehended the contending traditional forces that had struggled for supremacy in Austria's history, and that, in their transmuted cultural forms, continued both to trouble and enrich Austrian modernism at the turn of the century as it strove to transcend historicism along with the historical past. In his intellectual development as in his career, Mahler identified to some degree with all the conflicting currents, but surrendered to none.

A CHILD of his time and culture, Sigmund Freud was from his earliest years engaged with history and the great struggles that composed it. His value systems were initially imparted by his intense religious education in the history of the Jews and, at school, in that of classical antiquity. "To the Egyptian Dig" (Essay Twelve) examines Freud's changing relationship to history in maturity. In youth and early manhood, he embraced it as a primary mode of understanding reality. Then he departed from it to construct in psychoanalysis a systematic understanding of man so universal as to be torn loose from historical moorings. Finally, in his last years, he returned to history to accomplish, in the face of Nazism, a task of compelling social and personal importance.

Even in the creation of the new system that made him the most influential architect of Vienna's special contribution to modernism, psychologism, Freud could use from his own dreams materials of history that he could transform into examples of personal psychodynamics. When he came to project his system upon the nature and function of society, it was as a psycho-archeology of cultures as such, dehistoricized. The character of specific historical cultures kept reappearing in Freud's thinking, however, as he tried both to understand his own place as Jew, liberal, and scientist in his world and the conflict of values that bedeviled the contemporary world. Clio was in eclipse in psychoanalysis, but she had not vanished from Freud's mental life. The essay seeks to indicate both the variety of cultures that played a role in his consciousness and the trajectory of his concerns with them as he reached and then retreated from the high-water mark of his modernism in his explorations of bi-sexuality.

In the last years of his life, Freud was confronted by an overwhelming historical reality, the rise and triumph of National Socialism. It confirmed his worst psychoanalytic prophecies about the return of repressed collective aggression and the fragility of an enlightened civilization. It also forced him back to consider the historical cultures that entered so vitally into his childhood historical formation. In his last major work, *Moses and Monotheism*, Freud not only resumed thinking with history, but became a historicist himself. The book marks for us a return to the historicism rejected by his modernist psychologism. For Freud it represents a two-fold homecoming: to the Jewish culture of his fathers and to the European liberal universalism of his early social environment. It also celebrates the contemporary alliance between enlightened German gentiles and Jews to rescue European civilization from Hitler's relapse into barbarism, as Moses had rescued the Enlightenment tradition of Egypt by transforming the Jews into agents of gentile high culture, of *Geistigkeit* (mind and spirit). Once again in the aging Freud, historicism was serving as a model to confront the uncongenial present with an assignment for the future, as historicism had so often done in the nineteenth century.

Freud, Mahler, and Loos: all shared in shaping the modernist turn taken in Viennese high culture in the fin-de-siècle. Yet the relation of their breaks with the past were of different kinds and degrees. Freud, whose explorations of the unconscious and the role of sexuality so clearly undermined historicism, nevertheless continued to struggle in his life and thought with the traditional conflict between the Jewish and Enlightenment rationalism he consciously espoused and the gentile, largely Catholic sensuous culture which he found, through all his powerful resistances, so deeply attractive. Mahler's extraordinary catholicity of spirit enabled him to embrace much of both of the two traditional cultures of Austria, Baroque and Enlightenment, even while, as participant in Die Jungen's rebellion, he absorbed Nietzschean philosophy and made a vernacular multiculturalism his own. He resolved the dualism of past and present into the complex plural cohesions of a fragmented modern world. Only Loos can, in hindsight, clearly be defined as a modernist of rupture. Yet he too was firmly anchored in the Enlightenment tradition, the culture of Reason and the Word. Surely it proved easier to stop thinking with history than to escape its continuing power in culture.

How shall we understand the special quality of emergent Viennese modernism, with its ambiguous mixture of self-conscious rupture and transmuted tradition? Perhaps Arno Mayer's conception of "the persistence of the Old Regime," which he used so effectively to illuminate the role of aristocracy in the crisis of European international politics before World War I, can shed its light on the sphere of culture as well. Vienna's two traditions of Grace and the Word did not survive the breakthrough of modernism in culture intact. But they left their Old Regime stamp on the post-historicist, secular culture of modernism, to enrich its forms of feeling and to trouble its intellectual and social harmony.

As AN Afterword, I have added an essay that, exceptionally in this collection, focuses on thinking *about* history rather than *with* it. "History and the Study of Culture" attempts to locate the enduring characteristics of the historian's ancient craft as a form of knowing. It was conceived in our postmodern moment when, in academic culture, disciplines that had lost or jettisoned history as no longer usable for their particular contemporary missions have begun to seek connection to it once more. In a conference called "History and . . . ," scholars of disciplines other than history—philosophy, literature, anthropology, etc.—were brought together to explore the value of history to their work. As one of two historians present, I was to examine the relation of history to the study of culture, a common concern of all.

History can only exist in a symbiotic relationship with other disciplines. By virtue of its untheoretical, associative character, it depends on them for its analytic concepts. Nor does history have a particular subject matter of its own. Virtually the only stable center of the historian's armamentarium is the simple calendar that determines what came before something, what came after. In relation to the calendar's order of things, historians have throughout the ages woven together explanatory principles and evidences of past experiences or events to produce their configured patterns on the loom of time. This devotion to the ordinance of time—however variable its intensity—has given solidity and strength to Clio's weaving from Herodotus to the present. In its emphasis on the processes of change and transformation in culture, history offers reciprocal benefits to the other disciplines on which it depends. This final essay attempts to show, on the one hand, how simple are the fundamentals of the historian's craft and, on the other, how the inconstant and changing interests of historians in culture vary with their own historical situation, their shifting relationship to their society, its structures and its problems. Here again, I found myself thinking about history by thinking with it.

TWO

The Author:
Encountering History

MY FIRST ENCOUNTER with the world of learning took place, if family account is to be believed, when I entered kindergarten in Scarsdale, New York. To break the ice among the little strangers, my teacher, Miss Howl, asked her pupils to volunteer a song. I gladly offered a German one, called "Morgenrot." It was a rather gloomy number that I had learned at home, about a soldier fatalistically contemplating his death in battle at dawn. The year was 1919, and America's hatred of the Hun still ran strong. Miss Howl was outraged at my performance. She took what she called her "little enemy" by the hand and marched him off to the principal's office. That wise administrator resolved in my interest the problem of politics and the academy. She promoted me at once to the first grade under Mrs. Beyer, a fine teacher who expected me to work but not to sing.

Was this historical episode a portent of my life in the halls of learning? Hardly. But it was my unwitting introduction to the interaction of culture and politics, my later field of scholarly interest.

WHEN I taught European intellectual history at Berkeley in the early 1960s, I devoted a portion of my course to the way in which the same cultural materials were put to different uses in different national societies. One day, I gave a lecture on William Morris and Richard Wagner. The intellectual journeys of these two quite dissimilar artist-thinkers involved stops at many of the same cultural stations. Morris began by using Arthurian legend to champion a religion of beauty, then became an enthusiast for Norse mythology and folk art, and ended a socialist. Wagner traversed much the same itinerary as Morris, but in the reverse direction, starting as a social radical, then reworking Nordic sagas, and ending, with the Arthurian hero *Parsifal*, in a pseudo religion of art.

In the midst of delivering my lecture, I suddenly saw before me a picture from my childhood that I thought to be by Morris. (The picture proved to be the work of George Frederick Watts, then close to the Pre-Raphaelites.) It was "Sir Galahad," a painting that hung in color reproduction on the middle landing of the staircase in our family's house. Here was a beauteous knight in the best Pre-Raphaelite manner: a figure in burnished armor with a sensitive, androgynous face, mysteriously shrouded in misty bluish air.

After the lecture, I recalled how my mother loved that picture, how indeed she loved Morris's "Defense of Guenevere," and the literature of the Victorian medieval revival from Scott onward. Not so my father. He poured contempt on that feminine Sir Galahad. Now Wagner's *Lohengrin* or the *Nibelungenlied*—that was a medievalism he could embrace. Father not only loved Wagner's music, he believed in Siegfried the sturdy mythic socialist, as interpreted by G. B. Shaw in "The Perfect Wagnerite," and in the anti-feminist interpretation of Wagner of that curmudgeon radical, H. L. Mencken. Mother accorded a hard-won tolerance—no more—for the Teutonic longueurs of Wagner's operas, but none for the abrasive virility of Mencken or my father's Shaw.

Recalling hot parental arguments on such matters, I suddenly realized that, in contraposing Morris and Wagner in my teaching, I had hardly left the family hearth. Freud would say that, here in the midst of my professional work as an historian, I was addressing in sublimated form a problem of the family scene. In any case, the episode brought home to me the power of my family in shaping the cultural interests and symbolic equipment with which I came to define my life. They in turn were purveyors of the cultural history in which they participated.

As far as I know, my parents had no deliberate idea of pushing me toward an academic career. Autodidacts both, they respected learning, but what they cultivated was not scholarship but a kind of natural intellectuality. The concerts, theaters, and museums that were their recreation became the children's education. They fostered our musical interests not just with private lessons but by taking us with them into their choral societies. On my father's two-week vacations we went by rail and ship on intensive sight-seeing trips: to New England historic sites such as Concord or the old ports of Maine; Civil War battlefields where my grandfather had fought in a New York German regiment; the great cities of the East and Midwest from Philadelphia to St. Paul.

Along with all the elite cultural equipment, my parents introduced us children, through their lives as well as by precept, to the realm of politics. My father, son of a German-born cigar maker, inherited the radical propensities that went with that socially ambiguous trade. As a young New Yorker, father had campaigned for Henry George and Seth Low in their mayoral races, and followed the radical freethinker Robert Ingersoll. World War I made father, despite his profession as banker, a lifelong socialist. His deep-seated hostility to America's entry into the war—both as an anti-imperialist and an ethnic German—gave his political orientation, though still progressive in substance, a bitter, alienated quality by the time I came along in his forty-fifth year. I inherited a marginal's sensibility from him as a German. When my mother, who, unlike my father, was Jewish, encountered unpleasant social prejudice during my high-school years, I acquired a second marginal identity. Perhaps this sense of marginality, imposed by history, enhanced history's fascination for me and shaped my attitude toward it, at once wary and engagé. For me as for my parents, politics acquired particular importance, both as a major determining force in life and as an ethical responsibility.

~

IN 1932 I entered Columbia College. From Seth Low Library the statue of Alma Mater looked upon a space that contained the principal tensions of the university's life. In the foreground was 116th Street, New York City's bisecting presence at the center of the campus. On the south side of the street stood the Sun Dial, a great sphere of granite, Columbia's Hyde Park Corner. Here were held the rallies for Norman Thomas, who swept the student presidential poll in 1932. Here I took the Oxford Oath, pledging never to support my government in any war it might undertake. Here too I watched in ambivalent confusion as anti-war sentiment slowly turned into its own opposite, militant anti-fascism, after Hitler occupied the Rhineland and Mussolini invaded Ethiopia. Political radicalism then bore no relation to university rebellion; it only invigorated the university's intellectual life.

In Columbia's strongly defined academic culture, Clio still presided over much of the curriculum. It is hard for us to remember in our day of disciplinary differentiation and autonomy how much all subjects were then permeated with an historical perspective. Having deposed philosophy and become queen of the world of learning in the nineteenth century, Clio, though not as glamorous as she had been, still enjoyed pervasive influence. She dominated the only compulsory course for under-graduates, a two-year introduction, Contemporary Civilization in the West. It was designed in the spirit of the New History of the early twentieth century, that amalgam of pragmatism, democracy, and social radicalism that James Harvey Robinson, Charles Beard, and John Dewey had injected into Columbia's university culture. The course presented us in the first year with three textbooks in modern European history: one economic, one social and political, and one intellectual. Our task was to generate out of these materials a synoptic vision of the European past, leading in the sophomore year to analysis of the American present.

The structure of undergraduate major programs also reflected the primacy of history as a mode of understanding in contrast to the intra-disciplinary analytic and theoretical concerns that tend to govern the program in most fields of the human sciences today. The programs in literature, philosophy, even economics, were saturated with the historical perspective on human affairs.

I avoided a history major, which I felt would tie me down. Instead, I enrolled in Columbia's two-year humanities Colloquium, which allowed one to construct one's own program. Colloquium was centered in great books seminars conceived in a more classical spirit than usual in the university's prevailing pragmatist culture. The seminars were team-taught by truly outstanding young faculty members, such as Moses Hadas and Theodoric Westbrook, Lionel Trilling and Jacques Barzun. Watching their play of minds on the texts awoke in me for the first time a sense of the sheer intellectual delight of ideas.

The thought of an academic vocation, however, was slow in coming. Actually, I aspired to a career in singing, which I had studied since high-school days. By my junior year, the sad truth grew upon me that my voice simply had not the quality to support a career in *Lieder* and the kind of Mozart roles I dreamt of. In the same year, I enrolled in young Jacques Barzun's course in nineteenth-century intellectual history. Barzun simply overwhelmed his few students with the range of the subject and the brilliance of his exploration of it. At work on his biography of Hector Berlioz, Barzun injected much musical material into his course. While I shared with my classmates the exciting experience that this course turned out to be, I drew one rather personal conclusion from it: intellectual history was a field in which my two principal extra-academic interests—music and politics—could be studied not in their usual isolation, but in their relationship under the ordinance of time. I was ready to pursue it.

Yet something held me back. I felt myself to be an intellectual, interested in ideas; but could I be a scholar? Oddly enough, my Columbia
experience offered no basis for an answer. As an undergraduate, I had
only once been asked to prepare a research paper. Written exercises
took the form of essays, oriented toward appreciation and interpretation
of an issue or a text, with no particular attention to the state of scholarship or to the marshaling of empirical material to sustain a point of
view. I found scholarly works often uninteresting; and when they truly
impressed or captivated me, I found them daunting, far beyond my
powers to emulate.

The hue of resolution thus sicklied o'er by the pale cast of doubt, I
sought advice. It was arranged for me to see Charles Beard, who was
attending the American Historical Association's 1935 convention in New
York. Perched on the bed in his overheated room in the Hotel Pennsyl-
vania, Beard poured forth his scorn for the pusillanimity and triviality of
a historical scholarship that had lost all sense of its critical function in the
civic realm. He gave me a formula for a fine scholarly career: "Choose a
commodity, like tin, in some African colony. Write your first seminar
paper on it. Write your thesis on it. Broaden it to another country or two
and write a book on it. As you sink your mental life into it, your liveli-
hood and an esteemed place in the halls of learning will be assured."

The second counselor to whom I turned, Lionel Trilling, then in the
fourth of his six years as an instructor in a still basically anti-Semitic
Columbia University, almost exploded at me. What folly to embark, as a
half-Jew, upon an academic career in the midst of depression! Thus both
of my gloomy advisors spoke out of personal experiences that confirmed
the gap between the high calling of learning and some seamier realities
of the academy. Neither, however, could touch my central doubt, which
was about my own fitness for scholarly research. There seemed no solution to that but to put it to the test. When I entered Harvard Graduate
School in the fall of 1936, it was in a receptive spirit, but hardly with a
strong vocation.

❦

To PASS from Columbia to Harvard was to enter another world—socially,
politically, and intellectually. My undergraduate stereotypes of the two
institutions doubtless led me to exaggerate their differences. But stereotypes can have roots in realities. The very physical structure of Harvard

seemed to express a conception of the relation between university and society different from that of Columbia.

Harvard was in the city but not of it. Where Seth Low Library looked upon the city street, Widener Library faced the Yard, a green space walled off from the surrounding town. The Harvard houses, with their luxurious suites, dining halls with maidservants, separate libraries, and resident tutors, expressed a unity of wealth and learning in which each lent luster to the other. Whatever its social elitism, Harvard was, as Columbia was not, a citadel of learning seemingly impervious to political tensions. Harvard had no Sun Dial, no central space for student rallies. The students must have felt no need for one. If politics had a presence here, it did not meet the newcomer's eye. I was glad, given my self-doubts about a scholarly career, to take advantage of the opportunity that the university's calm environment offered for submersion in the work of learning.

The form of instruction at Harvard differed even more strikingly from Columbia's than its architectural form. At Columbia, we thought of our instructors as teachers, guides in the exploration of texts to make us generate intellectual responses. At Harvard, the instructors were more like professors, learned authorities dispensing their organized knowledge in lectures. The prevailing nineteenth-century idea of history, with its strong architecture of development and narrative structure, reinforced the authoritative lecture mode.

Thanks to the man who became my advisor and mentor, William L. Langer, I had no chance to follow the narrow road of Charles Beard's sardonic counsel about the strategy of the specialist. Langer urged me to take not just one seminar, but many, to gain experience in a variety of historical research techniques: economic, diplomatic, intellectual, and social. Seminar experience—especially with Langer—slowly dispelled my misgivings about a life of research, and gave me the much-needed intellectual discipline to pursue it. The greatest impact on my scholarly outlook and value system came not from the seminars in modern history, but from an intensive exploration of Greek history with William Scott Ferguson. Despite the fact that I was a modernist without usable Greek, Ferguson took me on for an in-depth tutorial. Each week I went to his house for a two-hour discussion of the books he had assigned, ranging from the anthropology of prepolitical tribes to Aristotle's Athenian Constitution or the structure of Roman rule in Greece. For my general examination I prepared a special subject on Aristophanes under Ferguson's guidance—an exercise that enabled me for the first time to ground a whole literary *oeuvre* in a field of social power. Ferguson's critical tutelage really opened my eyes, as the field of classics has done for so many, to the possibilities of integrated cultural analysis. It also remained with me as a model of pedagogic generosity.

The comparative quiet of Harvard's political scene that I found on my arrival in 1936 soon changed. After 1938, when America began to face the menacing international situation in earnest, political concern became more general and intense within the university—and in me. Divisions on the issue of intervention ran deep, and many of us, young and old, felt impelled to debate it publicly. When political passions run strong, the relation between one's obligations to the republic of letters and to the civic republic can become seriously conflated. Two personal experiences at Harvard brought this problem home to me.

The first occurred in 1940 in History I, the freshman course in which I served as a graduate teaching assistant. Its professor, Roger B. Merriman, a New England blueblood and a colorful, salty personality of the old school, was passionately devoted to aristocratic Britain. He believed, along with a few other staff members, that instructors had a public responsibility to get in there and tell the little gentlemen what the war was all about, to make them realize the importance of America's intervention. A few of us, across the often bitter barriers of political division, joined hands to resist the use of the classroom as an instrument of political indoctrination. My two partners in this effort, who were on different sides from me on the war issue, were Barnaby C. Keeney, later the first director of the National Endowment for the Humanities, and Robert Lee Wolff, who became professor of Byzantine history at Harvard. Quite aside from the principle involved, the experience of History I taught me how shared academic values could sustain friendships that political differences might destroy.

The second experience, of an intellectual nature, left a permanent mark on my consciousness as an historian. The graduate history club had organized a series of what were called, in jocular tribute to communist terminology of the day, "cells," in which the student members prepared papers on problems that were not being dealt with in regular seminars. My cell took up the problem of contemporary historiography. We inquired into historical work in different countries as it evolved under the impact of recent history. I examined German historians under the Weimar Republic and the Third Reich, not merely in terms of the political pressures upon them, but also in terms of the way in which specific cultural traditions in historiography, in confrontation with a new present, led to new visions of the past. I was astounded to discover that some of the most nationalist historians justified their doctrinaire nationalism by an explicit philosophic relativism. The value of this exercise in the sociology of knowledge was not only in understanding the work of historians of other nations. It also sensitized me and my fellow apprentices in history to the fact that we too live in the stream of history, a condition that can both enhance and impede the understanding of the past. Above all, it made us aware as our elders, in their positivistic faith in objectivity, were not of distortions that can result from our positions in society.

THE Research and Analysis Branch of the Office of Strategic Services, which I joined a few months before Pearl Harbor, has been rightly known as a second graduate school. My own intellectual debt to my colleagues there—especially to the German emigrés and to a stellar group of economists, some Keynesian, some Marxist—is not easy to calculate. The whole experience, however, taught me that, much as I enjoyed contemporary political research, I was not by temperament a policy-oriented scholar.

When I was released from service in 1946—over thirty, the father of two children, without a Ph.D.—I found what proved to be an ideal teaching post at Wesleyan University. I was to stay for fourteen years. Of all my mature educational experiences, that of Wesleyan probably had the strongest impact on the substance of my intellectual life and my self-definition as an historian. Basic to both were the larger shifts in America's politics and academic culture in the late forties and fifties. I would have encountered them in any university. But only a small college could have provided the openness of discourse that made it possible to confront the cultural transformation across the borders of increasingly autonomous disciplines. At Wesleyan in particular, thanks to President Victor Butterfield's selection of imaginative faculty members at the war's end, an atmosphere of vital critical exploration prevailed. From my colleagues I received the multidisciplinary education for the kind of cultural history I soon felt drawn to pursue.

In the first two years at Wesleyan, I had no sense of either the intellectual dilemmas about to appear or the new horizons that opened with them. Like most returning veterans, whether students or professors, I felt only a joyful sense of resuming academic life where I had left it five years before. The freshman Western Civilization course that I was asked to teach had just been introduced at Wesleyan by assistant professors fresh from Columbia. For me it was a throwback to my own freshman year fourteen years earlier. Teaching four sections, I had more than enough opportunity to explore the riches of the course. Once again I encountered there, in all its optimistic fullness, the Enlightenment premise that the progress of mind and the progress of state and society go hand in hand, however painful the tensions and interactions may sometimes be.

In framing an advanced course in European nineteenth-century history, I also returned to a prewar pattern to explore the relationship between domestic national histories and international development. Even my European intellectual history course, though fairly original in its comparative national approach to the social history of ideas, bore the stamp of the American neo-Enlightenment in which I had been formed at home and at Columbia. Its central theme was the history of rationalism and its relation to political and social change. Viable enough for constructing an architecture of intellectual development before the mid-nineteenth century, the theme proved less and less useful as the twentieth century approached, when both rationalism and the historicist vision allied with it lost their binding power on the European cultural imagination.

In the face of the fragmentation of modern thought and art, I fastened on Nietzsche as the principal intellectual herald of the modern condition. He stood at the threshold between the cultural cosmos in which I was reared and a post-Enlightenment mental world just then emergent in America—a world at once bewildering, almost threatening, in its conceptual multiplicity, yet enticing in its openness. After Nietzsche, whirl was king, and I felt rudderless. The conceptual crisis in my course set the broad question for my later research: the emergence of cultural modernism and its break from the historical consciousness.

While in my teaching I tested the dark waters of modern culture, my research was still cast in terms set by my political experience and values from the years of the New Deal and the war. I could not bear, after five years of engagement with National Socialism in the OSS, to resume my dissertation on its intellectual origins, despite a substantial prewar investment in the subject. Instead I turned to German Social Democracy as a thesis topic, and concurrently, to a more general study of the problem of

modern Germany. Behind both lay a pressing concern with the direction
of world politics. The two superpowers were in the process of creating
through their occupation policies two Germanies in their own images:
one socialist and antidemocratic, the other democratic and antisocialist.
Accordingly, the saw-toothed course of the divide between East and
West in German politics ran between the two working-class parties,
Communist and Social Democratic. Before World War I, these two
groupings had been part of a single party committed to both socialism
and democracy. Why had that unity failed to hold together? What was
the historical dynamic that made democracy and socialism incompatibles
in Germany? Contemporary questions surely stimulated my historical research, though they did not, I hope, determine its results. I realize now
that I was writing not only analytic history, but a kind of elegy for a once
creative movement that history had destroyed.

Parallel to the historical work on German Social Democracy, I explored directly the contemporary problem of Germany and American
policy toward it for the Council on Foreign Relations. There I had an
experience of the life of learning quite different from that of either government or academia. The members of the Council's German Study
Group, headed by Allan Dulles, were intelligent, influential members of
America's business and political elite. Most of them viewed German policy not as an area in which, as in Austria or Finland, some kind of accom-
modation was to be sought with the Soviet Union, but as a counter in the
fundamental conflict between the two powers. I continued to believe in
the goal of a unified but permanently neutralized Germany. That policy,
which had been espoused by the OSS group with which I had worked,
still seemed to me the only way of redeeming in some measure the dam-
age of the Yalta accord and of preventing the permanent division of Europe. Although the Council generously published my analysis of the German problem, it rejected my policy recommendations. It was my last
fling at influencing U.S. policy from within the establishment.

The swift transformation of the East-West wartime alliance into the
systemically structured antagonism of the Cold War had profound consequences for American culture, not the least for academic culture. It was
not simply that the universities became a prey to outer forces that saw
them as centers of Communist subversion. The breakup of the broad,
rather fluid, liberal-radical continuum of the New Deal into hostile camps
of center and left deeply affected the whole intellectual community. The
political climax of that division was Henry Wallace's presidential cam-

paign in 1948, in which I myself was active. The bitter feelings it left in its wake only served to conceal a more general change in climate by which most intellectuals were affected, namely the revolution of falling expectations in the decade after 1947. The coming of the Cold War—and with it, McCarthyism—forced a shift in the optimistic social and philosophic outlook in which liberal and radical political positions alike had been embedded.

Wesleyan was a wonderful prism through which these changes were refracted. Several liberal activists of the social science faculty, including nonreligious ones, turned to the neo-Orthodox Protestantism of Reinhold Niebuhr to refound their politics in a tragic vision. Young scholars in American studies transferred their allegiance from Parrington and his democratic culture of the open frontier to the tough moral realism of Perry Miller's Puritans. For undergraduates, a new set of cultural authorities arose. Jacob Burckhardt, with his resigned patrician wisdom in approaching problems of power, and the paradoxical pessimism of Kierkegaard elicited more interest than John Stuart Mill's ethical rationalism or Marx's agonistic vision. Existentialism, a stoical form of liberalism, came into its own, with Camus attracting some, Sartre others, according to their political persuasions.

Nothing made a greater impression on me in the midst of this transvaluation of cultural values than the sudden blaze of interest in Sigmund Freud. Scholars of the most diverse persuasions to whom my own ties were close brought the tendency home. Two of my teachers turned to Freud: the conservative William Langer used him to deepen his politics of interest; while the liberal Lionel Trilling, now battling the Marxists, espoused Freud to temper his humanistic rationalism with the acknowledgment of the power of instinct. Nor can I forget the day in 1952 when two of my radical friends, the Wesleyan classicist Norman O. Brown and the philosopher Herbert Marcuse, suddenly encountered each other on the road from Marx to Freud, from political to cultural radicalism. Truly the premises for understanding man and society seemed to be shifting from the social-historical to the psychological scene.

All these tendencies pointed American intellectuals in a direction that Europeans, with the exception of the Marxists, had gone half a century before: a loss of faith in history as progress. At a less credal level, but one actually more important for the world of learning, history lost its attractiveness as a source of meaning. Formalism and abstraction, refined internal analysis, and a new primacy of the theoretical spread rapidly from one discipline to another as all turned away from the historical mode of understanding of their subjects. For intellectual history, this tendency had two consequences, one relating to its educational function, the other to its scholarly method.

Students now came to intellectual history expecting consideration of thinkers no longer studied in the disciplines to which they belonged. Thus in philosophy, the rising Anglo-American analytic school defined questions in such a way that many previously significant philosophers lost their relevance and stature. The historian became a residuary legatee at the deathbed of the history of philosophy, inheriting responsibility for preserving the thought of such figures as Schopenhauer or Fichte from oblivion. In economic thought, a similar function passed to intellectual history as the economists abandoned their historical heritage of general social theory and even questions of social policy to pursue an exciting new affair with mathematics.

An opportunity for intellectual historians, you say? Yes and no. We were simply not equipped to assume such responsibilities. At best we had paid little attention to the internal structure of the thought with which we dealt. We had a way of skimming the ideological cream off the intellectual milk, reducing complex works of art and intellect to mere illustrations of historical tendencies or movements. The new ways of analyzing cultural products developed by the several disciplines revealed such impressionistic procedures as woefully inadequate. The historian thus faced two challenges at once: to show the continued importance of history for understanding the branches of culture whose scholars were rejecting it; and to do this at a moment when the historian's own methods of analysis were being revealed as obsolete and shallow by the very ahistorical analytic methods against which he wished to defend his vision.

For me, the issue first came to focus in dealing with literature. When I charged my Wesleyan friends in the New Criticism with depriving literary works of the historical context that conditioned their very existence, they accused me of destroying the nature of the text by my excess of relativization. One irritated colleague invoked Archibald MacLeish: "A poem should not mean, but be." But he taught me how to read literature anew, how the analysis of form could reveal meanings to the historian inaccessible if he stayed only on the level of ideas, of discursive content. Other colleagues in architecture, painting, theology, etc., similarly taught me the rudiments of formal analysis so that I could utilize their specialized techniques to pursue historical analysis with greater conceptual rigor.

By the fifties, the problems I have thus far described—the blockage in my course after Nietzsche, the changes in politics with the external and internal Cold War, the dehistoricization of academic culture, and the need for higher precision in intellectual history—all converged to define my scholarly agenda. I resolved to explore the historical genesis of the modern cultural consciousness, with its deliberate rejection of history. Only in a circumscribed historical context, so it seemed to me, could a common social experience be assessed for its impact on cultural creativity. Hence, a city seemed the most promising unit of study. Like Goldilocks in the house of the three bears, I tried out several—Paris, Berlin, London, Vienna—in seminars with Wesleyan students. I chose Vienna as the one that was "just right." It was indisputably a generative center in many important branches of twentieth-century culture, with a close and well-defined intellectual elite that was yet open to the larger currents of European thought. Thanks to my Wesleyan colleagues, I had acquired enough intellectual foundation to embark upon a multidisciplinary study.

In 1959, when I was on leave at the Center for Advanced Study in the Behavioral Sciences at Stanford, a Berkeley colleague asked me to take over his course in intellectual history for two weeks. The class, although over 300 strong, had a spirit of collective engagement and responsiveness that I simply had not encountered before. I was seized by the feeling that Berkeley, with its bracing intellectual atmosphere, was the place I had to be. Ironically enough, I had turned down an offer there only four years before without even visiting the Berkeley campus. Throwing shame and protocol to the winds, I called a friend in the history department to ask if the job was still open. Fortunately it was.

To pass from Wesleyan to Berkeley in 1960 was surely to move from academic *Gemeinschaft* to academic *Gesellschaft*. Wesleyan, with its intimate and open interdisciplinary discourse, had helped me to redefine my purposes as a scholar. Berkeley influenced the direction of my historical work much less. But it forced me to think through issues that I had not considered since Harvard: the relation of the university to contemporary society, and my vocation as a teacher. The crisis of the sixties presented them in depth and urgency.

As a public university, Berkeley was, of course, especially vulnerable to the pressures of both state and society. When I arrived there in 1960, the shadow of the oath crisis of the fifties and the McCarthy years still lay heavily upon the faculty. Moreover, 100-year-old regulations barring political and religious speakers and campus political organization were still in force. Devised to protect the university's immunity from outside pressures of state and church, these rules had become under current conditions nettlesome restrictions of academic freedom. Until 1964, however, it was not students but faculty members who took the lead in pressing the issue of free speech. My department, for example, unanimously agreed to make a test case of the restrictive rules by inviting Herbert Aptheker, a self-proclaimed communist historian with a Ph.D. and solid publications, to address its graduate colloquium. When the administration, as it had to do, refused permission for the speaker and denied the department the funds to pay him, we took the colloquium off campus and held it in a church hall to dramatize our point: that a responsible educational function had, in the University of California, to be conducted as an unauthorized off-campus activity.

In another action, when a well-funded right-wing group conducted a statewide campaign of "education in Communism" in the towns of California, the History Department offered a public lecture series on comparative Communism to counteract propagandists masking as scholars. Our historians, of widely different political persuasions and with varied regional expertise, demonstrated to a large public by their example how the university could serve society by intellectualizing in analysis and rational discussion its most burning public problems.

With the civil rights movement and the Vietnam War, American politics took a new turn, with profound consequences for the university. The pressure on it came not only from the right and the establishment, as in the fifties, but from the left and those with social grievances as well. This led at Berkeley to a shift in university attention from academic freedom and autonomy—a primary concern of the faculty—to political rights and the freedom of university members to pursue on campus their causes as citizens—a primary concern of students. In a liberal society, academic freedom and civic freedom are interdependent, but they are not the same. The first relates to the universal republic of letters, the second to the limited body politic. The recognition each must pay the other produces a delicate balance, easily upset when contestants locked in political struggle begin to see the university as a weapon or an obstacle. This is what happened at Berkeley. Political rights having been too long denied in the name of academic immunity, academic autonomy began to be put at risk in the name of political rights.

I became deeply involved as a minor actor in the ensuing crisis, serving first on the Emergency Executive Committee of the Academic Senate, then as Chancellor's officer for educational development. Let me say only that I went through the same rhythm of anguish, illusion, hope, and disabusement that is so often the lot of participants in intense social crises. I realize now, on reflecting back, that once again my outlook and actions were marked by a kind of basic archetypical mental disposition to synthesize or unify forces whose dynamics resist integration. An ironic thrust seems to have characterized my intellectual work: in my book on Social Democracy, I had tried to comprehend socialism and democracy in a single perspective. In my intellectual history of Vienna, I had sought to integrate politics and culture in substance, historical and formal analysis in method. Now, in the crisis of university and society, I tried to reconcile academic autonomy and antiwar activism in educational policy, faculty authority, and educational renewal.

Those who experienced the university crisis will know how searing the sense of dissolution can be, even if tempered now and again by a sense of future promise. I certainly had hopes that a stronger university community would issue from the crisis, and drew strength from the fine group of collaborating colleagues who shared my convictions about both free speech and educational reform. But in the conflict-laden environment, two other, less homogeneous entities made the situation bearable: my department and my classes.

The history department was deeply divided over the issues of university policy; more, it contributed articulate spokesmen to almost every shade of opinion in the Academic Senate. Yet when the department met on academic business, its divisions on personnel or curricular problems did not follow those in Senate meetings on university issues. I could expect to find in a colleague who had opposed me on the Senate floor a staunch ally on a department matter. Professional ethos and collegiality remained intact. How different it was in other departments, such as politics and sociology, where methodological divisions tended to coincide with and reinforce political faction! My classes, buoyant and intellectually engaged through all the troubles, also were a continuous source of stability. However, the pressures of the crisis caused me to rethink my teaching.

Once, after a final lecture in intellectual history, I had an experience that gave me food for thought. My students gave me the customary round of year-end applause. After all the difficulties of that year, I floated out of the lecture room on cloud nine. Then, as I walked down the corridor, I heard a girl behind me say to her companion, in a voice heavy with disgust: "And they call that a dialogue!" The remark jerked me back to earth. Beneath it lay two problems: first, student hunger for closer relations with the instructor, always present to some degree, but intensified by the unrest into a widespread rejection of the lecture system as "impersonal." Second, the passage of the student revolt from politics to culture. The gap that had opened between generations in both moral and intellectual culture was real—and in fact, wider than that in politics. How to bridge that gap, and make it possible for the professor of one generation to deal with new questions arising in another: that was the problem my jaundiced critic raised for me. It crystallized my interest in new educational forms suited to the mass university.

To bring my ideas of the intellectual tradition into a new relation to students' questions, I restructured my course on polycentric lines. While I continued to present my interpretation of intellectual history in the lectures, I displaced the locus of instruction into a series of satellite seminars. These were organized on topics defined not by me but by graduate teaching assistants. I asked them to deal with the same thinkers as I presented in my lectures, but left each free to choose texts of those thinkers more suited to the particular theme each had selected. They came up with themes I could not have thought of at the time, such as "The Costs of Freedom," or "The Idea of the Feminine in European Thinking." The graduate T.A. thus became a mediator between my professional discipline and standards in which he had a vocational stake, and the concerns of the new generation of which he was a part. All gained by the enlargement of the T.A.'s authority. The satellite seminar not only helped satisfy the felt need for dialogue, which in fact any section system might provide; it also set up a healthy dialectic between the interpretive scheme of my lectures and the ideas and existential concerns of the students reflected in each seminar's special theme.

As I followed the intellectual yield of the seminars, I was made aware of the deep truth of Nietzsche's observation that a new need in the present opens a new organ of understanding for the past. Many ideas that have become more widespread, such as Foucault's, first arose for me there. The satellite seminar system was adopted by a few others both in Berkeley and Princeton, and was effective for its time. In the mid-seventies, however, when deference to the canonical in matters intellectual and social quiescence returned, it lost its appeal for graduate assistants. Well suited to its time, its time soon passed. In education as in scholarship, one must live in the provisional, always ready to acknowledge obsolescence and to adapt the forms of instruction to changes in both culture and society.

∽

I WENT to Princeton in order to save, if possible, my scholarly work. It was not the fault of the University of California, which I dearly loved, that I invested so much psychic energy in institutional life and in my teaching. But, given a tendency to neglect research for the other claims on the academic man, I could not resist the temptation of an appointment at Princeton University coupled with a half-time fellowship for three years at the Institute for Advanced Study.

At Wesleyan in the fifties, in response to the impact of the rightward shift of postwar politics and the dehistoricization of academic culture, I had redefined my mission and method as an interdisciplinary intellectual historian. At Berkeley in the sixties, a university under the double pressure of America's conservative establishment and a recrudescent youthful left, I grappled in thought and action with finding the right relation between university and society. Part of a strong group of intellectual historians at Berkeley within a department of great diversity, I felt I was doing the work of my guild when I tried to adapt my subject to the intellectual and existential needs of a new generation of students.

At Princeton in the seventies, the center of my vocation shifted somewhat, from inside the history department to the humanities as a whole. Here again, a change in academic culture led me to redefine my function. Fundamental to it was the polarization of the social sciences and the humanities from each other. That process, which had begun in earnest in the fifties, now reached a new intensity. The concern with aggregate, depersonalized social behavior on the one side, and the concern with linguistic and structuralist textual analysis independent of any social context on the other did not simply diminish the relevance of history to both groups. Their mutually exclusive conceptual systems also penetrated the discipline of history itself. Social historians, seeking the "otherness" of past cultures or of classes neglected in previous historiography, became more interested in the static cross section of culture in the manner of anthropologists than in the dynamics of continuous transformation. At the other end of the spectrum, among intellectual historians, Hayden White lifted intellectual history clear of its social matrix by analyzing historiography as a literary construct. Synchronic recovery of a static slice of the past at one end of the spectrum, humanistic theory of forms at the other: these recapitulated within history itself in the seventies the loss of interest in process and transformation that had marked the new academic culture outside history in the fifties. In my Princeton history department, the dominant orientation was toward the social sciences.

I am no theorist and no methodologist. My way of addressing the problem of polarization in the *sciences humaines* and in history itself was through teaching—but this time not alone, and not purely within history. A small group of Princeton faculty from different departments joined me in devising an undergraduate interdisciplinary program called European Cultural Studies. Its regnant idea was to bring to bear on the same objects of study the separate lights of social scientists, historians included, and humanists—the groups that elsewhere were pulling so far apart. All courses in the program were taught in two-person teams—hopefully one social scientist and one humanist. Few social scientists other than social historians could be induced to join the program. But the seminars did establish a field of discourse relating the social and ideational worlds to each other, despite the autonomism of our academic culture. In a more personal sense, teaching over some years with scholars in philosophy, architecture, Russian, German, and French literature made of my last teaching decade a quite new learning experience. From one of the seminars, on Basel in the nineteenth century, issued a research project with my teaching partner, a study echoing the concern of my Berkeley years: the relation between university culture and social power.

During much of my scholarly life, I worked to bring the arts into history as essential constituents of its processes. In the last years, I have reversed the effort, trying to project historical understanding into the world of the arts, through work with museums, architecture schools, and critical writing for the larger public. The venue may change, the forms of one's engagement alter as one grows older and the world changes. Preparing this account, however, made me realize all too clearly that I have not moved very far from the issues that arose in my formative years, when, under the pressures of history, the value claims of intellectual culture and the structure of social power first appeared in a complex interaction that has never ceased to engage me.

PART ONE

Clio Ascendant:
Historicist Cultures in
Nineteenth-Century
Europe

THREE

The Idea of the City
in European Thought:
Voltaire to Spengler

DURING two hectic centuries of social transformation, the problem of the city pressed relentlessly upon the consciousness of Europe's thinkers and artists. The response of the intellectuals to this pressure was infinitely varied; for social change brought in its train transformations in ideas and values more protean than the alterations in society itself.

No one thinks of the city in hermetic isolation. One forms one's image of it through a perceptual screen derived from inherited culture and transformed by personal experience. Hence the investigation of the intellectuals' idea of the city inevitably carries us outside its own frame into myriad concepts and values about the nature of man, society, and culture. To chart in its proper context the changing idea of the city since the eighteenth century far transcends the bounds of the possible in a brief paper. I can do no more than present a few major strands of thought on the city, in the hope that the resulting pattern may suggest further lines of investigation.

One may, I believe, discern three broad evaluations of the city in the past two hundred years: the city as virtue, the city as vice, and the city beyond good and evil. These attitudes appear among thinkers and artists in temporal succession. The eighteenth century developed out of its philosophy of Enlightenment the view of the city as virtue. Industrialism in the early nineteenth century brought to ascendancy an antithetical conception: the city as vice. Finally there emerged, in the context of a new subjectivist culture born in the mid-nineteenth century, an intellectual attitude that placed the city beyond good and evil. No new phase destroyed its predecessor. Each lived on into the phases that succeeded it, but with its vitality sapped, its glitter tarnished. Differences in national development, both social and intellectual, blur the clarity of the themes.

Moreover, as the decades pass, strands of thought once seen as antithetical merge to form new points of departure for thought about the city. In
the history of the idea of the city, as in other branches of history, the
novel fructifies the old more often than destroys it.

॰ℳ₺

SURELY it was the unspoken assumption of the great middle class in the
nineteenth century that the city was the productive center of man's most
valued activities: industry and higher culture. This assumption was an
inheritance from the preceding century, an inheritance so powerful that
we must devote some attention to its character. Three influential children of the Enlightenment—Voltaire, Adam Smith, and Fichte—had
formulated the view of the city as civilized virtue in terms congenial to
their respective national cultures.

Voltaire sang his first lauds of the city not to Paris, but to London.
London was the Athens of modern Europe; its virtues were freedom,
commerce, and art. These three values—political, economic, and cultural—spring from a single source: the respect of the city for talent.

> Rival of Athens, London, blest indeed
>   That with thy tyrants had the wit to chase
> The prejudices civil factions breed.
>   Men speak their thoughts and worth can win its place.
> In London, who has talent, he is great.[1]

London was for Voltaire the fostering mother of social mobility against
the fixed hierarchical society.

The virtues he found in London, Voltaire soon generalized to the
modern city as such. His views of the city form a belated chapter in the
Battle of the Books, of Ancients versus Moderns. Voltaire wielded his
rapier smartly against the defenders of a vanished past, of the golden age
of Greece and the Christian garden of Eden. Why should mankind exalt
the poverty-stricken Greeks?—or Adam and Eve with their matted hair
and broken fingernails? "They lacked industry and pleasure: Is this virtue? No, pure ignorance."[2]

Industry and pleasure: these two pursuits distinguished urban life for
Voltaire; together they produced "civilization." The urban contrast between rich and poor, far from holding terrors for the *philosophe*, provided
the very basis of progress. Voltaire modeled his rich man not on the

captain of industry, but on the spendthrift aristocrat pursuing a life of ease in the city, a true child of the pleasure principle. Voltaire described his *mondain*'s luxurious rococo *hôtel*, with its exterior "ornamented by the striking industry of a thousand hands."[3] He savoured the rich man's daily rounds, his life of refined sensuality: the *mondain* rides in a handsome gilded carriage across imposing city squares to an assignation with an actress, then to the opera and a lavish meal. Through his sybaritic mode of existence, this squandering *bon vivant* creates work for countless artisans. He not only provides employment for the poor but becomes a model to emulate. Aspiring to the life of civilized ease led by their betters, the poor are encouraged to industry and parsimony, and thus improve their state. Thanks to this happy symbiosis of rich and poor, elegant ease and thrifty industry, the city stimulates progress in reason and taste and thus perfects the arts of civilization.[4]

Despite his rather bourgeois stress on the city as a force for social mobility, Voltaire regarded the aristocracy as the crucial agency in the progress of manners. The removal of the nobles to the city, especially in the reign of Louis XIV, brought a "sweeter life" to the uncouth townsman. The gracious wives of noblemen formed "schools of *politesse*," which drew the urban young people away from the life of the pothouse, and introduced good conversation and reading.[5] Voltaire thus viewed the culture of the new city somewhat as, in our day, Lewis Mumford and others have seen the planning concepts which inspired it: as an extension of the palace. But where Mumford found Baroque despotism—a strange combination of "power and pleasure, a dry abstract order and an effulgent sensuality," coupled with a deterioration of life for the masses—Voltaire saw social progress.[6] Not the destruction of community, but the diffusion of reason and taste to individuals of all classes: such was the function of the city for Voltaire.

Like Voltaire, Adam Smith attributed the origin of the city to the work of monarchs. In a wild and barbarous feudal age, the cities, needed by the kings, were established as centers of freedom and order. The city thus laid the foundations for progress in both industry and culture: "When [men] are secure of enjoying the fruits of their industry," Smith wrote, "they naturally exert it to better their condition and to acquire not only the necessaries, but the conveniences and elegancies of life."[7] For Voltaire, the advent of the nobility civilized the towns; for Smith, the town civilized the rural nobility and at the same time destroyed feudal lordship. The nobles, "having sold their birthright not like Esau for a mess of pottage in time of hunger and necessity, but in the wantonness of plenty for trinkets and baubles . . . , became as insignificant as any substantial burgher or tradesman in the city."[8] The city leveled nobles down and burghers up, to produce a nation orderly, prosperous, and free.

The dynamic of civilization thus lay in the city for Smith no less than for Voltaire. Yet both as economist and as moralist, Smith committed himself less fully to urbanism than Voltaire did. He defended the city only in its relationship to the country. The exchange between raw material and manufacture, between country and town, formed for him the backbone of prosperity. "The gains of both are mutual and reciprocal." But Smith regarded mobile capital as essentially unstable and, from the point of view of any given society, untrustworthy. "[A] very trifling disgust," wrote Smith, "will make [the merchant or manufacturer] remove his capital and . . . all the industry which it supports from one country to another. No part of it can be said to belong to any particular country, till it has been spread over the face of that country, either in buildings, or in the lasting improvements of lands."[9] The urban capitalist is thus a rather unpatriotic nomad. Although the city improves the countryside by providing a market and manufactured goods, although it enriches mankind by making possible the transcendence of animal needs, its enterprising denizens are socially unreliable, labile.

Other vices of a subtler sort accompany the urban virtues: "unnaturalness and dependence." Smith maintained that "to cultivate the ground was the natural destination of man." Both by interest and by sentiment, man tended to return to the land. Labor and capital gravitated naturally to the relatively risk-free countryside. But above all, the psychic satisfactions of the planter surpassed those of the urban merchant or manufacturer. Here Adam Smith showed himself an English preromantic: "The beauty of the country, . . . the pleasures of the country life, the tranquillity of mind which it promises and, wherever the injustice of human laws does not disturb it, the independency which it really affords, have charms that more or less attract everybody."[10] The city stimulated, the country fulfilled.

Smith pressed his psychological prejudices even at the expense of his economic logic when he argued that the farmer considered himself an independent man, a master, while the urban artificer felt always dependent on his customer, and thus unfree.[11] If the virtue of the city was that of the stimulus to economic and cultural progress, it did not afford the sense of security and personal freedom of the farmer's life. Adam Smith's model for the "natural" return of men and capital to the land was North

America, where primogeniture restricted neither personal freedom nor economic progress.[12] Here alone city and country stood in their proper relationship. The city stimulated thrift, wealth, and craft; it thus provided the artificer with the wherewithal to return to the land and to fulfill himself ultimately as an independent planter. Thus even this great champion of laissez-faire and of the city's historic role expressed that nostalgia for the rural life which was to characterize so much of England's thought on the city during the nineteenth century.

The intellectuals of Germany took little interest in the city until the early nineteenth century. Their indifference was understandable. Germany had no dominant capital in the eighteenth century to correspond to London or Paris. Her cities fell into two basic classes: on the one hand, there were surviving medieval towns, such as Lübeck or Frankfurt, still centers of economic life but with a rather sleepy traditional bourgeois culture; on the other hand, there were new Baroque political centers, the so-called *Residenzstadt*, such as Berlin or Karlsruhe. Paris and London had concentrated political, economic, and cultural power in their hands, reducing the other cities of France and England to provincial status. In divided Germany, the many political capitals coincided only infrequently with the many economic or cultural centers. German urban life was at the same time more sluggish and more variegated than that of England and France.

The generation of great intellectuals that arose at the end of the eighteenth century in Germany elaborated its ideas of freedom against the arbitrary power of the princes and the stultifying conventionality of the old burgher class. In neither dimension was the role of the city as an active element of progress of central concern to them. Against the atomizing and dehumanizing impact of despotic state power, the radical German humanists exalted the communitarian ideal of the Greek city-state.

During the Napoleonic Wars, Johann Gottlieb Fichte broke with the retrospective classical ideal to formulate a view of the city which governed much of German thought in the nineteenth century. Fichte adopted from Western thinkers the notion of the city as the culture-forming agent par excellence. But where both Voltaire and Smith attributed the development of the city to the freedom and protection granted it by the prince, Fichte interpreted the German city as a pure creation of the *Volk*. The Germanic tribes which fell under the sway of Rome became victims of Western *raison d'état*. Those which remained untouched in Germany perfected their primitive virtues—"loyalty, uprightness (*Biederkeit*), honor, and simplicity"—in medieval cities. "In these [cities]," Fichte wrote, "every branch of cultural life quickly developed into the fairest bloom."[13] To the branches of culture recorded positively by Voltaire and Smith—commerce, art, and free institutions—Fichte added yet another: communitarian morality. Precisely in the last, the German folk soul expressed itself. The burghers, in Fichte's eyes, produced "everything which is still worthy of honor among the Germans." They were neither made civilized by aristocrats and enlightened monarchs as in the view of Voltaire, nor motivated by self-interest as in the view of Smith. Inspired by piety, modesty, honor, and above all by a sense of community, they were "alike in sacrifice for the common weal." The German burghers had shown for centuries that, alone among the European nations, Germany was "capable of enduring a republican constitution." Putting history to a new use, Fichte called the age of the German medieval city "the nation's youthful dream of its future deeds, . . . the prophecy of what it would be once it had perfected its strength."[14]

In his glorification of the city as civilizing agent, Fichte thus added several new dimensions. The city in his vision became both democratic and communitarian in spirit. The medieval city took on the sociocultural characteristics assigned by other German thinkers—Schiller, Hölderlin, and the young Hegel—to the Greek polis. Fichte thus fortified the self-consciousness of the German bourgeoisie in its struggle for nationalism and democracy with a concrete model from its own history, a lost paradise of its own creation to regain. And with it, enemies to combat: the princes and the immoral state. The bloom of the city had been "destroyed by the tyranny and avarice of the princes, . . . its freedom trodden under foot" until Germany had sunk to its lowest ebb in Fichte's age, when the nation suffered the imposition of the Napoleonic yoke.[15] While he did not disvalue the role of the city in commerce, Fichte rejected Smith's "swindling theories about . . . manufacturing for the world market" as an instrument of foreign power and corruption.[16] Fichte had neither Voltaire's appreciation of the role of aristocratic luxury in urban culture-building, nor Smith's fear of the city entrepreneur's rootlessness. By extolling the burgher-city as a model ethical community, Fichte introduced ideal standards for the later critique of the nineteenth-century city as a center of capitalist individualism.

The stronger survival in German society permitted Fichte to develop notions which differed in their historical import from the ideas of the city held by his French and English predecessors. For Voltaire and Smith, who thought of history as a process, the city possessed virtues making for social progress; for Fichte, the city as community incarnated virtue in a social form. Fichte could use the past to formulate an ideal goal for the future, but had no notion of how the ideal was related to a process for its realization.

❧

EVEN while the idea of the city as virtue was being elaborated during the eighteenth century, a countercurrent began to make itself felt: the idea of the city as vice. The city as seat of iniquity had, to be sure, been fair game for religious prophets and moralists since Sodom and Gomorrah. But in the eighteenth century, secular intellectuals began to raise new kinds of criticisms. Oliver Goldsmith deplored the destruction of England's peasantry as mobile capital extended its sway over the countryside. Unlike Adam Smith, he saw accumulating wealth produce decaying men. The French Physiocrats, whose notions of economic well-being centered upon maximizing agricultural production, eyed the city with suspicion. One of their leaders, Mercier de la Rivière, presented what seems like a deliberate transformation of Voltaire's urban gentleman riding gaily to his assignation: "The threatening wheels of the overbearing rich drive as rapidly as ever over stones stained with the blood of their unhappy victims."[17] Social concern for the prosperity of the peasant freeholder brought anti-urbanism in its wake, no less surely in Mercier's Europe than in Jefferson's America. Other intellectual currents only reenforced developing doubts about the city as "civilizing" agent: the pre-Romantic cult of nature as a substitute for a personal God, and the sense of alienation that spread among the intellectuals as traditional social loyalties atrophied.

By the end of the eighteenth century, the spendthrift rich and the industrious artisans of Voltaire and Smith became transformed into Wordsworth's getters and spenders, equally wasting their powers, equally alienated from nature.[18] The rationality of the planned city, so prized by Voltaire, could appear to William Blake to impose "mind-forged manacles" on both nature and man. How different is Blake's poem, *London*, from Voltaire's earlier paean of praise:

> I wander thro' each charter'd street,
> Near where the charter'd Thames does flow,
> And mark in every face I meet
> Marks of weakness, marks of woe.[19]

Before the full consequences of industrialization were made manifest in the city, the intellectuals had already begun that revaluation of the

urban environment which has not yet run its course. The reputation of
the city had become entangled with concern over the transformation of
agrarian society, with the fear of "mammonism," the cult of nature, and
the revolt against mechanistic rationalism.

To this emergent view of the city as vice, the spread of industrialism in
the first decades of the nineteenth century gave a powerful new impetus.
As the promise of the beneficent operations of natural law in economic
life became transformed into the findings of the "dismal science," so the
hopeful mutual identity of interest of rich and poor, town and country
turned into the warfare between Disraeli's "two nations," between the
insouciant wealthy and the depraved slum dwellers.

What the romantic poets had discovered, the prose writers of the English social realist school in the 1840s described in its specific urban setting. The city symbolized in brick and grime and squalor the social crime
of the age, the crime that more than any other preoccupied the intelligentsia of Europe. The *cri de cœur* first raised in Britain spread eastward
with industrialism until, a hundred years after Blake, it found voice in the
Russia of Maxim Gorki.

Were poverty, squalor, and upper-class hardheartedness novae in the
urban universe? Assuredly not. Two developments account for the fact
that the city in the early nineteenth century became the stigmatic symbol
of these social vices. First, the dramatic increase in the rate of urbanization and the establishment of the jerry-built industrial town dramatized
urban conditions which had hitherto passed unnoticed. Second, this negative transformation of the social landscape came against the background
of Enlightenment expectations, of optimistic historical thinking about
the progress of wealth and civilization through the city such as we have
seen in Voltaire, Smith, and Fichte. The city as symbol was caught in the
psychological trammels of disappointed hopes. Without the dazzling picture of the city as virtue, inherited from the Enlightenment, the image of
the city as vice could hardly have achieved so firm a grip on the European mind.

The critical responses to the industrial urban scene may be loosely
distinguished between archaistic and futuristic. Both responses reflected
an acute consciousness of history as the medium of social life, with the
present located in a trajectory of change. The archaists would abandon
the city; the futurists, reform it. The archaists, such as Coleridge, Ruskin,
the Pre-Raphaelites, Gustav Freytag in Germany, Dostoievsky, and
Tolstoy, firmly rejected the machine age and its modern megalopolis. In

their respective ways, all sought a return to agrarian or small-town society. The utopian socialists in France, such as Fourier with his phalansteries, and even the syndicalists showed similar anti-urban traits. For the archaists, the good life simply could not be lived in the modern city. They revived the communitarian past to criticize the grinding competitive present. Their vision of the future involved, to a greater or lesser degree, the recapture of a preurban past.

It is my impression that the failure of nineteenth-century urban architecture to develop an autonomous style reflected the strength of the archaistic current even among the urban bourgeoisie. Why, if railway bridges and factories could be built in a new utilitarian style, were both domestic and representational buildings conceived exclusively in architectural idioms antedating the eighteenth century? In London even the railway stations struck archaic poses: Euston Station sought in its façade escape to ancient Greece, St. Pancras to the Middle Ages, Paddington to the Renaissance. This Victorian historicism expressed the incapacity of city dwellers either to accept the present or to conceive the future except as a resurrection of the past. The new city builders, unwilling to face directly the reality of their own creation, found no aesthetic forms to state it. This was almost as true for Napoleon III's Paris, with its strong tradition of controlled architectural continuity, as for Wilhelmian Berlin and Victorian London with their more flamboyant historical eclecticism. Mammon sought to redeem himself by donning the mask of a preindustrial past that was not his own.

Ironically, the true archaistic rebels against the city, whether esthetic or ethical, found the medieval styles they advocated caricatured in the façades of the metropolis. Both John Ruskin and William Morris bore this cross. Both turned from an archaistic estheticism to socialism, from the classes to the masses, in the search for a more promising solution to the problems of industrial urban man. As they did so, they became somewhat more reconciled to modern industrialism and to the city. They passed from archaism to futurism.

⁂

THE futuristic critics of the city were largely social reformers or socialists. Children of the Enlightenment, they found their faith in the city as civilizing agent severely strained by the spectacle of urban misery, but their melioristic thrust carried them over the chasm of doubt. The thought of

Marx and Engels shows in its most complex form the intellectual adaptation of the progressive outlook to the era of industrial urbanization. Both revealed in their early writings a Fichtean nostalgia for the medieval artisan, owner of his means of production and creator of his entire product. In 1845, the young Engels, in his *Condition of the Working Classes in England*, described the plight of the urban poor in terms little different from those employed by the English middle-class urban reformers, social novelists, and parliamentary commissioners of the 1840s. Engels described the industrial city realistically and indicted it ethically, yet offered no serious solution to its problems. Neither he nor Marx, however, suggested that the clock be turned back; nor did either support the "model community" solutions so favored by the nineteenth-century utopians.

After nearly three decades of silence on the urban problem, Engels once again turned his attention to it in 1872, treating it now in the context of matured Marxian theory.[20] While still rejecting the industrial city existentially, he now affirmed it historically. Where the domestic worker who owned his home was chained to a given spot as victim of his exploiters, Engels argued, the urban industrial worker was free—even though his freedom was that of a "free outlaw." Engels scorned the "tearful Proudhonist's" looking backward to rural small-scale industry, "which produced only servile souls. . . . The English proletarian of 1872 is on an infinitely higher level than the rural weaver of 1772 with his 'hearth and home.'" The driving of the workers from "hearth and home" by capitalist industry and agriculture was not, in Engels's view, retrogression, but rather "the very first condition of their intellectual emancipation." "Only the proletariat . . . herded together in the big cities is in a position to accomplish the great social transformation which will put an end to all class exploitation and all class rule."[21]

Engels's attitude toward the modern city paralleled exactly Marx's attitude toward capitalism; both were equally dialectic. Marx rejected capitalism ethically for its exploitation of the worker and affirmed it historically for socializing the modes of production. Similarly, Engels excoriated the industrial city as the scene of labor's oppression, yet affirmed it historically as the theater par excellence of proletarian liberation. As in the struggle between big capital and small entrepreneurship Marx espoused the former as the "necessary" and "progressive" force, so in the struggle between urban and rural production, Engels favored the industrial city as the purgatory of the fallen peasant or small-town artisan, where both were to be cleansed of servility and both were to develop their proletarian consciousness.

What place would the city occupy in the socialist future? Engels shied away from concrete blueprints. Yet he was convinced that a start must be made toward "abolishing the contrast between town and country, which has been brought to its extreme point by present-day capitalist society."[22] Late in life, Engels resurrected in his discussion of the city of the future the anti-megalopolitan outlook of the utopian socialists. He saw in the model communities of Owen and Fourier the synthesis of town and country—and lauded this synthesis as suggesting the social essence, though not the form, of the living-unit of the future. Engels' anti-megalopolitan stance was clear: "To want to solve the housing question while at the same time desiring to maintain the modern big cities is an absurdity. The modern big cities, however, will be abolished only by the abolition of the capitalist mode of production."[23] Under socialism, the "intimate connection between industrial and agricultural production," and "as uniform distribution as possible of the population over the whole country ... will ... deliver the rural population from isolation and stupor" and bring the blessings of nature into city life.[24] Engels refused to specify his ideas of population centers more precisely, but his whole argument suggested a strong affinity to the small-city ideal common to urban reformers since the close of the nineteenth century.

Where Adam Smith, on the basis of a theory of reciprocal urban and rural development, had seen the city man's fulfillment in a return to the land as an individual, Engels envisaged socialism as uniting the blessings of town and country by bringing the city to the country as a social entity; and conversely, nature to the city. In the course of three decades, his thought had passed from ethical rejection of the modern city, through historical affirmation of its liberating function, to a transcendence of the urban-rural debate in a utopian perspective: the synthesis of urban *Kultur* and rural *Natur* in the town of the socialist future. Though bitterly critical of the contemporary city, Engels rescued the idea of the city by integrating its very vices into his historical process of social salvation.

A new generation of continental writers in the 1890s expressed views not far removed from Engels's. Unlike the English social novelists of the 1840s, they thought neither of preindustrial life as bliss nor of Christian-ethical solutions to modern urbanism as viable. Émile Zola, in his trilogy *Trois villes*, painted Paris as a sink of iniquity. The Christian message was too weak and corrupted to regenerate modern society; neither Lourdes nor Rome could help. The cures must be found where the disease centered: in the modern metropolis. Here, out of degradation itself, would arise the humanistic moral and scientific spirit to build a new society. Émile Verhaeren, an active socialist as well as an avant-garde poet, showed the modern *villes tentaculaires* sucking the life's blood out of the countryside. Verhaeren shared with the archaists a strong feeling for earlier village and town life, but the horrendous vitality of the city had turned the archaistic dream into the modern nightmare-actuality of bigotry and emptiness which ruled in rural life. The last cycle in his poetic tetralogy, entitled *Dawn*, showed that the industrial energies which, for a hundred years, had dragged man into oppression and ugliness, were also the key to redemption. The red light of the industrial mills betokened the dawn of the regenerated man. The red revolution of the masses would work the transformation.[25]

Were the archaists then dead by the end of the century? No. But they flowered in more fateful blooms, the *fleurs du mal* of totalitarian nationalism: Léon Daudet and Maurice Barrès in France, the proto-Nazi litterateurs in Germany. Condemners of the city all, they assaulted not the city as vice, but its people as vicious. The liberal urban rich were at best the allies of the Jew; the urban poor were the depraved and rootless masses, supporters of Jewish materialistic socialism. Back to the provinces, the true France, cried the neo-rightist French! Back to the soil where blood runs clear, cried the racist Germans! The German proto-Nazis—Langbehn, Lagarde, Lange—joined to their cult of peasant virtue the idealization of Fichte's medieval burg. But where Fichte used his archaic model to democratize German political life, his successors employed it for a revolution of rancor against liberalism, democracy, and socialism. Fichte spoke for a middle class on the way up; his proto-Nazi successors, for a petty bourgeoisie which felt itself on the way down, crushed between big capital and big labor. Fichte exalted the communitarian city against the despotic *Residenzstadt*; his successors, against the modern metropolis. In short, where Fichte wrote in hope as a communitarian rationalist, the proto-Nazis wrote in frustration as blood-and-soil irrationalists.

The second wave of archaism may be most easily distinguished from the first by its lack of sympathy for the city man as victim. The sympathetic attitude had passed by 1900 largely to the futurists, the social reformers or revolutionaries who accepted the city as a social challenge and hoped to capitalize its energies. The remaining archaists viewed the city and its people not with tears of pity but with bitter hatred.

How does the idea of the city as vice in 1900 compare with that of the city as virtue a century before? For the futurists of 1900, the city possessed vices, as for Voltaire and Smith it had possessed virtues. But those vices, the futurists believed, could be overcome by the social energies born of the city itself. The neo-archaists, in contrast, had fully inverted Fichte's values: for him the city had incarnated virtue in a social form to be emulated; for them it incarnated vice, and was to be destroyed.

∌

SOMEWHERE about 1850, there emerged in France a new mode of thought and feeling which has slowly but forcefully extended its sway over the consciousness of the West. No agreement yet exists on the nature of the great sea change in our culture ushered in by Baudelaire and the French Impressionists, and given philosophical formulation by Nietzsche. We know only that the pioneers of this change explicitly challenged the validity of traditional morality, social thought, and art. The primacy of reason in man, the rational structure of nature, and the meaningfulness of history were brought before the bar of personal psychological experience for judgment. This great revaluation inevitably drew the idea of the city into its train. As virtue and vice, progress and regression lost their clarity of meaning, the city was placed beyond Good and Evil.

"What is modern?" The intellectual transvaluators gave a new centrality to the question. They asked not, "What is good and bad about modern life?" but, "What *is* it? What true, what false?" Among the truths they found was the city, with all its glories and horrors, its beauties and its ugliness, as the essential ground of modern existence. Not to judge it ethically, but to experience it fully in one's own person became the aim of the *novi homines* of modern culture.

Perhaps we can most readily distinguish the new, modernist attitude from older ones by examining the city's place in relation to the ordinance of time. Earlier urban thinking had placed the modern city in phased history: between a benighted past and a rosy future (the Enlightenment view) or as a betrayal of a golden past (the anti-industrial view). For the new culture, by contrast, the city had no structured temporal locus between past and future, but rather a temporal quality. The modern city offered an eternal *hic et nunc*, whose content was transience, but whose transience was permanent. The city presented a succession of variegated, fleeting moments, each to be savoured in its passage from nonexistence to oblivion. To this view the experience of the crowd was basic: all its individuals uprooted, each unique, all conjoined for a moment before the parting of their ways.

Baudelaire, by affirming his own deracination, pressed the city into the service of a poetic of this modern life-attitude. He opened vistas to the city dweller which neither lamenting archaist nor reforming futurist had yet disclosed. "Multitude and solitude: [these are] terms that an active and fertile poet can make equal and interchangeable," he wrote.[26] He did so. Baudelaire lost his identity, as the city man does, but he gained a world of vastly enlarged experience. He developed the special art he called "bathing himself in the crowd."[27] The city provided a "drunken spree of vitality," "feverish joys that will always be barred to the egoist." Baudelaire regarded the poetic city dweller as cousin to the prostitute— no longer an object of moralistic scorn. The poet, like the prostitute, identified himself with "all the professions, rejoicings, miseries that circumstances bring before him." "What men call love is a very small, restricted and weak thing compared with this ineffable orgy, this holy prostitution of a soul that gives itself utterly, with all its poetry and charity, to the unexpectedly emergent, to the passing unknown."[28]

For Baudelaire and the fin-de-siècle esthetes and decadents who followed him, the city made possible what Walter Pater called "the quickened, multiplied consciousness." This enrichment of personal sensibility, however, was bought at a terrible price: detachment from the psychological comforts of tradition and from any sense of participation in an integrated social whole. The modern city had, in the view of the new urbanite artists, destroyed the validity of all inherited integrating creeds. Such creeds had been preserved only hypocritically as historicist masks of bourgeois reality. To the artist fell the duty of striking off the masks in order to show modern man his true face. The esthetic, sensuous—and sensual—appreciation of modern life became in this context only a kind of compensation for the lack of anchorage, of social or credal integration. Baudelaire expressed this tragically compensatory quality of the esthetic acceptance of urban life in desperate words: "The intoxication of Art is the best thing of all for veiling the terrors of the Pit; . . . genius can play a part at the edge of the tomb with a joy that prevents it from seeing the tomb."[29]

To live for the fleeting moments of which modern urban life was com-

posed, to jettison both the archaistic and the futuristic illusions, could
produce not only reconciliation but also the wracking pain of loneliness
and anxiety. The affirmation of the city by most of the decadents had the
character not of an evaluation, but of an *amor fati*. Rainer Maria Rilke
represented a variant of this attitude; for while he conceded the city's
fatality, he evaluated the city negatively. His *Book of Hours* showed that, if
art could veil the terrors of the pit, it could disclose them too. Rilke felt
imprisoned in "the cities' guilt," whose psychological horrors he described with all the passion of a frustrated reformer:

> But cities seek their own, not others' good;
> they drag all with them in their headlong haste.
> They smash up animals like hollow wood
> and countless nations they burn up for waste.

He felt himself pinioned in the stone grip of the city, and the result was
anguish, "the anguish deep of cities monstrous grown." The city here,
though surely not beyond good and evil, was a collective fatality that
could know only personal solutions, not social ones. Rilke sought his
salvation in a poetic neo-Franciscanism, which negated in spirit the
empty fate—the "spirally gyration"—which urban man called progress.[30]
Despite his clear social protest, Rilke belonged rather to the new fatalists
than to the historical archaists or futurists; for his solution was psychological and metahistorical, not socially redemptive.

Let us not fall into the error of some critics of the modern city by
ignoring the genuine joie de vivre that the esthetic acceptance of the
metropolis could generate. In reading the sophisticated urbanites of the
fin de siècle one cannot but sense a certain affinity to Voltaire. For example, take Richard Le Gallienne's "London":

> London, London, our delight,
> Great flower that opens but at night,
> Great city of the midnight sun,
> Whose day begins when day is done.
>
> Lamp after lamp against the sky
> Opens a sudden beaming eye,
> Leaping a light on either hand,
> The iron lilies of the Strand.[31]

Le Gallienne expressed the same delight in the vital gleaming city as
Voltaire. To be sure, the source of radiance was different: sunlight bathed

Voltaire's Paris; nature glorified the work of man. Le Gallienne's city, in contrast, defied nature with mock-bucolic iron lilies and gaslit midnight suns. Not art but artificiality was celebrated here. Pleasure-seeking nocturnal London blotted out its grimy day. The Blakean meter of Le Gallienne's poem—was it intentional?—recalled Blake's workaday London, the gray historical transition from Voltaire's brilliant daylight to Le Gallienne's garish night-light. The night-bloom of London—as Le Gallienne showed he knew in other poems—was a flower of evil. But in an urban world become fatality, a flower's still a flower. Why should a man not pluck it? Voltaire's pleasure principle still had life in the fin de siècle, though its moral force was spent.

However marked their differences in personal response, the subjectivist transvaluators were at one in accepting megalopolis with its terrors and its joys as the given, the undeniable ground of modern existence. They banished both memory and hope, both the past and the future. To endow their feelings with esthetic form became the substitute for social values. Although social criticism sometimes remained strong, as it did in Rilke, all sense of social mastery atrophied. The aesthetic power of the individual replaced social vision as the source of succor in the face of fate. Where the social futurists looked to the redemption of the city through historical action, the fatalists redeemed it daily by revealing the beauty in urban degradation itself. What they saw as unalterable, they made endurable in a stance strangely compounded of stoicism, hedonism, and despair.

BAUDELAIRE and his modernist successors unquestionably contributed to a new appreciation of the city as a scene of human life. Their esthetic revelation has converged with the social thought of the futurists to issue in richer and more constructive thinking about the city in our century. Since this form of thought is generally familiar, I shall close instead on another more somber intellectual synthesis, one which drove to its ultimate extreme the idea I have been discussing: the city beyond good and evil. This idea—with its historistic equivalent, the city as fatality—achieved its fullest theoretical formulation in the thought of Oswald Spengler, and its practical realization at the hands of the German National Socialists.

In his conspectus of civilization, Spengler brought together in the most sophisticated way many of the ideas of the city we have traced here. The city was for him the central civilizing agency. Like Fichte, he viewed it as an original creation of the folk. Like Voltaire, he called it the perfector of rational civilization. Like Verhaeren, he observed it suck the life out of the countryside. Accepting the psychological analyses of Baudelaire, Rilke, and Le Gallienne, he regarded modern urban humanity as neo-nomadic, dependent upon the spectacle of the ever-changing urban scene to fill the void of a desocialized and dehistoricized consciousness. With all these affinities to his predecessors, Spengler differed from them in the most crucial area: he transformed all their affirmations into negations. This most brilliant historian of the city hated his subject with the bitter passion of the fin-de-siècle neo-archaists, the frustrated anti-democratic rightists of the lower middle class. Though he presented the city as fatality, he clearly welcomed its demise.

The German National Socialists shared the attitudes of Spengler—though surely not his richness of learning. The example of their urban policies illuminates the consequences of the fusion of two of the strands we have discussed: neo-archaist values and the notion of the city as a fatality beyond good and evil.

Translating neo-archaist notions into public policy, the Nazis began their rule with an active policy of returning the urban population to the holy German soil. They tried both permanent resettlement of urban workers on the land, and the education of urban youth in rural labor service.[32] Their anti-urbanism did not, however, extend to Fichte's cherished medieval cities. Although the Nazi movement originated in a *Residenzstadt*, Munich, it chose medieval Nuremberg as the appropriate site for its annual party congress. The demands of the modern industrial state, however, could only be fulfilled in an urban setting. The Nazis, while excoriating the "pavement literature" of the 1920s, and branding urban art as decadent, brought out in their city building all the elements which the urban critics had most strongly condemned. Was the city responsible for the mechanization of life? The Nazis slashed down the trees of Berlin's Tiergarten to build the widest, most monotonously mechanical street in the world: the Achse, where rurally regenerated youth could ride their roaring motorcycles in black-uniformed formation. Was the city the scene of the lonely crowd? The Nazis built huge squares in which the crowd could intoxicate itself. Had the city man become deracinated and atomized? The Nazis made him a cog in a huge machine. The hyper-rationality which the neo-archaists deplored reappeared in the

Nazi parade, the Nazi demonstration, the organization of every aspect of life. Thus the whole cult of rural virtue and the medieval, communitarian city revealed itself as ideological veneer, while the reality of anti-urban prejudice brought the vices of the city to an undreamt-of fulfillment: mechanization, deracination, spectacle and—untouched behind the great squares of men on the march one knew not where—the still-festering slums. Truly the city had here become a fatality for man, beyond good and evil. The anti-urbanites had brought to fruition the very features of the city they had most condemned. For they were themselves children of the unreformed city of the nineteenth century, victims of an Enlightenment dream gone wrong.

NOTES

1. "Verses on the Death of Adrienne Lecouvreur," translated by H. N. Brailsford in his *Voltaire* (Oxford, 1947), 54.

2. Voltaire, "Le Mondain" (1736), in *Oeuvres complêtes* (Paris, 1877), 10:84.

3. Ibid., 83.

4. Ibid., 83–86. Voltaire here secularizes the traditional medieval view of the division of function between rich and poor in the social economy of salvation. In the medieval view, the rich or "noble" were saved by their generosity, the poor by their sufferings. Each was necessary to activate the virtues of the other. Voltaire introduced into this static symbiosis the dynamic of social mobility. (Cf., for a Baroque statement of the traditional view, the ideas of Abraham a Santa Clara analyzed by Robert A. Kann, *A Study in Austrian Intellectual History* [New York, 1960], esp. 70–73.)

5. Voltaire, *Le siècle de Louis XIV*, 2 vols. (Paris, 1934), chap. 3, 43–44.

6. Lewis Mumford, *The Culture of Cities* (New York, 1938), 108–13, 129–35. For a more differentiated analysis of the development of the modern city, see Martin Leinert, *Die Sozialgeschichte der Grosstadt* (Hamburg, 1925), vol. 3, *passim*.

7. Adam Smith, *The Wealth of Nations* (New York, 1937), 379.

8. Ibid., 390–91.

9. Ibid., 395.

10. Ibid., 358.

11. Ibid., 359. The farmer likewise depends, in Smith's theory, on his customer, for only the sale of his surplus enables him to purchase city-made necessities. In a free market economy all are interdependent.

12. Ibid., 392–93.

13. J. G. Fichte, *Reden an die deutsche Nation* (Berlin, 1912 [?]), 125–26.

14. Ibid., 127, 128.

15. Ibid., 126.

16. Ibid., 251.

17. Quoted from Mercier de la Rivière's *Tableau de Paris* in Lewis Mumford, *The Culture of Cities* (New York, 1938), 97.

18. William Wordsworth, "The World," in *Oxford Book of English Verse* (Oxford, 1931), 609.

19. William Blake, "London," in *The Portable Blake*, edited by Alfred Kazin (New York, 1946), 112.

20. "The Housing Question," in Karl Marx and Friedrich Engels, *Selected Works* (2 vols., Moscow, 1958), 1:546–635.

21. Ibid., 563–64.

22. Ibid., 588.

23. Ibid., 589.

24. Ibid., 627–28.

25. Cf. Eugenia W. Herbert, *The Artist and Social Reform* (New Haven, 1961), 136–39.

26. Baudelaire, "Short Poems in Prose," *The Essence of Laughter*, edited by Peter Quennell (New York, 1956), 139.

27. Cf. Martin Turnell, *Baudelaire: A Study of His Poetry* (London, 1953), 193.

28. Baudelaire, *Essence of Laughter*, 139, 140.

29. Ibid., 147–48.

30. Rainer Maria Rilke, *The Book of Hours*, translated by A. L. Peck (London, 1961), 117–35.

31. Quoted in Holbrook Jackson, *The Eighteen Nineties* (London, 1950), 105.

32. Frieda Wunderlich, *Farm Labor in Germany, 1810–1945* (Princeton, 1961), 159–202, *passim*.

FOUR

History as Vocation in Burckhardt's Basel

BASEL in the nineteenth century can best be understood as a viable anachronism. Surviving from the medieval era as a city-state, it managed to maintain a substantial measure of its political autonomy and much of its patrician-dominated social structure. From the Renaissance era it retained a humanistic cultural tradition within a new world of powerful modern nation-states, big cities, big business, and technological culture. Determination to remain small was essential to the Basel elite's successful defense of its civic tradition and, for a long time, its social power. In a modern world that worshiped growth as health and bigness as bounty, especially in cities, Basel long resisted expansion. In 1780 it had about 15,000 inhabitants—only 15 percent more than in 1600. In 1848 it had 25,000. Only slowly in the second half of the nineteenth century did the resolution of the entrenched merchant oligarchy weaken under the temptations of new economic opportunities and the pressures of sociopolitical demands from below to meet the conditions for urban expansion. Yet not until 1880 did Basel's population pass the 80,000 mark.[1]

Basel stubbornly tried to cling not only to the scale but also to the character of a polis, a free city. The historian Jacob Burckhardt expressed the outlook of the Basel oligarchy to which he belonged as a general proposition: "The small state exists so that there may be one spot on earth where the largest possible proportion of the inhabitants are citizens in the fullest sense of the word."[2]

History and geography had schooled Basel well for its adaptive defense of its ancient civic tradition against modernity. Situated at the elbow of the Rhine between the navigable portion of the river and the Alpine passes to Italy, the city had always enjoyed an enviable position on Europe's greatest commercial highway. The reverse side of this economic advantage, however, was political and strategic vulnerability. Trade routes easily became the roads of war. Basel lay on the boundary between some of the deepest and strongest divisions of Europe: between the French and German language and cultural communities, between the often warring and expansionist French monarchy and the Holy Roman Empire, between Protestantism to the north in Germany and Catholicism to the west in France. Amid conflicting forces, all more powerful than itself, Basel learned to live by a paradoxical combination of sophisticated cosmopolitanism and narrow localism. Open in commerce and culture, the city-state was closed and aloof in its civic self-definition. Access to citizenship was tightly controlled, often requiring generations of family residence, in the interest of the guild corporations and a small oligarchy that held its power through the guilds.

To safeguard its position among stronger neighbors, Basel avoided war and eschewed alliances wherever possible (even when it sold mercenaries). Instead the city developed a remarkable capacity and reputation for mediation between conflicting states, cantons, or communes. In 1501, when Basel joined the Swiss Confederation, the constitutional contract (*Bundesbrief*) forbade the city the use of armed force in intra-Swiss disputes and at the same time enjoined it to use its diplomatic skill as broker and peacemaker in conflicts among other Confederation members. Basel's sons preserved their right to be themselves by learning the minds and ways of their neighbors and using the understanding thus acquired to avoid friction and to moderate conflict. The city's behavior in the Reformation was characteristic. Although it adopted the new Reformed faith, it exercised in 1529 its creative diplomacy to prevent the Catholic cantons from going to war with the Protestant ones, establishing for Switzerland the principle, not always honored in practice, of confessional peace based on local choice. It was a principle Europe would adopt only after another century of devastating religious wars.

⁂

BASEL's practical, irenic cosmopolitanism found early reinforcement in a culture of humanism that became crucial to the city's whole subsequent development. The University of Basel, founded in 1454, became a center of Christian humanism and a place of confluence of Italian and French learning. Characteristically integrating economic opportunity and intellectual values, Basel also became in the sixteenth century a center of paper production and, more important, one of Europe's leading scholarly publishing centers. While members of the university community became involved in editorial functions, the printers were admitted to university lectures to enhance their understanding of Latin texts. It was this vigorous culture of the book that attracted Erasmus to make Basel his home for much of the last two decades of his life. Erasmus himself exercised a powerful and lasting, if informal, influence on the city's intelligentsia. His kind of humanism, with a stronghold in the university and a foothold in the patriciate, tempered the zealotry of the Reformation, sparing the city the worst, though not all, of the fratricidal consequences of the religious crisis. A glance at the culture heroes of the great Swiss cities tells us much: Zurich remembers the militant Protestant leader Zwingli as the refounder of the city; Geneva recalls stern Calvin; Basel looks back to the compromising Catholic humanist Erasmus.

While in many ways Basel resembled other patrician-controlled imperial free cities of the Germanies, it was unique in the high value assigned by its elite to humanistic culture. It was unique also among free cities— especially those of the Rhineland—in maintaining until modern times a university as radiating center of its specifically civic values. The profession of learning, from the sixteenth century onward, was prized among the merchant families as the priesthood was in Ireland. By the nineteenth century no self-respecting patrician family could be without its "Onkel Professor." True, in the eighteenth century the university sank to a low ebb in both size and quality. The professors were chosen almost exclusively from local families. They were elected from a slate of three candidates by lot, as were other officials under Basel's narrow collegial constitution. Despite a few intellectual dynasties of high caliber, such as the Bernoullis in math and science and the Burckhardts in philology and theology, the local patriciate's monopoly of academic posts had cost the university its European stature by the time of the French Revolution.

After the trauma of the Revolution, when Basel's ancient political culture had been threatened by the centralized Helvetic Republic and Napoleon, the patriciate set about refounding the city and its own power in it on a more solid basis. Restoration in the Basel context meant not only the return to power of the ruling elite but also the deliberate reanimation of the humanist cultural tradition as the center of the civic ethos. To accomplish this objective the university was seen as the primary instrument. A reform commission was instituted in 1813 to reconstitute the university on modern lines.[3] The reformers had a choice of new models: the French one of the *grandes écoles*, to produce functional professionals for the modern state—architects, bureaucrats, teachers, natural scientists, and so on; or the German university, as revitalized by Humboldt's educational countermovement to cultivate the citizen of *Bildung*, a new human person of moral and aesthetic sensibility, creativity, and sharpened understanding. Although the Basel commission was staffed with several French-style rationalists, they too were by local tradition sympathetic to the Humboldtian alternative, which easily prevailed in their recommendations.

The reformers did not, however, restore autonomy to the university. Patricians though they were, they had learned the lesson of the deterioration of the university when it was an uncontrolled preserve of the professors from their own class. The reformers built university government directly into civil government, in a way that must be unique in the annals of both politics and learning. As Rome had two consuls, so Basel had two burgomasters. Of these, one also served as chancellor of the university. Since turnover in this office was low, continuity in university leadership was ensured. The burgomaster-chancellor had to be academically qualified and had to enjoy the confidence of the faculty. Of the four incumbents from 1803 to 1874, three were professors as well as city council members (*Ratsherren*). All were, of course, unpaid public officials, wealthy members of the elite enjoying the highest esteem among both citizens and academics—rather like James Bryant Conant at Harvard and in Boston. They combined, as one of the historians of the university said, "scientific culture, the gift of statesmanship, and *Baseler Civismus*."[4] The burgomaster-chancellorship was no mere honorific post like the chancellorship of Oxford. The holder of the office chaired a three-man committee (*Kuratel*) that supervised curriculum and prepared recommendations of faculty appointments for the city's Educational Council (*Erziehungsrat*), which he served as president. Faculty members played an advisory role in the appointment of professors, but no more. Final authority was vested in the Small Council of the city government, in which the great patrician families predominated until the city government was democratized in 1874.

One of the faculty reformers expressed well the revitalized ethos of civic humanism: "The meaning and nature of man is first revealed in the state. . . . But the determining condition of the state is freedom, in which every energy [*Kraft*] can develop itself without restraint, and the mind [*Geist*] can make itself effective in its activity undisturbed."[5] *Civismus*, as the Baselers like to call public spirit, and *Wissenschaft* went hand in hand.

Two consequences flowed almost at once from this organization of the university, one affecting the character and ethos of the faculty, the other shaping the very substance of Basel's creative contribution to European thought. I shall briefly sketch the first and then illustrate the second with the individual cases of two historians of culture, Johann Jakob Bachofen and Jacob Burckhardt.

Scarcely had the new university statutes been put into effect in 1818 than the post-Napoleonic political reaction began to harden its grip on intellectual life in Germany to the north. As liberal professors were dismissed or began to think of fleeing government repression in German—especially Prussian—universities, Basel fished in the troubled waters, winning a fine catch of front-rank academic talent. C. J. Jung's grandfather, who came on the recommendation of Alexander von Humboldt, reformed the medical faculty, while another émigré, the Germanist Wilhelm Wackernagel, reinvigorated the philological curriculum. There were genuine radicals among the new German appointees, too, such as Karl Follen, later founder of German study at Harvard, who was wanted in Prussia for his association with the student militants of the *Burschenschaften*. Conservative Basel gave him house room and more. On his behalf, for the first time in history, Basel stood up to powerful Prussia. The city government resisted both the threats of Prussia and the pressures of the anxious Swiss Confederation and refused to extradite the "subversive" professor. From that time forward Basel had the reputation of giving refuge to maverick foreign professors, including "heaven stormers." Even the leading families, normally known for the closed character of their society, welcomed such professors into their homes.

Political reaction in the Germanies, and especially the rise of Prussian *Realpolitik*, gradually changed the definition of the scholar's function in Germany, with important consequences for the culture of Basel. In response to the French Revolution, Humboldt and the Prussian reformers had developed a neohumanistic cultural ideal which, through school and university, was to make ethically sensitive citizens of Prussian subjects. Beginning with the reaction, however, and increasingly as the *Machtstaat* progressed, the vocation of learning for citizens was transmuted into the profession of science for the state. The professor became not the purveyor of humanistic culture but the learned specialist. Such were the premises on which Germany's positivistic scientific eminence was built.

Basel took another road in defining science as vocation. Just as the Prussians were abandoning Humboldtian neohumanism, Basel espoused it heart and soul. Education, not specialized production, became the aim of scholarship. The Basel professor after the reform was not just a university scholar and teacher. He was a *praeceptor urbis* in the fullest sense of the term. The 1820s university reform involved him in a demanding outreach program, animated especially by the theologian Wilhelm de Wette. Professors were expected to offer public lectures. They also edited journals aimed at the amateur. To their crucial lectures, such as inaugural lectures or rectoral addresses, the whole town was invited—and many came. For faculty members—especially the young and the newcomers—the presence of the general public at such occasions could be intimidating. Thus, the young theologian Franz Overbeck wrote to his colleague Friedrich Nietzsche before his inaugural address: "Tuesday I must speak in the great hall [*aula*]. Here the whole city is invited. Naturally, it's no laughing matter."[6] Above all, the members of the philosophical faculty were expected to teach in the *Pädogogium*, the public preparatory school, as part of their regular teaching load. What this burden could amount to is made clear in the case of Nietzsche's obligations in the summer semester of 1870: two three-hour lecture courses and a seminar at the university and, at the *Pädagogium*, a six-hour course in Greek tragedy and six hours of Latin and Greek language instruction—a total of twenty hours.[7] In short, the Basel *homo academicus*, though a free, protected, and socially appreciated intellectual explorer, was at the same time a kind of home missionary whose vocation was to develop cosmopolitan *Bildung* in allegiance to the local scene. The first generation of neohumanist scholars, reinforced by Prussian émigrés, enthusiastically put this commitment into place. The second, those who matured in the 1830s, were reared in it.

As luck would have it, just when Basel adopted fully the German idealist scholarship of *Bildung*, European *Wissenschaft* was becoming geared into the requirements of the modern nation-state. Connected as it was with the defense of a tradition of the polis and the power of its patriciate, Basel's neohumanism was socially anachronistic. Yet by virtue of its critical *prise de position* in relation to scholarship's subservience to the more common state structures of modern power, it can also be seen as culturally futuristic, formulating anti-positivistic ideas that became widespread only in our century.

No act of civic or cultural will could prevent the political and economic forces of nineteenth-century Europe from penetrating Basel. Under the contagious impact of the French liberal revolution of 1830, the underprivileged of Basel's Catholic rural-artisan countryside revolted against Protestant patrician rule. The oligarchy's attempt to repress the insurgent populace failed, and urban Basel (*Stadt*) had to accept the secession of rural Basel (*Basel-Landschaft*) as an independent canton. Then, in the 1840s, while liberalism grew in strength within Basel, challenging the ancient elitist political regime, the city-state's political autonomy was further reduced by the reorganization of the Swiss Confederation on more centralistic and democratic lines. At the same time the advent of railroads knit Basel's economy more strongly to neighboring France and Germany, while industrialization, especially after 1850, changed the social basis of Basel's industry from a traditional artisanate to a modern working class. Here, too, demographic and democratic pressures weakened the deferential society from within, even as Basel's great industrial neighboring states communicated the tremors of their crises of growth in the revolutions of 1848 and the wars of unification and national rivalry of the midcentury decades.

❦

To THE internal and external challenges to their embattled patrician way of life, Basel found intellectual and psychological defenses, if not political ones. Elsewhere in Europe cultural responses to the trauma of modern social change came from free or deracinated intelligentsia, often artists; in Basel they came from academic intellectuals, from professors. Two of these Basel academics can serve us to acquire some sense of the relation between their role definitions as civic scholars and the intellectual substance of the work that they bequeathed to posterity.

J. J. Bachofen, historical anthropologist, and Jacob Burckhardt, cultural historian, were born to the Basel patriciate, and were educated by the first generation of neohumanists. Where their teachers were tempered optimists, fulfilled in their mission, the younger men had to endure the change in the conditions of patrician power which robbed the idealism of their elders of its social promise and its philosophic force. Bachofen and Burckhardt, each in his own way, did battle to rescue humanistic science-as-vocation from what they saw as the new academic servants of power. Each found a way to reanimate the humanistic legacy by injecting into it a new, quasi-aesthetic form of social understanding and a stoic intellectual stance.

Johann Jakob Bachofen (1815–87) most vividly dramatizes in his life and thought the pressures of the nineteenth century on the patrician consciousness. Scion of one of Basel's wealthiest families, which made its fortune, as did the Burkhardts, in the manufacture of silk ribbons, Bachofen studied both law and philology in German universities as well as in Basel. He began his career in legal work, both scholarly and practical. In 1841 the City Council appointed him to a teaching post in the law faculty of the university. The liberals, however, increasingly strong since the patrician failure to prevent the independence of rural Basel in 1833, launched a press campaign against the young man's appointment, branding it as "the result of illegitimate preferment and special family influences." At this slight to his talents and integrity Bachofen took deepest offense; he refused both title and university salary. A year later the City Council persuaded him to accept the office of professor, although he would not accept the salary. Then, in 1844, he changed his mind again: he gave up his professorship and became a private scholar.[8] Bachofen continued to perform other civic duties. He played an important role for the university as a member of the municipal committee, the three-man *Kuratel*, that controlled it. He also served as a judge for several decades. But the hostile charge of patrician nepotism, with its inevitable reflection on his competence as a legal scholar, had struck a wound that would not heal. Bachofen not only withdrew from his formal academic career but, in 1845, also resigned his seat on the Great Council—an extraordinary step for a patrician only thirty years old.

Bachofen's civic disengagement did not imply diminished devotion to his native city. "One has firm roots only in one's native soil," he wrote. "The great experiences of life can be gone through only there, for the destinies of families and states are not played out in one life, but only in a whole series of generations following one upon the other."[9] He not only tolerated "boredom as always" in "our Lilliput,"[10] but he committed heart and mind to preserving and enhancing the humane values for which his city stood.

As a private scholar Bachofen embarked on a kind of exploration that would serve as cultural counterfoil to the modern politics and scholarship that threatened his polis and its humanist tradition. For inspiration in this scholarly mission Bachofen looked back to the Basel humanists of the fifteenth century and to the German scholars who, from Winckelmann through Creuzer, had defined out of the classical heritage the *Bildungsideal* in the era of Humboldt. For his intellectual targets Bachofen looked north too: his enemies were the new Prussian scholars—"the pygmies"—from Barthold Niehbuhr on, who turned classical learning from the cultural glory that was Greece to the political greatness that was Rome. "In our age," he wrote, "even men's minds have been put in uniform."

The great historian Theodor Mommsen incarnated for Bachofen all that he feared and despised in modern classical learning.[11] Nationalist, liberal champion of German unification under Prussia, Mommsen in his spectacular *History of Rome to the Death of Caesar* (1854–56) celebrated Rome as the state that, by combining just law and power, had succeeded in unifying ancient Italy. Bachofen saw in Mommsen's achievement only its contemporary essence. "Rome and the Romans are not Mommsen's real concern," he wrote. "The heart of the book is the application of the latest ideas of the times, . . . the apotheosis [in and through Rome] of the boundless radicalism of the new Prussia."[12]

Bachofen exhumed from the mists of prehistory another Rome to counterpose to Mommsen's naked, masculine power-state. Using myths and funerary sculpture of pre-Roman cultures and placing them in the light of his sensitive anthropological imagination, Bachofen recovered a prepolitical antiquity: the creative communities of the Sabines and the Etruscans, who charted the first perilous passage of mankind from raw nature to culture. Law appeared among these primitives not as a product of power to organize domination but as a manifestation of the spirit, to canalize and sublimate man's chaotic libidinal and violent instincts through religion and law. It was not the male of the species who accomplished this feat of community creativity, but the female. Woman, as the only visible source of new biological life, established the first system of law, *Mutterrecht*. It was a system of lineage and of family, enforced by codes of blood vengeance. Woman took these first steps in self-defense, to protect her child nurturing and to regulate unbridled sexual license. Matriarchy, succeeding to hetaeric promiscuity, sublimated natural love into the idea of the sacred and elevated procreative drives into marital bonding and religious culture. Through religious ritual and mystical exaltation, matriarchal society created an ennobling "erotic-spiritual culture." In the end, Bachofen maintained, the female principle limited the intellectual potentialities of man. The earth-mother principle was overcome by the sky-father principle, material and psychic nature by abstract and intellectual nature, Demeter by Apollo. "Motherright yields to the right of the state, *ius naturale* to *ius civile*. . . . Nowhere was patriarchal law so sternly carried through as in Rome."[13] But the ultimate fundamental service of woman to humankind remained: she founded culture to refine our nature, while the male created the state to rule it.

Bachofen did not, despite his hatred for imperial Rome and Prussian *Realpolitik*, deplore this victory of the male principle as such; for on it, in his view, the role of intellect and of the individualism necessary to the great achievements of European culture was ultimately based. But if his mind accepted the victors, his heart stayed with the vanquished: with the dead past, not the living present; with the culture of the mothers, not the civilization of the fathers; with the nurturing erotic bonding of community as against the rational regulations of society; with the religious care of souls rather than the state's promotion and protection of abstract rights.

If Bachofen succeeded in restoring a humanistic *Altertumswissenschaft* against the critical realism of the new German historical science, he did so on a terrain of the past which could not perform the moralistic educational functions of the earlier humanists. For the chthonic realm of the mothers, with its dark divinities, could scarcely match the pantheon of Olympian gods and heroes in providing ideal types for civic *Bildung*. In fact, Bachofen performed a more dangerous intellectual function in his historical anthropology. He opened the repressed world of eros and thanatos to the historical consciousness of modern man. He held up to sympathetic contemplation all the values that were sacrificed when the male-dominated state prevailed over the matriarchal order—love, religion, a sensuous spirituality, cultivation of life, pious acceptance of death. This inveterate patrician could not, as Nietzsche tried to do, draw strength from the realm of instinct for the regeneration of modern culture. Bachofen's archaizing vision could create elegiacally an appreciation for a world that was lost, reinforcing the values of nurturing culture against those of overmastering politics. But it could not refute the historical truth of the success of Mommsen's Rome. His lifetime scholarly polemic produced lament for the lost and an attitude of resignation, but not hope for its renewal.

DURING the 1850s, when Mommsen was producing his paean to political power in the Roman history and Bachofen his sympathetic re-creation of prepolitical culture in *Motherright*, Jacob Burckhardt was at work on *The*

Culture of the Renaissance in Italy. Perhaps the most important single contribution of Basel to European thought since Erasmus, Burckhardt's book addressed in historical terms the problem of the relationship of cultural creativity to social experience. The book can also be read, like Bachofen's, as part of the effort of the Basel intelligentsia to preserve its cosmopolitan tradition of *Bildung* under modern conditions that were hostile both to it and to the survival of the patriciate that had nurtured and sustained it.

In 1858 Bachofen, as a member of the *Kuratel*, drafted the invitation to Burckhardt to return from Zurich to his native city as professor of history. Bachofen expressed himself in terms well calculated to appeal to Burckhardt's civic idea of the intellectual's vocation. Not only did the faculty and the city officials enthusiastically wish him to return, Bachofen wrote to the younger scholar, but he had remained, thanks to his wonderful public lectures in the 1840s, "the darling of the [Basel] public." "Come back joyfully then, and help to develop intellectual life, to give it the freshness among us that—if we don't lose our courage—will still be granted it."[14] Could a Burckhardt resist such an appeal—a Burckhardt whose family had provided Basel with innumerable professors for its university and at least one of the city's two burgomasters for almost one hundred fifty years?

Burckhardt's acceptance should not surprise us, then. But the way in which he carried out his "office" of Basel professor really must excite our wonder. Where Bachofen withdrew from teaching to fight his battle for *Bildung* only through writing, Burckhardt self-consciously gave up publishing after his *Renaissance* appeared in 1860 and dedicated himself wholly to teaching his fellow Baselers at every level. His classes in the *Pädagogium*, the public prep school for the university, were as important to him as his university lectures. For the educated amateur in the Junior Merchants' Society or at the Basel Museum, Burckhardt lectured on subjects ranging from "The Art of Cooking of the Later Greeks" to "The Letters of Madame de Sévigné," preparing his polished presentations with the same careful research and organization of sources as other historical scholars devoted to their writing.[15] Everywhere Burckhardt's pedagogic aim was the same: to teach men how to understand history through contemplation and reflection. "Listen to the secret of things. The contemplative mood. . . ." He respected professional specialism for the accurate knowledge it produced but rejected it for its narrowness and its failure to seek wisdom: "How is the collector of inscriptions to find time for contemplative work? Why, they don't even know their Thucydides." (This barb is directed at Mommsen and his energetic organization of teams to collect Roman inscriptions in Italy. Bachofen, too, inveighed against this Prussianization of research.) Burckhardt avoided learned association meetings "where they go and sniff each other like dogs."[16] He prided himself, in research as in teaching, on being "an arch-dilettante," committed to nurturing amateurs to be reflective about their own historical experience by entering vicariously into the staggering varieties of life in the past, where each culture revealed another aspect of human nature and destiny. It was the "special duty of the cultivated person," he believed, "to broaden the picture of the continuity of world development in himself"[17] and, as a thinking participant-observer in the flow of history, to preserve it.

To this stubborn negator of the nineteenth century's articles of faith, historical process was far from synonymous with progress. Here Burckhardt was at one with Bachofen. Burckhardt's greater worldliness enabled him to see the changing configurations of history not with his colleague's bitter ethical regret or metaphysical despair but with a fine mixture of irony and otherworldly aesthetic wonder. Skeptical of progress, he avoided a necessitarian pessimism as well, accepting the openness of history as a changing scene of creativity and spiritual achievement ironically linked to malevolence, stupidity terror, and suffering. Such a concept of history's flow made it possible to cherish and even expand culture even while undergoing the traumas of social disorder and political defeat.

In *The Culture of the Renaissance* Burckhardt created a new kind of history much closer to the work of the anthropologist than to that of the traditional historian. Synchronic cross-sections replace diachronic phases or narrative sequences as the basic structural units of the book. Burckhardt examines Renaissance culture not dynamically for actions and events but statically for its character as a scene of interrelated aspects of human life and activity. Not narrative literature but stagecraft seems to offer Burckhardt the formal language for his historical *tableaux vivants*. In a series of great panels devoted to the nature and structure of politics, intellectual life, mores, and religious practices, he shows us the Renaissance, as he says, not in its motion (*Verlauf*) but in its states of being (*Zustände*). The sense of historical space supersedes that of historical time.

Yet Burckhardt has placed his spatial scene in a temporal frame that

lends it not only perspective but historical meaning. It is here that Burckhardt's concerns as a Baseler—community, the state, and cultural creativity—are brought into focus in his historical theater. At the back of
the Renaissance stage Burckhardt has hung a backdrop of medievalism;
in front of it a scrim of modernity through which we view it. At the
beginning of each part of the book the medieval backdrop is deftly
sketched in a few sentences. Burckhardt portrays it as a unified culture in
which politics and religion penetrate each other and in which the individual was conscious of himself only as part of a community organized
for the salvation of mankind. The Renaissance, seen against this medieval
backdrop, is an era of decadence, the end of medieval innocence and
unity, disintegrating as religion and politics separate, as pope and emperor divide. By the same token the Renaissance is also "a civilization
which is the mother of our own," an era in which, out of the destruction
of community, modern individualism, with its incredible self-consciousness, was born. The scrim of modernity sharpens our vision of the action
on the stage. In the new city-states and despotisms of Italy, "for the first
time we detect the modern political spirit of Europe, . . . often displaying
the worst features of an unbridled egotism, outraging every right, killing
every germ of a healthier culture." Yet in consequence and compensation
the creativity of man is activated: "a new fact appears in history—the
State as an outcome of reflection and calculation, the State as a work of
art."[18] That the state is not God-given but man-devised, an artifact posited against the chaos of existence, often brings new terrors in its train.
In the artistic world, however, creativity is also unleashed, this time in a
most positive way, to produce new and glorious images of man as the
medieval bonds of faith dissolve. Where Enlightenment historians had
associated the Renaissance flowering of art with social progress, Burckhardt connected it with ruthless political individualism and despotism,
the chaos of autonomous states that was Italy. Burckhardt's vision linked
the glory of cultural creativity with the curse of unconstrained self-asser-
tiveness that the decay of medieval unity released. Terror and beauty,
intellectual discovery and moral degradation went hand in hand at the
birth of "modern" culture, where individual competition replaced human
community and man became literally self-made. Such a view was beyond
progress and regression. In contrast to the elegiac ideas of Bachofen, who
lamented the lost "natural" culture of Italy's primordial mothers, Burckhardt offered his contemporaries, in the mirror of the Renaissance, an
image of the beginning of their own civilization in which neither hope

nor despair seemed justified. The warmest appreciation of man's achievements in the sphere of culture was interwoven with the most unsentimental sense of the realities of naked power. Such a complex and skeptical historical vision, harsh but sublime, could well accomplish the vocational aim of Burckhardt as *Wissenschaftler*, Basel-style: to make the man of *Bildung* in the threatening world of the mass state not smarter for tomorrow but wiser forever.

NOTES

1. Hans Mauersberg, *Wirtschafts- und Sozialgeschichte zentraleuropäisher Städte in neuerer Zeit,* . . . *Basel, Frankfurt a M., Hamburg, Hannover und München* (Göttingen, 1960), 26–30.

2. Quoted in Edgar Bonjour, H. S. Offen, and G. R. Potter, *A Short History of Switzerland* (Oxford, 1960), 338.

3. On the work of this commission and its results, see Edgar Bonjour, *Die Universität Basel* (Basel, 1960), chaps. 22, 23.

4. Ibid., 353.

5. Franz Dorotheus Gerlach, ancient historian, quoted ibid., 353.

6. Letter of Overbeck to Nietzsche, 13 March 1870, in Carl Albrecht Bernoulli, *Franz Overbeck und Friedrich Nietzsche, eine Freundschaft* (Jena, 1908), I, 30.

7. Curt Paul Janz, *Friedrich Nietzsche. Biographie*, 3 vols. (Munich, 1978–1979). I, 351.

8. Bonjour, *Die Universität Basel,* 549–50.

9. Quoted from Bachofen's autobiographical letter to F. C. von Savigny, legal historian, by Lionel Gossman, *Orpheus Philologus. Bachofen versus Mommsen on the Study of Antiquity.* Transactions of the American Philosophical Society 73.5 (Philadelphia, 1983), 17.

10. Bachofen letter to Rudolf Müller, 7 November 1879, in *Johann Jakob Bachofens Gesammelte Werke,* edited by Karl Meuli (Basel and Stuttgart, 1967), vol. 10, letter 300.

11. For Bachofen's antagonism to Mommsen, see Gossman, *Orpheus Philologus,* 21–41.

12. Quoted ibid., 29.

13. For a condensed statement of the nature of matriarchal culture and its passage to patriarchy, see Bachofen's introduction to "The Myth of Tanaquil," in *Myths, Religion and Motherright: Selected Writings of J. J. Bachofen,* Bollingen Series LXXXIV, paperback ed. (Princeton, 1973), 211–46.

14. *Kuratel* to Dr. J. J. Burckhardt, 24 January 1858, quoted in Bonjour, *Die Universität Basel,* 686.

15. A number of these lectures are collected in Jacob Burckhardt, *Kulturgeschichtliche Vorträge,* edited by Rudolf Marx (Stuttgart, 1959). See, for the circumstances, educational aims, and style of the lectures, Marx's "Nachwort," 419–45.

16. Jacob Burckhardt, *Letters*, selected, edited, and translated by Alexander Dru (London, 1955), 32.

17. Quoted in Marx, "Nachwort," in Burckhardt, *Kulturgeschichtliche Vorträge*, 442–43.

18. Jacob Burckhardt, *The Civilization of the Renaissance in Italy*, translated by S.G.C. Middlemore (London, 1951), 2.

FIVE

Medieval Revival and
Its Modern Content:
Coleridge, Pugin,
and Disraeli

KARL MARX opened his Communist Manifesto with an arresting, not to say chilling, announcement: "A specter is haunting Europe—the specter of Communism." By 1847, when the "social question" had become a major concern not only in industrial England but as far east as the Germanies, the specter of revolution indeed weighed heavy on the European consciousness. But there were other, older ghosts that stalked the land as well, sometimes allied with Marx's futuristic specter, sometimes in conflict with it. One of these is the concern of this paper: the specter—or spirit—of medievalism.

A ghost is a protean thing at best, and surely that is true of the haunting spirit of the Middle Ages. I shall say nothing of its first fitful appearances in eighteenth-century England as part of the taste for the exotic, the grotesque, and the sublime. My concern is rather with the historical invocation of the medieval past by three thinkers possessed of an urgent sense of England's riven present in the second quarter of the nineteenth century: a poet, Samuel Taylor Coleridge; an architect, Augustus Welby Pugin; and a novelist-politician, Benjamin Disraeli. These three very different intellectuals shared a tendency not characteristic of all Gothic revivalists: namely, to conceive English medieval civilization holistically, as an integrated culture, much in the way that German idealists interpreted the Greek polis. They saw in medieval England a comprehensive symbol of the good society—all that modern England was not. They drew upon the Middle Ages for norms with which to criticize one or another aspect of their own society; and, at their most extreme, they construed medieval civilization as a counterculture to be posited against modernity. Although none of our three thinkers-with-history produced a comprehensive pic-

ture of medieval England, all treated it as a paradise lost. All espoused a
somewhat similar Tory historical myth of the fall: Catholic Church corruption was the original sin. Tudor excess in breaking the economic independence of the Church magnified the consequence of sin. Whig
greed rooted it in the oligarchic aristocracy. And, finally, modern capitalism made the moral decay general and pervasive. On this ideological
trajectory of the ills of England, all three critics—the poet, the architect,
and the writer-politician—could agree.

Where our three thinkers differed was in the nature of redemption and
the means to attain it. For here the virtues of the past had to be adapted
to the realities of the present. In their respective areas of primary concern—the moral and social function of the intellectual class for Coleridge; the built environment for Pugin; practical social policy for Disraeli—each revealed the limits as well as the uses of his "medieval"
values. Paradoxically, the critical import of their medieval norms forced
forward their own modernity, propelling them to widen the gulf between
past and present that they had hoped to bridge. That the medieval ghosts
were sent back once more to the city of the dead, their mythic life petri-
fied as past history, was an unintended by-product of the work of these
medievalizing critics. But the nature of England's modernity was made
both clearer and richer by their intellectual ventures into archaism.

Three texts provide the substance for this sampling of England's medievalizing counterculture: Coleridge's *On the Constitution of the Church and
State* (1829), Pugin's *Contrasts* (1836, 1841), and Disraeli's *Sybil* (1845). The
boundaries so sacrosanct in intellectual life and study in today's world were
freely ignored by the members of our trio. Coleridge the poet produced
constitutional theory; Pugin the architect, a work of culture criticism. The
budding politician Disraeli used the novel as his means to articulate his
social ideas. The relations of the life of letters and that of public affairs,
traditionally well integrated in England, became more turbulent in the
early nineteenth century, when the deepening divisions in society were
refracted in thought. For in the face of the unprecedented overlapping
crises of democratization and industrialization, the very nature and function of culture in society became a burning issue. All three of our critics
addressed it with history, in ways contributing to its transformation.

⁂

COLERIDGE conceived his influential treatise, *On the Constitution of the
Church and State*, in the context of the agitation for Catholic emancipa-

tion, in order to clarify the rights and powers of religion in the civil order. Eager to hold the line against the Catholic Church as an institution, Coleridge nevertheless found himself exploring ways in which the social functions traditionally associated with religion could be expanded for his society. He sought to stake out a new division of power between economic forces and cultural ones in a modern polity. With an extraordinary mixture of history and logic, Coleridge adapted medieval forms to modern conditions and for modern uses.

In his tract, Coleridge presented the skeletal structure of English institutions of Church and State in essentially medieval dress, modified only to accommodate the Erastian powers of the king over both Church and State. Coleridge's Parliament is composed of "Major Barons" and "Minor Barons" (the latter also called "Franklins"); but also of a second group, representing "the mercantile, manufacturing, distributive and professional classes, under the common name of citizens," or "the burgesses." Instead of defining these groups in terms of status and function in the feudal manner, Coleridge strikes through his own screen of medieval nomenclature to identify them as two broad economic classes, according to their forms of private property. The barons major and minor constitute the landed interest; all the rest are the "personal interest," resting on "movable and personal possessions." i.e., on mobile capital in all its forms. Coleridge invents a medieval-sounding term to cover both forms of capital: "the Propriety." Into the hands of its possessors he consigned the legislative power.

The two forms of property perform for him two functions indispensable to the common weal: the landed interest assures "permanence"; the personal interest, "progression." "Permanence and progression": Coleridge's pairing is but one more among many such distinctions developed by nineteenth-century intellectuals in their concern to contain in concept the tensions and conflict between continuity and change, the party of order and the party of movement. St. Simon's "organic and critical powers," Comte's "order and progress," the whole series of dualisms cast up by German idealism as it entered the sphere of politics, are intellectual signs of the same strains in nineteenth-century history.

Far from any romantic communitarianism in his view of the state, Coleridge flatly stated that men "super-induced [i.e., built] the political relation on the social [one]," and "not for the protection of their lives, but of their property."[1] Similarly his idea of history was based, like that of Adam Smith, Hegel, or Marx, on the necessary and fundamental social tension between landed and mobile capital. In Coleridge's view, the English constitution had institutionalized that tension constructively in Parliament. He cheerfully recognized the primacy of property in the political sphere. But that did not end England's problem. All the values of civilization—spiritual, social, and cultural—that did *not* serve the interests of private property had, he thought, been sacrificed on its altar. To redress the balance, Coleridge called forth the spirit of what he called the National Church. This was both more and less than the "Church of Christ," with its concentration on the purely religious life. The National Church traditionally bore responsibility for our "cultivation," for "the harmonious development of those qualities and faculties that characterize our humanity." "We must be men," Coleridge wrote, "in order to be citizens."[2] For this purpose, the English nation had created a separate estate of the realm, the "clerisy," to take its place as a third estate beside the two estates (landowners and merchants) of the propertied classes.

Again Coleridge produced pseudo-medieval jargon in order to endow modern functions with the aura of tradition—or, conversely, to adapt ancient ways to answer modern needs. His word "clerisy" resonates, with deliberate ambiguity, of both past and present. The functions performed by the clergy in the past under the aegis of theology must be assumed in the modern world by a secular intelligentsia under the aegis of moral and social philosophy. As the clerisy, the intellectual class preserves and transmits the values of the nation, linking past and present. It serves to protect and cultivate the person as an ideal, not as a mere means. It teaches wisdom and learning for the good life, not mere instrumental knowledge as an avenue to power and property. Schooled in German idealism, Coleridge charges his clerisy with the promotion of what should be, as against what is. Coleridge unleashes his bitterest attacks against the "mechanic-corpuscular theory," "the mechanic philosophy"—his terms for the philosophy of Helvetius and his English disciple Jeremy Bentham. Inveighing against a "machinery of the wealth of nations made up of wretchedness, disease, and depravity of those who should constitute the strength of the nation," Coleridge called for the re-creation, in the clerisy, of a class of moral educators and protagonists of the national interest wholly independent of the propertied classes and their political power.[3]

But how could that independence from the power of property and the state be achieved for his clerisy? Once more Coleridge drew on medieval precedent. Just as Church lands had supported the clergy of yore, so a portion of national wealth must be set aside for the collective support of the clerisy. Coleridge called this fund the "Nationalty" (sic). Since it was committed to the national weal, it would serve as counterforce to the

"Propriety," the private and inheritable land and capital that was committed to serve individual interest. The great crime of the Tudor monarchs—to destroy the moral independence of the Church by turning over its lands to private propertied interests that controlled the State—would thus be reversed. And with it, the intellectuals of the realm would be freed of subservience to the propertied. Guardians of culture and morality, protectors of the weak, the clerisy would once more, as in the Middle Ages, have the corporate economic foundation to pursue in independence its ideal of service to the nation as a whole—especially in learning, education, and the social care of the poor.

Coleridge's constitutional theory rests firmly on the medieval distinction between the temporal and spiritual powers. But beneath his medieval-romantic jargon of barons, burgesses, and clerisy, one discovers a hard-nosed division of social functions resting on types of property. The basic functional division of state and church is resolved into an economic division between Propriety and Nationalty; i.e., between private and public property. Coleridge acknowledges the right of the Propriety to control state power. As a child of his time, he makes the best of the conflict between landed and mobile capital by associating with each, as Adam Smith had done, a function in the dynamic of orderly change: mobile capital to innovate, landed capital to stabilize. For those without property, there is no place in Coleridge's state, but there is *concern*. Here is where the clerisy comes in. For Coleridge, as for the German idealists who so deeply affected the structure of his thought, the idea must transcend the limitations of reality and, where need be, negate or transform it. Against the abuses of private property, he tried through the clerisy to mobilize in collective form the power of thought, which could posit an ideal community where none now existed. From the historical ghosts of a medieval clergy he distilled modern *Geist* (Mind), and concretized it in a modern intelligentsia, a critical, culture-bearing social class. Hegel had turned to the bureacracy to inject disinterested Geist into the world of interests. Coleridge proposed more: to create of dependent, isolated intellectuals an independent social class on an autonomous economic base. Thus he hoped to build into the constitution of the realm a disinterested countervailing power to mitigate the play of naked interests in favor of the general weal.

⁂

In 1836, six years after the aging Coleridge gave to the world his reflections on the constitution, Augustus Welby Pugin published *Contrasts*,

surely the most intemperate manifesto of the medieval revival.[4] The
young author (b. 1812) was an engraver and designer, recently turned
architect. Accordingly he expressed his ideas in visual form, to which his
writing was but an adjunct. The full title of Pugin's tract stated both his
message and his approach to it: *Contrasts: or, A Parallel between the Noble
Edifices of the Middle Ages and Corresponding Buildings of the Present Day;
Showing the Present Decay of Taste.* Unlike Coleridge, who tried to integrate past values and present realities, Pugin's "contrasts" were in fact
designed to separate them. Pugin embraced the past for its radical otherness, in the light of which the blighted modern world stood irretrievably
condemned. While Coleridge conflated religion and culture, Pugin, a
convert to Roman Catholicism, made his faith the sole source and guarantor of society's health. In the plates of *Contrasts*, he dramatized the
difference between a fifteenth-century society living by Christian truth
and a nineteenth-century society based on pagan, infidel, and Protestant
error. His text explained the history of the progressive corruption that
destroyed the English Catholic commonwealth.

Pugin pioneered in the idea that building was a statement of value,
reflecting the ethic of the builders. For him, as later for John Ruskin, the
beautiful manifested the good. Aesthetic preference, however, could
readily be legitimated by an ethical reading, and vice versa. Pugin integrated ethics and aesthetics, and pressed the combination into the service
of his Catholic faith by his picturesque renderings of fifteenth-century
civilization. Pugin grounded his religious apologetic for the nineteenth
century in the medieval sense of community, using images of the Gothic
built environment to convey it.

Pugin made his argument by paired pictures of medieval and modern
life in their respective spatial settings—as "right way" and "wrong way."
Contrasting types of poorhouses show the simple core of his argument
(Figure 5.1). The repressive discipline of the New Poor Law is expressed
in the closed geometric form of the Benthamite panopticon. The medieval almshouse, by contrast, is a confraternity of guiding superiors and
happy followers. The medieval physical facility is to strike us by its openness in form and its closeness to nature. Its component elements are
irregular in size and varied in design, yet freely articulated into a harmonious whole.

Stylistic contrasts also serve Pugin's point. The Classical and Gothic
styles express for him two conceptions of order, one legalistic and repressive, the other charitable. The Classical style, with its horizontal orienta-

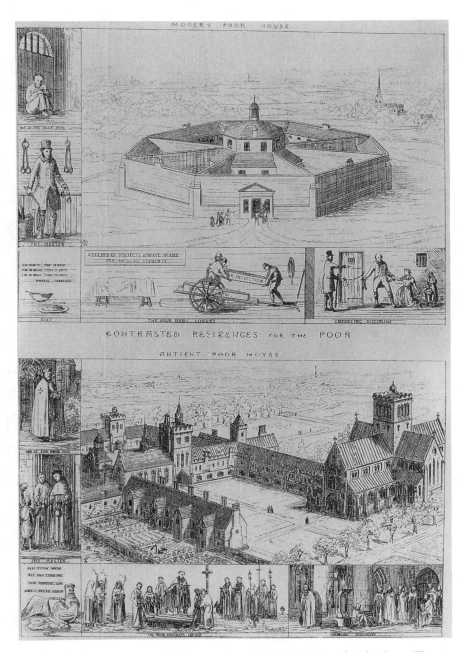

Figure 5.1. Augustus Welby Pugin, Contrasted Residences for the Poor. Top: "modern poor house"; bottom: "antient poor moyse."

tion, is pagan, pressing close to earth. Gothic or pointed architecture points to God, and vaults to heaven. It alone is Christian. Pugin carries this associative theme through his series of snapshot sketches.

In the public water conduits of Figure 5.2, the modern prosaic facility, located before the police station, is locked and guarded against the thirsty child. The beautiful medieval conduit draws the users to its elegantly recessed front. In two college gateways (Figure 5.3), Pugin uses every trick to produce the triumph of the medieval over the modern. A rich procession of clerics and scholars adorns the medieval scene, while tatterdemalion flâneurs and a commercial hawker set the scene outside the locked gate of modern King's College, London. The angle of vision through Christ's College gate in Oxford shows the handsome yard within, while at King's Pugin's perspective conceals from us that behind that gate too is a handsome court.

Finally, Pugin sketches his indictment of the cold factory city of 1840, which has replaced the lofty spires and trees of the "Catholic town" of 1440 with smoky chimneys and ugly factories (Figure 5.4). George Hersey has called this pair of drawings Pugin's masterpiece of architectural excoriation. The detailed identification of the buildings in the two cities shows us how the differentiated life-affirmation of holistic Christian culture has been broken into separate modern institutions to impose on man the instrumental grids of specialized, rational repression.

In his pictures of contrasting chapels (Figure 5.5), Pugin carries us into one of the points where religion and political authority converge. The modern royal chapel at Brighton, vulgar-classical in form, Protestant in content, shows the minister preaching the word *at* the passive people, while the royal family looks down upon him from above. In the ancient chapel at Windsor, the altar and the book are central, pointing upward to God. The people, led by the priest to the altar, are as one before Him, regardless of rank. We must not deduce from such egalitarian disposition of the worshipers in his court chapel any democratic impulses on Pugin's part. The reunification of divided Christians upon which Pugin implicitly believed community among Englishmen to rest was "rather to be obtained through the sacrifice of the altar and by midnight supplication than by the clamours of an election platform or the tumult of popular commotion." To which Pugin adds the ringing cry of the man of faith to the secular world: "Laus deo!"[5]

It was Pugin's sad fate as a religious believer to become a prisoner of his own apologetic. As the harmony and beauty of fourteenth- and

Figure 5.2. Augustus Welby Pugin, Public Water Conduits. Left: "St. Annes Soho"; right: "West Cheap Conduit, Thomas Ilam 1479."

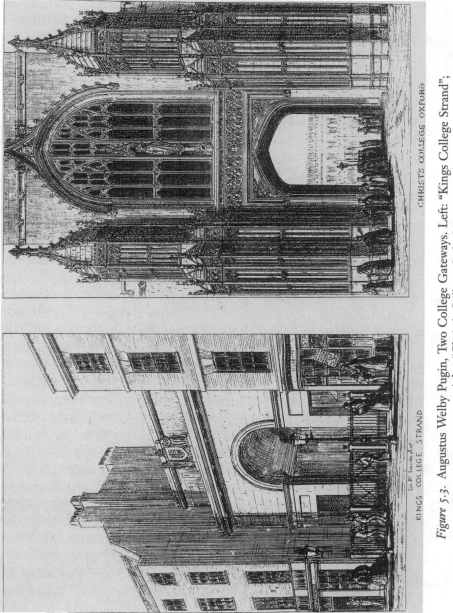

KINGS COLLEGE STRAND

CHRIST'S COLLEGE OXFORD

Figure 5.3. Augustus Welby Pugin, Two College Gateways. Left: "Kings College Strand"; right: "Christ's College Oxford."

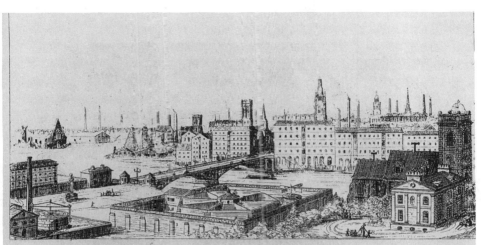

THE SAME TOWN IN 1840.

1. St. Michael's Tower, rebuilt in 1750. 2. New Parsonage House & Pleasure Grounds. 3. The New Jail. 4. Gas Works. 5. Lunatic Asylum. 6. Iron Works & Ruins of St. Maries Abbey. 7. St. Evans Chapel. 8. Baptist Chapel. 9. Unitarian Chapel. 10. New Church. 11. New Town Hall & Concert Room. 12. Wesleyan Centenary Chapel. 13. New Christian Society. 14. Quakers Meeting. 15. Socialist Hall of Science.

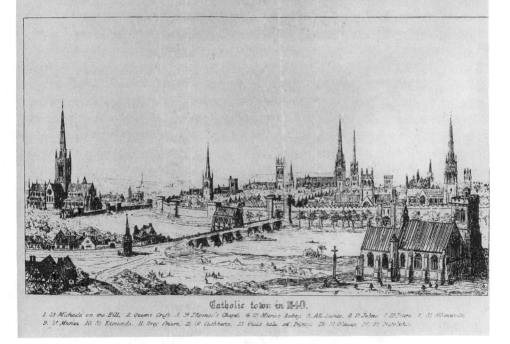

Catholic town in 1440.

1. St. Michaels on the Hill. 2. Queens Cross. 3. St. Thomas's Chapel. 4. St. Maries Abbey. 5. All Saints. 6. St. Johns. 7. St. Peters. 8. St. Alphage. 9. St. Maries. 10. St. Edmunds. 11. Grey Friars. 12. St. Cuthberts. 13. Guild hall. 14. Trinity. 15. St. Olaves. 16. St. Botolph.

Figure 5.4. Augustus Welby Pugin, Two Towns. Top: "The same town in 1840"; bottom "Catholic town in 1440."

CHAPEL ROYAL BRIGHTON

S.T GEORGE'S CHAPEL WINSOR

Figure 5.5. Augustus Welby Pugin, Two Chapels.

fifteenth-century English civilization was for him the embodiment of the
True Faith, so the True Faith became identified in Pugin's mind with the
cultural forms of that moment of the past. He fell victim to what Pope
Pius XII called "the Christian culture-illusion." Pugin as Roman Catholic could face his own time only as archaist, idealizing the past in total
contempt of the present.

Even the most intransigent archaist must have his attachment to the
here and now. Pugin clung to architecture itself. He addressed its potentialities in *Principles of Pointed or Christian Architecture* (1842). In *Contrasts*,
he had used the social and aesthetic virtues of medieval building impres-
sionistically to demonstrate the efficacy of faith and the sickness of the
modern age. In *Principles*, he inverted the procedure. He used the Christian virtues and practices he found in Gothic architecture to elaborate
general norms for architecture as such, with significant results for the
spatial culture of the future. True to his very secular principle that "the
history of architecture is the history of world," Pugin examined medieval
building forms for their purposes and the values they embodied. With an
ethical analytic, he produced an architectural aesthetic which shared several of the tenets of modern functionalism. Pugin's functionalism had two
aspects: one social, the other structural. The social aspect was the asser-
tion of the primacy of purpose in determining the form of the building.
As to structure, Pugin demanded candor in its disclosure—first, by
matching form and even ornament to its demands; second, by remaining
true to the properties of building materials.

To demonstrate the social-functional principle, Pugin drew on the example of English medieval universities and monastic complexes, with
their different-sized units for chapel, refectory, halls, and sleeping quarters. Here the ground plan took clear precedence over the claims of the
façades; function (he used an older term, "convenience") determined the
spatial forms. The surviving medieval university buildings of England,
with their ingeniously flexible plans, volumetric design, and differentiated fenestration patterns, illustrated Pugin's principle that "the external
and internal appearance of an edifice should be . . . in accordance with
the purpose for which it is destined."[6] Even ornament was to be judged
by the degree to which it was integrated as an "enrichment of the essential construction," with forms suiting that function.[7]

Pugin would not have been Pugin had he not thrown the book at the
"deceitful" architecture of Europe since the Reformation. He indicted
Christopher Wren's St. Paul's Cathedral for concealing its engineering,

its buttresses, behind a screening outer wall for the sake of appearance. ("One half the edifice is built to conceal the other.")[8] Nor did he exempt the "Gothic style" of his own day from the charge of falsehood. It too could be used as merely one of "the disguises" of his deceitful times in "the carnival of architecture," where buildings are "tricked out in the guises of all centuries." All fell to the modern error, said this enemy of Bentham, of "disguising rather than beautifying articles of utility."[9] For Pugin, Gothic building pointed the way out of the eclectic Babel of his age—but only insofar as it expressed the truth of the faith that had made England a community in the Middle Ages. Unable to find, and unwilling to search for, modern premises for the regeneration of culture as Coleridge had, Pugin nevertheless gave to architecture new criteria for defining its character and function in the modern world. Ironically, it was Pugin's fanatical conviction of the truth of his religious faith that enabled him to give to architecture a faith in its own functional truth.

<hr />

BENJAMIN DISRAELI, in his novel *Sybil* (1845), sang the praises of medieval England no less fervently than the other two members of our trio: yet we soon become aware that his was in fact a swan song, a romantic aria of medievalism, all but engulfed in the realistic orchestration that was to sustain it.

Sybil: or The Two Nations is a love story and a social allegory. It aims at redeeming England by wedding past ideal and present power. The love story takes the form of a double bildungsroman, in which each of the two principal characters is in effect educated by the other. For Disraeli, the central duality of his age is not spirit vs. matter as with Coleridge or Pugin, but class division. Hence, the union of his principal characters, Charles Egremont and Sybil Gerard, is to point to the reconciliation of Rich and Poor, the "Two Nations" of the novel's subtitle. The scenario itself, however, unfolds in ways which undermine its own intention, producing instead of class harmony a legitimation of class oppression. Almost in spite of himself, Disraeli shows how medievalism as an ideology was transformed from an historical critique of modern class society into one of its rhetorical instruments. The self-destruction of his novel records a modern social function of England's medieval ghosts before they returned to the tomb of history.

The action of the novel follows two trajectories: one is the unfolding of class struggle in the early years of Chartism, England's first great labor movement, down to its dramatic climax in a working-class riot in the North Country in 1842. The other plots the relations between the two lovers-to-be, and charts as it unfolds the shift in the social provenance of medievalizing idealism. Both actions, the social and the ideological, are presented with a wealth of acute spatial symbolism that ranges from Pugin's communitarian visions in architecture to Friedrich Engels's tough-minded portrayal of the modern factory city. To confront, as one must in reading *Sybil*, an amalgam of Sir Walter Scott's romantic sentimentalism with the reportorial prose of a parliamentary investigating committee taxes the modern literary sensibility, but the mixture suits Disraeli's political strategy. I shall confine myself here to the barest outline of the novel's double movement, ignoring its descriptive riches.

The story opens with a portrayal of idle, bored, irresponsible young aristocrats at a racing club—a picture designed to arouse the reader's outrage at the wealthy ruling class, the first of the two nations. Charles Egremont, the hero, is one of these drifters without aim—a descendant of a wily domestic in the entourage of Henry VIII who had founded the family fortune by despoiling Marney Abbey. The present Lord Marney, relating to his brother Charles like Cain to Abel, is a brutally self-interested landlord, a disciple of Helvetius—"arrogant, literal, hard." His suffering tenants and dispossessed yeomen are being pushed to rick-burning and other acts of desperation.

The second nation, that of the poor, we encounter first not, like the corrupt aristocracy, in its worst representatives, but through its finest types, in the Gerard family. They are wise, simple, virtuous Catholics, bearers of the great tradition of the good old England of the Middle Ages. Charles Egremont encounters them in the ruins of Marney Abbey, described in Puginian terms. Walter Gerard is of yeoman stock. He expounds—in terms which Coleridge too might have used—the virtues of the solicitous rule of the monastics. "They made the country beautiful, and the people proud of their country. . . ."[10] The poor are thus identified with the ancient faith, and with community, as opposed to modern social "aggregation." At twilight, from the starlit arch of the rose-grey ruins of the Abbey, emerges Gerard's daughter Sybil. Like "the fair phantom of some saint haunting the sacred ruins of the desecrated fain,"[11] Sybil incarnates the spirit of medieval idealty. Egremont is smitten, partly by the truth of the medieval social message, partly by the beauteous virtue of the messenger. Thus the cottage and the convent begin the education of the scion of corrupted modern aristocracy.

The weak, idealized female begins to inspire the male to use power responsibly. The social structure, however, intervenes to slow the progress of the courtship of ideality and power. Disraeli intrudes a third crucial factor in the struggle for harmony between rich and poor: mobile capital and its works, (Coleridge's forces of "progression,") as embodied in the raw industrial city of Mowbray. This disrupts the potential alliance between the two forces of the "permanence," the landlord and the yeoman. The city of Mowbray and the nearby mining and artisan metalworking communities produce an aggressive and rebellious poor, the Chartists. With these the yeomen Gerards, Sybil and her father Walter, become sympathetically associated.

The indifference of the rich produces the rebellion of the poor. But as the novel proceeds, Disraeli shifts the correlation between evil and class from the rulers to the ruled. Charles Egremont learns compassion and the virtues of Christian service from Sybil, but Sybil's hatred of ruling-class injustice blinds her to the animal aggression of the workers. Slowly, painfully, she learns from Charles's helpfulness to her imprisoned father that, in the words of Gilbert and Sullivan, "hearts just as pure and fair may beat in Belgrave Square as in the lowly air of Seven Dials." Slowly, painfully, Sybil, the saintly seraph from the past, also learns about the structure of social reality and modern working-class brutality. The dynamic of social struggle reverses the reader's initial perceptions and compels a transfer of sympathy from the oppressed worker to the embattled, physically threatened propertied class—as Sybil has to do.

At the novel's end, Disraeli embeds in both tracks of his plot, the social one and the bildungsroman, the historical outcome of medieval revival. The social action culminates in a revolt of the masses at Mowbray. The workers slip out of the control of Stephen Morley and the moderate Chartists. Running amok, a drunken, violent mob storms and burns Mowbray Castle, the seat of the aristocrats of industrial wealth and mobile capital. In vain does gentle, Christian Sybil exhort the wild workers to desist. They are as deaf to her pleas as the ruling classes were to the workers' plight. In this *lutte finale*, the fate of the Gerards, father and daughter, presages the end of the autonomous medieval social creed they so ideally represented in their lives and character. Father Gerard, the finest leader of the Mowbray Chartists, is shot by Lord Marney, the worst leader of the forces of property. Sybil, who tries in vain to exercise her spiritual power to tame the raging workers, has to be rescued by

Charles. Thus the mediating role of the characters who best embody medieval values for Disraeli ends in either death or dependence.

The end of the bildungsroman and the love story confirms the social result—and more. Lord Marney, Charles's older brother and the most ruthless of the rich, is stoned to death by the mob. His slaying paves the way for his brother Charles, educated now to social responsibility by Sybil, to inherit the family title, wealth, and power. Meanwhile, by one of those wonderful trick endings beloved of Victorian novelists, Sybil is revealed to be the true heir of the land and titles that the Mowbrays had usurped and had used to build their industry-based fortune. Thus our spiritually rich poor girl is miraculously metamorphosed into a plutocrat of the blood. Thus too the marriage of Sybil and Charles symbolizes not, as one had been led to expect throughout the novel, the marriage of the Two Nations, Rich and Poor, but the wedding of two kinds of capital, landed and industrial, the basis of what is classically known as the Victorian Compromise. Of course the marriage also represents the integration of power with spirit. Charles has learned public virtue from Sybil's example; she has come to understand political reality from Charles's.

Is this the end of medievalizing ideology? Disraeli the politician might have said "No," for he might have envisaged the spread of the creed of medieval paternalism on a broad front among the ruling classes. But Disraeli the writer presents a more pessimistic perspective. The action ends in successful repression and the restoration of threatened property. Order is restored, and with it the split between the Two Nations is ratified. Charles, the new Lord Marney, has taken to wife the saintly Sybil as a conscience to temper harsh reality, but she serves only to adorn Charles's power with the cloak of medieval spirituality, rather as—to the disgust of medievalizers like Pugin and Ruskin—medieval forms were used to screen Victorian railway stations.

Though Charles's heart is in the right place, he has no idea how to tackle the condition of England question. Indeed, the one practical proposal for the relief of class conflict in the novel is the model factory of a Catholic paternalistic employer Disraeli describes the plan of the factory complex. The chic factory building is Gothic in architectural style, with lofty groined arches in the workroom. But to the extent that its spatial layout places the employer's house in the center, the vantage point for surveillance of the hive, Disraeli's ideal "medieval" factory conforms rather to the design of utilitarian Jeremy Bentham's panopticon, and would confirm Foucault more readily than Pugin.

Disraeli, more deliberately than Coleridge and Pugin, tried to absorb the medieval ideal into the world of modern social reality. He used the idea of the medieval paradise lost to devastating critical effect, precisely because his capacity to see and record the complex chaotic society of England in the 1840s was so honest and so strong. But because he accepted the primacy of modern social power in ways that the more romantic Coleridge and Pugin could not, he deflated the medieval ideal to a rhetorical adornment of the rule of property. In so doing, he exposed the revived medieval spirit as truly a ghost, which could contribute to a critique of modernity but could offer no means to change it.

Let me end this paper as it began, with the help of Karl Marx. The founder of Communism once observed that when men produce revolutionary changes, they screen themselves from their own frightening innovations by dressing themselves in the cultural clothing of a past to be restored. That, perhaps, is what, in their comprehensive projection of medieval culture as a norm, our three authors were engaged in. Marx illustrated his point with the English Revolution of the seventeenth century, in which the revolutionaries identified themselves with the angry ethics of the Hebrew prophets. But when the Restoration came, when "the real aim . . . of bourgeois transformation of English society had been accomplished," the gains were consolidated on a frankly empirical philosophic base. The Old Testament spirits were dispelled. In Marx's words, "Locke supplanted Habakkuk."[12]

All our three characters had modern aims as they did their thinking with medieval history to redeem England—Coleridge as theorist of a new autonomous role for the intellectual class, Pugin as functional spatial designer, Disraeli as pioneering ideologist of Tory democracy. But only Disraeli, as a tough, realistic writer and as political actor, exposed the medieval culture critique as in the end a ghost, even as he tried to harness it to serve his modern purposes of raising the public consciousness of the aristocracy as a reforming ruling class.

NOTES

1. Samuel Taylor Coleridge, *On the Constitution of the Church and State according to the Idea of Each* in Professor (N. N.) Shedd, ed., *The Complete Works of Samuel Taylor Coleridge*, 7 vols. (New York, 1853), 6:76.

2. Ibid., 51.

3. Ibid., 64–67.

4. A second edition, with additional plates contrasting the state of towns in medieval and modern times, was published in 1841. It was reissued in facsimile in

1969 by the Humanities Press (New York) and Leicester University Press, with an introduction by Henry Russell Hitchcock.

5. Augustus Welby Pugin, *An Apology for the Revival of Christian Architecture* (London, 1843), 51.

6. A. Welby Pugin, *The True Principles of Pointed or Christian Architecture* (London, 1853), 35–36, 43–46.

7. Ibid., 2.

8. Ibid., 4.

9. Ibid., 22.

10. Benjamin Disraeli, *Sybil: or The Two Nations*, Oxford World Classics (London, 1939), 64.

11. Ibid., 65, 68

12. Karl Marx, *The Eighteenth Brumaire of Louis Bonaparte*, in Karl Marx, *Selected Writings*, edited by David McLellan (Oxford, 1977), 301.

SIX

The Quest for the Grail:
Wagner and Morris

IS IT JUSTIFIED to yoke together two artists so different as Richard Wagner and William Morris? By what warrant shall one compare a musician with a designer and craftsman, a German nationalist with an English socialist, a child of the age of Metternich with a son of the Victorian era twenty-one years his junior? All these incomparabilities make an effort at reciprocal illumination suspect. Yet history often reveals patterns in seemingly disparate phenomena. Although Wagner and Morris were indifferent to each other's work and even to each other's existence, they were joined by many ties. Both became artists in an era when art was changing its function in European culture; when, no longer expressing the dominant values of society, art began to advance its own values, sometimes in the guise of a vanished past, sometimes in the garb of a hoped-for future. Both Wagner and Morris quested for the future in the relics of the past. Both thought with history about their function as artists in their times.

There was scarcely a fund of tradition drawn upon by Wagner as poet-musician that his younger contemporary did not also appropriate as poet-designer. Arthurian legend, Minnesang, Norse or Germanic myth, and—more concretely historical—the medieval artisan ideal: both men exploited all of these in confronting the problems of modernity. Although children of the so-called Age of Realism, they scrupulously avoided contemporary materials as subject of their art. Revolutionaries in aesthetic expression, they were conservatives in their search for spiritual anchorage. Wagner and Morris rang their German and English variations on a common theme of nineteenth-century culture: disenchantment with modern civilization. Each sought for a vision by which the ills of his age might be cured.

In their quest for that vision, these two romantics traveled the same road in reverse directions. Wagner and Morris began their intellectual journeys at what seem like opposite ends of the road, crossed in a dead center of historical despair, and continued to the starting point of the other voyager. To trace that course may perhaps reveal a few of the hidden threads which bind together art and social change in the dense texture of nineteenth-century life.

⟋⟍

WILLIAM MORRIS (1834–1896) began his intellectual career where Wagner was to end: infatuated with medieval Christianity. When Morris went up to Oxford in 1853, the Catholicizing tendencies of the Oxford Movement had just reached their height. Swept out of what he called the "rich establishmentarian Puritanism" of his family by a newfound friend, Edward Burne-Jones, Morris developed a passion for medieval Christendom. An aspirant to Anglican Holy Orders, Morris avidly read the new Oxford theology, and in 1854 almost took the fashionable and fateful step to Rome. He joined the Plain Song Society, devoured medieval history, and became engrossed in medieval art. Culture soon began to speak more strongly than Faith. Ruskin's *Stones of Venice*, demonstrating the superiority of free Gothic work-forms over the tyranny of ancient and modern rational design, provided a theoretical basis for the late romantic medievalism of Morris and his friends.

Morris's group, which, in college style, had begun informally and was known as "the set," reorganized itself more earnestly as "the Brotherhood." The members, most of whom were destined for the clergy, pledged themselves to celibacy and the conventual life. The religious bond among them, however, was ambiguous. They loved the holy more because it was beautiful than because it was true. They saw the ills of the world not in the Christian fashion as the perduring consequence of sin, but as the special product of modern history, the result of commercial civilization. Most of the Brotherhood were sons of industrial Birmingham (Morris himself was the child of a well-to-do London businessman), and as such perhaps in the quite usual revolt against their utilitarian parents. Whatever their motives, the brothers launched what Burne-Jones called "a crusade and holy warfare against the age." The knights of the grail offered them a peculiarly appealing model, combining religious idealism and aestheticism, aristocratic style and romantic service. Burne-Jones advised Morris to learn "Sir Galahad"—presumably Tennyson's—by heart, "as he is to be the patron of our order."[1]

In his writings, young Morris idealized the Middle Ages as a romantic refuge for the starved modern imagination. G. B. Shaw, a devoted admirer of Morris, was always uneasy about his literary archaism. Shaw characterized Morris's energetic and lifelong medieval story writing as an attempt to restore Don Quixote's burnt library. There was justice in the charge. Morris and the Pre-Raphaelites despised Cervantes as "an abominable Philistine" who destroyed medieval romance by creating Don Quixote, "an insult to beauty and chivalry."[2] Morris's writing, however, reflects only the romantic and less original part of his quest.

More fruitfully, Morris interpreted medievalism as committing him to rejuvenate the modern environment by reviving craft culture. A kind of aesthetic Luddite, he directed his "holy warfare" against the factory and its products, against the whole wretched environment of industrial England. He set out to restore what he saw as the medieval unity between artist and artisan, art and craft, beauty and utility. On leaving college, he first studied architecture, then turned, under Rossetti's influence, to painting, and finally to an incredible range of handicrafts—house furnishings, wallpapers, textiles, and the like—to restore imaginative handiwork. Through the revival of crafts Morris hoped to restore both joy to the worker and beauty to the scene of modern life. With prodigious energy, Morris instructed himself in the decorative crafts. Like Diderot when he worked on the great dictionary of arts and crafts for his Encyclopedia a century before, Morris went to the workroom as well as to the library to learn the skills he sought. Where Diderot looked for the most modern mechanized techniques that he might spread them, Morris pursued the dying craft arts that he might save them. Diderot fought for an economically liberating technology against an inhibiting ancient way of work; Morris, for a psychologically gratifying ancient way against an enslaving new technology. Both were equally zealous learners of the crafts that would redeem.

From religion to the romantic-aesthetic brotherhood, then on to the workshop: so Morris's journey ran. With some of his friends, Morris in 1859 built a model home for himself, the Red House on Bexley Heath. His first and last *Gesamtkunstwerk* (total work of art), Morris embodied in it his medieval ideal of a unified, simple house, posited against what he called "the age of makeshift" and the eclectic Victorian home. The architect Philip Webb planned the building on simple, spacious lines, and assisted Morris in designing the furniture, from cabinets to candlesticks. Burne-Jones, Ford Maddox Brown, and Rossetti painted walls and cupboards with illustrations from classical and medieval romance, while the ladies of their circle embroidered tapestries. Though medieval in aspiration, the Red House was modern in conception: a bold precursor of unified design—from floor plan to ashtray in a single, almost tyrannically harmonious conception of the house beautiful.

In 1861, Morris established the Firm, a partnership to produce craft products on a paying basis. For two decades, the Firm's products sold well, and influenced the taste of the well-to-do.[3] But Morris drew decreasing psychological satisfaction from this sort of success. For every Morris chair or tapestry sold, England was stained by another jerry-built housing development. The fair vision of the grail, of an England redeemed by revived crafts, seemed incommunicable. Like Don Quixote's windmill, the factory was too strong. Morris fell into personal depression and social pessimism.

"Dreamer of dreams, born out of my due time, why should I strive to set the crooked straight?"[4] In this mood, Morris took refuge in poetic fantasy. In the late sixties, he produced a collection of tales entitled *The Earthly Paradise*. The collection expressed, as his perceptive daughter observed, "the melancholy of an unquiet mind, standing on the verge of some infinitude, waiting and listening."[5] The tales are far removed from reality. Ifor Evans has described well the author's approach to capturing the remote quality of the life of fantasy: "He himself dreams that a group of men set out for a distant dreamland, and then within that scheme they tell tales to each other, many of them dreams, some dreams within dreams."[6]

Among the tales that Morris tells is *The Hill of Venus*. It is the same story that Wagner set to music in *Tannhäuser*, celebrating the triumph of profane love over the consciousness of sin.

Most of *The Earthly Paradise*, however, is dominated by a more somber mood, one reflected in a line which came to epitomize Morris in the Victorian mind, "the idle singer of an empty day." The usually vital Morris here came uncommonly close to Baudelaire's ennui, or to Wagner's musical rendering of Schopenhauer's deathly metaphysical dream-reality in *Tristan und Isolde*. By the end of the 1860s, the holy crusader against the ugliness of his age seemed to be seeking refuge in art rather than in transforming his world by means of it.

੬⊬

Wagner's development in the equivalent part of his career ran a different course but terminated in a similarly airless dead center of ontic malaise.

Born in 1813, two decades before Morris, Wagner grew up in a society whose problem was not the utilitarian ethos and industrial ugliness but personal liberty; his target accordingly was not the factory, but the state. Though Wagner and Morris built their heavens out of much the same materials, they had quite different hells.

Wagner began as a late-born child of the Sturm und Drang, the Promethean flamboyance of which had psychological relevance in the stillness of Metternich's Germany. The young musician's enemies were the traditional ones of the creative German intellectual: the philistines of his own burgher class and the rationalistic, absolute state. These two enemies joined in upholding convention, and convention was what the young Wagner attacked on every front. He fought it in music and in literature, in politics and in love. Because he saw convention as having in Reason its strongest ally, Wagner became the lifelong enemy of Reason. Accordingly, he began his revolt not, like Morris, for the beautification of life, but for the liberation of instinct; not as a medievalizing Romantic conservative, but as a semi-Bohemian revolutionary. In one of his earliest operas, *Das Liebesverbot*, Wagner celebrated the rehabilitation of the flesh in a vindication of "unrestrained sensuality" against "puritanical hypocrisy." Shakespeare's *Measure for Measure* gave Wagner his plot; but he altered it to allow the victory of love over law to be accomplished by a revolution rather than by a princely judgment.[7] In *Rienzi*, he glorified the Renaissance tribune of the people as a Promethean democrat and revolutionary hero.

In *Lohengrin* (1845), Wagner brought together three themes that dominated his early concerns: sexual fulfillment, folk freedom, and the redeeming hero. Lohengrin, son of Parsifal the grail-knight, is the artist as self-conscious redeemer. He *has* the grail and its vision; his quest is for fulfillment through serving others and being loved. It is politics that makes this possible: corruption in the court of Brabant results in injustice to Elsa, the embodiment of womanhood. "Elsa," Wagner tells us, "is the unconscious, the unvolitional, in which Lohengrin's conscious, volitional being yearns to redeem itself." As woman, she is "the *un*conscious, *un*volitional in Lohengrin"; but, as princess, she is a political victim. "Elsa the Woman," Wagner says, "made me a full-fledged revolutionary. She was the spirit of the folk, in whom I too, as artistic human being, was yearning for my redemption."[8]

What shall we make of this astonishing identification of the female and the folk? Both were the inactive element, the victims, and at the same time potential receivers of the seed. The folk, like the woman, had healthy instinct and the capacity to become ennobled, but lacked conscious will. The folk, like the woman, was passive, held in thrall by the political order, awaiting a redeemer. Lohengrin is that redeemer, but he can accomplish his work only on his own terms: that he be unconditionally loved, like a child, regardless of his origins or attributes. Neither the woman nor the folk are ready to accept the artist knight of the grail. The redeeming mission of the artist in society fails; he is the frustrated victim of incomprehension. But Wagner tells us that, through writing the tragedy, he shifted his own identification from the rejected Lohengrin to the fallible but unfulfilled Elsa-folk.[9] The self-pitying male egoist found the link between eros and society.

Wagner's early years, in pre-1848 Germany, allowed him to relate the fate of art to folk-revolution in ways not possible for an Englishman in the mid-century. Intellectually advanced but socially retarded, Germany had no concrete mass movements of the lower classes before the Revolution of 1848. Hence the as-yet-unconscious masses—for Wagner no less than for Marx—could be assigned universal historical tasks and characters without reference to their sleepy present. The lack of dynamic popular reality allowed the fantasy of the radical intelligentsia full sway. For Wagner, this meant that the folk would provide the social material to realize the artist's dreams of a restoration of "wholeness" to man. In mid-century England, on the other hand, the working classes had already acquired a sufficient clarity of definition and consciousness of aim to be something more than the stuff that dreams are made on. Trade unionism and Chartism appeared on the stage even before Morris went to school. In the 1870s and 1880s, when Morris sought to relate his art to politics, he both could and necessarily had to reckon with social forces already formed and organized. While English conditions imposed narrower limits on the political imagination than did German ones, they also gave Morris a social base for the active realization of his values. And in his early years, the more homogeneous social climate among intellectuals in England gave Morris a Brotherhood in his crusade. Young Wagner as redeeming grail-knight, like so many intellectuals in his fragmented country, wandered and served alone.

Still committed to a heroic concept of individuality, Wagner was swept up in the rising tide of democratic nationalism in the late 1840s. His most important ideas on the nature of drama and its relation to society took shape during the Revolution of 1848. Wagner welcomed the revolution with the most naive confidence that a new and happier world would spring from it. Falling under the influence of Feuerbach, Wagner turned from the grail to the Greeks to find the right relationship between art and society. Like Schiller and Hegel, Hölderlin and Marx, Wagner saw the Greek polis as an historical archetype of community, a lost paradise to be regained. Greek drama expressed the oneness, the wholeness of that community: "[T]he drama was the sum and substance of all that could be expressed in the Greek nature; it was—in intimate connection with its history—the nation that stood facing itself in the art-work, that became conscious of itself."[10] The Greek polis and Greek drama rose and fell together. When the polis fell, the drama fragmented into the many arts which had composed it: music, poetry, dance, and the visual arts. These all then acquired their separate existence, just as the individuals in an atomized polis did. Wagner set himself the task of reviving holistic drama, which was part of the larger task of making a community out of coldly rationalistic modern society. That is the origin of his Gesamtkunstwerk, less simple and far more pretentious than Morris's archaizing house beautiful.

Greek drama, in Wagner's view, was conservative because it reflected the community and its experience of life. Modern art must be revolutionary: it must present in ideal form a unified community which does not exist in broken modern society. Drama in Greece reflected community; drama today can only live in opposition to society. It must *create* community by serving as model for it. Only "the great revolution" can restore the unified art-work as a mirror of society. Both art and politics must strive for the same end: "the strong and beautiful man, to whom revolution shall give his strength and art his beauty."[11]

What Morris aimed at only in his last, socialist years, Wagner proposed in 1848: to link the political future of mankind and the future of art in indissoluble union. The drama was the only possible model to make of enslaved mankind a community of artists. Morris's crafts could be practiced in the here and now, insinuated into present-day society. Wagner's ideal drama could only live in constant contradiction with contemporary social reality. Drama must be an art of the future; with the disordered present, it could only live in tension. It would have to cut through the external realities of an age of false authority and materialism to the suppressed folk, to the buried communal consciousness, the spirit of the people.

In the pursuit of this subliminal folk-soul, Wagner was drawn to German myth, and especially to the *Nibelungenlied*. Shaw, who admired Wagner as much as he did Morris, interpreted the Ring operas simply as an allegory of revolutionary radicalism. Siegfried, said Shaw, is Wagner's friend Bakunin.[12] If this interpretation is too pat, certainly Shaw's larger, central thesis about Wagner's view holds firm: that the ancient myth pointed an accusing finger at the materialistic and hypocritical order of present-day society. In the person of a vital, young, and innocent folk-hero from the past, Wagner celebrated a German *renovatio* in the future.

The defeat of 1849 left Wagner profoundly disillusioned. He re-worked his *Nibelungen* materials in more pessimistic directions. He re-placed the heroic optimism of the early version of the Ring with an ending in doom and gloom. The Gesamtkunstwerk lost its paradigmatic and specifically social character. Wagner's later works relate less to his-torical possibility than to passional necessity. He shifted from history to metaphysics. From other defeated exiles, Wagner discovered Schopen-hauer, who sealed the development in him which, as he was himself aware, the revolution manqué had prepared.[13] Wagner transformed the metaphysical conception of Schopenhauer's Will—blind cosmic en-ergy—into a psychological one: compulsive instinct. *Tristan und Isolde* was conceived in this mood of postpolitical ontic despair, in which only the claims of libido have life. The communal eros has become confined to the personal, sexual. One can feel the birth of depth psychology out of the spirit of frustrated liberal idealism. In *Tristan*, music drama be-comes a theater of the psyche.[14] Id and ego, eros and reality are in hostile array. The state appears not as unjust or corrupt, as in *Lohengrin* or *Siegfried*, but as a symbol of eternal social restraint upon our emo-tional life. Fulfillment lies not in regeneration, but in death. The whole drama is a farewell to time and space, and thus to history. Nietzsche's phrase, "Und alle Lust will Ewigkeit" (And all desire wishes eternity), suits *Tristan und Isolde* well. In no work of art is the organized world of reality so drastically contraposed to the world of wish and of dream, of instinct and of love. The linkage of instinct and folk, so strong in *Lohengrin* and *Siegfried*, has disappeared without a trace. Psyche and society are in hopeless disjuncture, in absolute opposition.

Tristan und Isolde is one of the most sophisticated works of European art, and it is perhaps not right to relate it to Morris's rather simple *Earthly Paradise*. Yet the moods of the two are strikingly similar. Wagner's disillusion with politics and Morris's disappointment with the results of his aesthetic crusade had produced similar states of mind in both men. Morris's description of his own intention is like the plight of Tristan and Isolde in the realm of King Mark:

> . . . Pardon me
> Who strive to build a shadowy isle of bliss
> Midmost the beating of the steely sea.[15]

The heavy feeling of doom, the sweet scent of death, the dreamy quality of life, the affirmation of night from which Morris's lovers, like Wagner's, wake "from delight unto the real day void and white";[16] above all, the total abandonment of the historical world as a field of action: these join the German composer of metaphysical despair with England's idle singer of an empty day. This was their common *mezzo del camin'*.

❧

NORSE mythology served Wagner as the vehicle for his most massive commitment as artist to the revitalization of political and cultural life in 1848. Under the impact of defeat, his modification of the *Ring*'s libretto in the direction of political pessimism marked Wagner's transition from social politics to psychological metaphysics. In William Morris's intellectual development, Norse mythology played just the opposite part: instead of the last stage before the plunge into despair, it was the first step out of defeat and world-weariness.

In 1868, Morris took up the Icelandic language, and became enamored of Norse sagas. Henceforth he devoted years to translating and reworking them. Even more than Wagner, Morris found in Old Norse life the model of community existence. Here was a culture that had learned to face poverty and adversity with directness, courage, and good-humored acceptance. And the ancient heroism still survived! Visiting modern Iceland, Morris found it still undistorted by the crippling machine, by ugliness and slums. The Icelanders faced grinding poverty, but, said Morris, that "is a trifling evil compared to inequality of classes."[17]

There was no "aristocracy" here. Even kings in the Norse sagas shared the common life, making sails and working in the fields. Morris's enthusiasm knew no bounds: "glorious simplicity of the terrible and tragic. . . ." "Delightful freshness and independence of thought of them, the air of freedom which breathes through them, their worship of courage (the great virtue of the human race), their utter unconventionality took my heart by storm."[18]

The discovery of community, of collective, heroic folk strength smoothed the transition for Morris, as Shaw observed, from "the facile troubadour of love and beauty into the minstrel of strife and guile, of battle, murder and death."[19] There was a contemporary ingredient too. Like Wagner, Morris moved the problem of gold and greed into the center of *Sigurd the Volsung*, his version of the Siegfried saga. Iceland, ancient and modern, had shown him the value of collective struggle over the aesthetic isolation of the Brotherhood and the Firm. The erstwhile knight-errant of "the holy, the beautiful and the true" thus girded himself for the active life of democratic working-class politics.

As Morris passed from his metaphysical despair into Wagner's world of myth and politics, Wagner for his part was passing back over Morris's earlier course. In *Die Meistersinger von Nüremberg* (completed in 1867) Wagner returned to history once more, seeking relief from the pain of life so sorely felt in *Tristan*. The model was neither chivalric nor heroic now, but medieval burgher. Like Morris in the period of the Firm, Wagner was drawn to the medieval commune, where social, economic, and artistic life were one. This model allowed Wagner a new form of archaizing critique of the modern world. But again, as in *Lohengrin*, the misunderstood artist is at the center of the world. Wagner's old enemy, convention, appeared once more in *Die Meistersinger*, in the character of Beckmesser, who represented the classical, contrapuntal tradition in music. The opera also conjoined historical nostalgia with a new brutality against the establishment in scenes of brawling apprentices and the "healthy" mauling of Beckmesser. Small wonder that this was Hitler's favorite opera!

If Wagner, like Morris, extolled the medieval guild, he embraced it for different reasons. Morris's crusade was for creative work, Wagner's for the artist's right to social recognition for his personal genius. Morris's medieval heroes of art were, like Ruskin's, anonymous workers. In *Die Meistersinger*, the hero is the artist as *Führer* of the artisan; Wagner honors the guildsmen only because they recognized that German art must be an élite, personal expression, and *not* merely a social craft. For Wagner the gap between art and the common life was widening as for Morris it was narrowing.

~

IN HIS final phase, Morris went out into the modern social arena. Wagner turned inward to explore the modern soul. Both remained the dreamers their romantic heritage had made of them. But as each in his late years assumed something of the youthful concerns of the other, he illuminated those concerns in a new and modern light. Wagner in his last decade reached the point where Morris had begun his quest: the redemption of the world through art, as expressed quasi-religiously in the legends of the grail. In the late 1870s Morris finally arrived at Wagner's conviction of the 1840s: that art could be regenerated only by revolution. Each artist found an appropriate institution to project his final vision. What the Bayreuth Festival was to Wagner, the Hammersmith Socialist Society was to Morris: a center for a brotherhood of redeemers.

Since his first years of exile after 1848, Wagner had projected a theater for the German people, through which it could become conscious of its own essential nature. As the project grew, he came to think of it, as he said, as "an art-Washington," "something absolutely new," deliberately remote from the workaday cities and the corruption of materialistic German culture. Finally, in 1876, the Bayreuth summer opera house was opened. Here Wagner's great dramas, mirrors of the German spirit, would restore wholeness to divided modern man. Here the magic of art would weld together a mythical, archetypal community that allowed the audience of votaries to escape, as Wagner said, "this world of lying, fraud, hypocrisy and legalized murder," "the toil and trouble of life, for the sake of its loftiest ends."[20]

Like the customers of the craft products of Morris's Firm, those of Bayreuth were too often wealthy followers of fashion rather than true believers. At the opening of the opera house in 1876, Nietzsche recoiled in disgust at the well-to-do middle-brows who composed the audience: "The whole idle rabble of Europe had been brought together.... I recognized nothing any more . . . not even Wagner."[21] Wagner became high priest of a cult. His patron, Ludwig II of Bavaria, hailed him as such in fitting language at the opening of the first festival: "an artist by the grace of God, who came into this world to purify, bless and redeem it."[22] Wagner himself accepted the assignment.

He provided not the restoration of "wholeness" to all classes of society that he had aimed at in his early years, but a theatrical psychotherapy for the cultivated operagoer. Bayreuth became not the model of a new society, a restored Greek theater, but the center of a new cult. As in Morris's early Oxford Brotherhood, art was the center of the faith, rather than faith the center of the art. Wagner the artist offered a communal rite to remove the votary from the pressures of space and time, from the pain and corruption of modern life.

Beyond all that is thinkable as concept, the tone-poet seer reveals the inexpressible to us: we [dimly] sense, yes, we feel and see that even this seemingly inescapable world of Will is only a [transient] condition, disappearing before the one [truth]: "I know that my redeemer liveth."[23]

In "the knowledge of the decadence of the human race," we purify ourselves and restore our innocence by "submerging ourselves in the element of . . . symphonic revelation which can count as a consecrated, purifying religious act."[24]

As once the Greeks had developed community drama out of religious ritual, so at Bayreuth Wagner developed a quasi-religious community out of theatrical ritual. Even the strongest myths he used—those of Siegfried and Parsifal—did not incorporate a belief held by the society. They only posed suggestively a truth of wholeness which modern man could accept as aspiration but not embrace as creed. Wagner's art could no more posit a surrogate religion than it could earlier create a new community. All the depth-psychological shock tactics of modern musical stagecraft could not transcend the limits of virtuality to which art is by its nature condemned. The grail in the theater could enchant and bewitch but it could not redeem.

Wagner's last glorious achievement, *Parsifal*, is redolent with the pseudoreligiosity of Bayreuth, but it far transcends it. Nietzsche truly missed the mark when he cried out in anger, "What you hear is Rome: Rome's faith without words!"[25] What in fact you hear is the opposite: Rome's words without faith. *Parsifal* illuminates modern man neither through social message nor religious faith, but through a musical statement of depth psychology. Parsifal, the innocent fool, redeems the guilty world by discovering his Oedipal self.

The political world is completely absent from *Parsifal*—for the first time in any Wagner opera. In all his previous works, Wagner rendered the ordered world of the state in a specific musical idiom. In *Tristan* its character is especially sharply drawn: a diatonic world of space, a marked and metrical world of time. Against the strong grid of this harmonic, tonal, regular day-world, the lovers' life of passion plays, chromatic and almost keyless, surging and rhythmic. *Tristan* dramatizes a battle between personal, instinctual wish and social, rational reality. Within Tristan and Isolde, the struggle eventuates in a total victory of id over ego, even unto death. Conscience, super-ego, plays almost no role. In *Parsifal*, by contrast, there is no political state; in fact no outer reality at all, i.e., no world of ego; the only society is the mystical Brotherhood of the Grail. The dualities in *Parsifal* are not Wagner's earlier ones: heart and reason, freedom and slavery, love and social greed, love and the state, id and ego. His dramatic tension is now both more archaic and more modern: in religious terms, which dominate the text, between guilt and redemption; in Freudian terms—and these dominate the music—between super-ego and id. The social scene of action has been narrowed to a brotherhood whose members are spiritually sick and psychologically paralyzed. The drama has no external action, only internal transfiguration. Even the scenery dissolves the coordinates of spatial reality. In dreamlike transmutations deserts become gardens, a scenic analogue of transubstantiation, the mystery of the grail.

The drama of Parsifal is not a religious exploration but a depth-psychological one. It centers upon the ambiguous relationship of love as sexual drive and love as social conscience. The technique of the seductress, Kundry, is to exploit mother-love, the Oedipal vulnerabilities of Parsifal, to undermine the childish innocence of her victim. In some of the sweetest yet most penetratingly sickish music ever written—*luxe, calme et volupté*, Wagner's admirer Baudelaire might have called it—the temptress almost ensnares Parsifal by identifying herself dreamlike with his mother. Asking Parsifal to think of his father, she implants her nearly fateful kiss as "the last greeting of maternal blessing: love's first kiss." In resisting the Oedipal crime, Parsifal's sexual temptation becomes transfigured into diffused libido, socially redemptive rather than instinctually gratifying. The ecstasy of sex and the ecstasy of religious passion are shown to be convertible; the magic of art works the transformation.

In the deep psychological world of *Parsifal*, there are virtually no deeds. History is left off the stage; only psychic states have life, in shifting planes of memory and hope. Leaden music represents the guilt-sick present and its cure lies in regression. One goes forward only by going back: historical regression into the medieval past for the ideal of redeeming service; psychological regression into pre-Oedipal innocence for the strength to purify the fallen brotherhood with a diffuse and oceanic sense of love. Wagner-Parsifal becomes the psycho-therapeutic artist-redeemer. No wonder Thomas Mann's and Freud's contemporaries worshiped at Wagner's shrine. No wonder that, despite the cult of Bayreuth, they stood in awe of him, both for his insight into the modern condition of moral pessimism and psychological introversion, and for his powers in translating the ancient arts of religious redeemers into the modern religion of aesthetic redemption.

THE end of Morris is more simply told. The young religious aesthete became an old revolutionary—just the reverse of Wagner. Morris spent his last decade as *spiritus rector* of the Hammersmith Socialist Society. He turned over the large weaving room of his Hammersmith house as a meeting hall for the society. After the meetings on Sunday night, Morris entertained the votaries of the new religion of Marxian socialism. Burly workers would join young intellectuals such as Yeats or Shaw for a supper at the broad bare oaken table of the great designer. Agitation became the center of the old man's life.

Did Morris's dream of medieval beauty evaporate in the strenuous years of socialist struggle? For the answer one need only read his utopian novel, *News from Nowhere* (1890). Here again is the "dreamer of dreams, born out of my due time." Morris fills out the socialist future with that romanticized picture of the Middle Ages so characteristic of the era of his youth. He imagines future London, the London of 1962: a congeries of small villages again. Factories are no more. There is salmon running in the Thames, and men spend their time in the creative play of happy artisans. The Houses of Parliament are a dung market, their erstwhile powers taken over by local motes. The costumes are fourteenth-century and charming; the language of the good folk is Morris's own neo-Chaucerian. Above all, socialist England is a community—a community such as Morris discovered in Norse mythology, but gentler; a community such as the early Wagner loved to dream of, but more playful; a community such as England's postwar new-town planners, children of Morris, hope to create to redeem industrial civilization.

Neither Wagner nor Morris succeeded in conquering the dragons they had sallied forth to slay: the English factory or the German state. But the visions they had on their Quixotic quest, penetrating visions into the social and psychological needs of nineteenth-century civilization, live into our own day.

NOTES

Valuable assistance and suggestions in the preparation of this essay were provided by my wife, Elizabeth, and Mr. John Rockwell.

1. For Morris's Oxford years, see J. W. Mackail, *The Life of William Morris*, 2 vols. (London, New York, Bombay, 1901), 1:28–66.

2. George Bernard Shaw, "William Morris as I Knew Him," in May Morris, *William Morris, Artist, Writer, Socialist*, 2 vols. (Oxford, 1936), 2:xxviii.

3. The Firm decorated rooms in St. James Palace and a model dining room for the Victoria and Albert Museum.

4. *The Earthly Paradise*, in William Morris, *Collected Works* (London, 1910–1915), 3:1.

5. May Morris, *Morris*, 1:399.

6. B. Ifor Evans, *William Morris and His Poetry* (London, 1925), 97.

7. Richard Wagner, *My Life*, 2 vols. (New York, 1911), 1:101–2; idem, "Eine Mitteilung an meine Freunde," in *Gesammelte Schriften und Dichtungen*, edited by Wolfgang Golther, 10 vols. (Berlin, etc. [1913]), 4:254–55.

8. Wagner, *Gesammelte Schriften*, 4:301–2.

9. Ibid., 302.

10. Quoted in Ernest Newman, *Wagner as Man and Artist* (New York, 1924), 184.

11. Ibid., 183–84.

12. [George] Bernard Shaw, *The Perfect Wagnerite* (Chicago and New York, 1905), 57.

13. Wagner, *My Life*, 2:614–17.

14. See especially Francis Fergusson, *The Idea of a Theater* (Princeton, 1949), chapter 3, "*Tristan und Isolde*: The Action and Theater of Passion," *passim*; Joseph Kerman, *Opera as Drama* (New York, 1959), 192–216.

15. Morris, *Works*, 3:2. For the best analysis of Morris's "poetry of despair," see E. P. Thompson, *William Morris* (New York, 1961), 140–62.

16. Thompson, *William Morris*, 156. In *Tristan und Isolde*, the persistent problem of the lovers is to banish the day-world. Act II, where they succeed in this, is a night-act; Act III opens with the victory of day: a shepherd's plaintive song; a hot, still air; an empty sea; an atmosphere heavy with foreboding.

17. Ibid., 222.

18. Ibid., 219–20.

19. Shaw, in May Morris, *Morris*, 2:xxxvii.

20. P. A. Loos, *Richard Wagner* (Bern, 1952), 487–88; Ernest Newman, *Life of Richard Wagner*, 4 vols. (New York, 1933–1946), 4:705, 101.

21. Quoted in Loos, *Wagner*, 489.

22. Newman, *Life*, 4:482.

23. Wagner, *Gesammelte Schriften*, 10:250–51.

24. Ibid., 250.

25. Loos, *Wagner*, 205.

SEVEN

Museum in Contested Space:
The Sword, the Scepter,
and the Ring

AUSTRIA'S CONSTRUCTION of a capital complex within an existing city was surely one of the great achievements of nineteenth-century urban planning and bureaucratic imagination. To modern eyes, Vienna's circular Ringstrasse district, with its splendid monumental buildings of politics and culture and its vast, luxurious apartment blocs, appears as a coherent urban *Gesamtkunstwerk* (total work of art). The many styles of its buildings seem welded into a harmonious unity by the common commitment to monumentality and the agreed symbolic meanings of style in the lexicon of historicism shared by their makers. Even to its builders, the very modernity of the Ring consisted in its syncretic mastery of the diverse historical traditions that preceded it.

Yet what conflict lies concealed and congealed in the buildings of the Ringstrasse! Through much of its development the area was contested space. Many a building in it, and the site it occupies, was the outcome of a struggle among the subgroups that composed the ruling élite in their attempts to shape a swiftly changing Austrian politics. Into the built environment they projected their claims to power and their cultural values. To the phases in that struggle this essay is addressed—not for the first time in my writing,[1] but with a new point of entry and, as a consequence, a new interpretation. The cultural historian Johan Huizinga once observed that historical thinking sometimes resembles a floral bouquet: to add a single flower of another form or color to the bouquet can alter its whole character and impact. Such has been the case for me in reexamining the development of Vienna's capital in the mid-nineteenth century after I discovered, as the new flower in the bouquet, the Kunsthistorisches Museum. In the great complex of the Ringstrasse, the Kunsthistorisches Museum, along with its sister, the Naturhistorisches Museum

across the square, had a certain pride of place, both spatially and symbolically. Spatially linked in the minds of its patrons and designers to the
Hofburg, the museums represented symbolically the extension of the ancient dynastic patrimony of art and science, of a huge cabinet of curi-
osities, from the court to the people of the modernized Empire.

I shall say nothing of the Museum's definition either in content or in
form. My concern here is rather with the assignment of space to it, and
the changes in the organization of buildings around it that gave it a new
meaning and function in socio-political conflict resolution. Through the
Kunsthistorisches Museum, the politics of space itself became aestheticized as the politics of culture became neutralized.

❧

THE premise for the development of the Ringstrasse area as a compact
representative space was, in a way, Austria's backwardness. Into the nineteenth century, Vienna's ancient defense system had survived. Its broad
glacis, separating the inner city from the suburbs, provided a vast belt of
open land on which a new capital area might be built (Figure 7.1).

Well before the Revolution of 1848, the bourgeois city fathers of
Vienna had tried through recourse to the courts to win the right to build
on the glacis to relieve the economic and population pressure on the
inner city. In vain; Emperor Francis I simply forbade the city government from bringing suit. After the Revolution, the situation of those who
wished to expand the city grew even worse. The military establishment,
smarting from its eviction from Vienna by the liberal insurgents in Octo-
ber 1848, became more intransigent than ever about its control of the
glacis. Where its earlier rationale for the defense system was protection
against the foreign foe, the army redefined it now in terms of the protection of the emperor against his rebellious subjects. The army, in the early
1850s the most influential interest group in the emperor's entourage,
closed its grip on the glacis area, drawing new plans for its military employment against urban insurrection. This included the construction of
huge new barracks (1854–1857) and an arsenal (1849–1855), located
near railway stations for swift reenforcement of the capital's garrison.
True, a broad belt boulevard on the glacis—what became the Ringstrasse—was now espoused by the military for the rapid deployment of
troops. Thus the Ringstrasse was motivated in the same way as the bou-
levards of Napoleon III's Paris. But the walls were to remain intact, the
glacis left clear as a field of fire.[2]

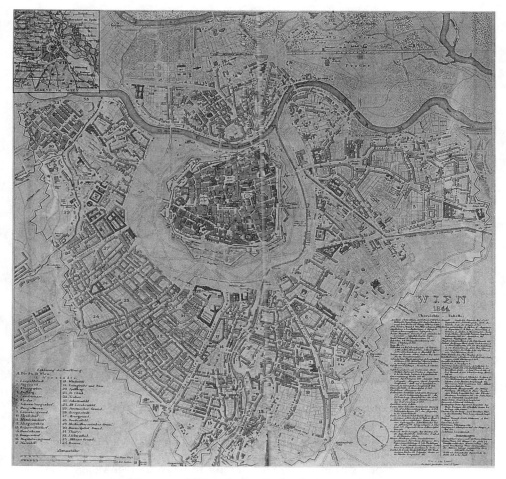

Figure 7.1. Vienna before Redevelopment, 1844.

Important for our concerns, however, was that the military party joined
to its urban building program for defense a cultural one: the projection of
its own image and values through a museum. Beginning in 1856, a *Waffen-
museum* (Museum of Arms—later called *Heeresmuseum*, Military Museum)
was added to the new arsenal. Only the best of architecture could ade-
quately serve the representational purposes of the builders. The army
commissioned Theophil Hansen, whose classicism was soon to make him a
favorite of the liberals, to provide it with a lavish Byzantine romantic
building. Conceived in a triumphalist spirit to celebrate the army as guardian of the Empire, the museum contained a hall of military leaders (Feld-
herrnhalle) with commissioned statues of commanders, and a hall of fame
(Oesterreichische Ruhmeshalle) decorated with painted battle scenes. In
the entrance hall the busts of four modern generals (Haynau, Win-
dischgrätz, Radetzky, and Jelačić) were placed over the grand staircase.
Their common glory consisted in suppressing the Revolutions of 1848.[3]

It was thus under the sway of the sword that there was launched a
postrevolutionary cultural politics through monumental building, soon to
characterize the Ring as a whole, even while the army blocked civilian
claims to use the precious space of the glacis for such purposes. Meanwhile, the emperor added his weight to the public glorification of military virtue with the erection on the Äussere Burgplatz—now the Heldenplatz—of the statues of Archduke Charles, victor over Napoleon at
Aspern, and Prince Eugene.[4]

The other pillar of restored absolutism in the 1850s was, of course, the
Church. Appropriately, the first nonmilitary institution to be built on the
glacis was the Votivkirche. Financed by public subscription to commem-
orate the escape of Emperor Francis Joseph from an assassin's dagger in
1853, the new church was to serve as a patriotic shrine and, like West-
minster Abbey, as a burial place for national heroes. Also serving as
church for the garrison of Vienna, it represented the unity of scepter,
cross, and sword against what Vienna's Archbishop Cardinal Rauscher
called "the mortally wounded tiger of the Revolution."[5] When the archbishop used those words at the laying of the cornerstone of the Votivkirche in April 1856, a concordat with major concessions to the Church
was already in place. The Restoration atmosphere had reached its height.

WITHIN the state bureaucracy and in the city, however, pressures were
already at work in the mid-1850s that would usher in a new phase in the

development of the capital. Neo-absolutism was more than restoration and repression; it aimed also at the modernization of the monarchy. Alexander Bach, the interior minister whose tough, imaginative policies dominated the postrevolutionary decade, envisaged a highly centralized, transnational, bureaucratic state. He sought to blunt the dangerous political potential of liberalism and nationalism by fostering the economic and cultural interests of the bourgeoisie that could also strengthen the state. In the centralistic scheme of things, the city of Vienna acquired a new meaning. Even in the constitution imposed by the emperor in March 1849, the status of Vienna was explicitly defined in terms that transformed and enlarged the ancient dynastic concept of *Residenzstadt* into that of a centralizing state capital (*Reichshauptstadt*). "Vienna is the capital of the Empire and the seat of the imperial power," the Constitution said.[6]

The logical parallel to political centralization was cultural centralization. Vienna must become the focus and radiating center of a transnational, pan-Austrian, modern consciousness. Traditional institutions of the court—theater, museums, opera—must reach out to the public of the whole empire to create a uniform culture. Where court institutions for this task were inadequate or nonexistent, the state must fill the void. Thus Bach tried to establish an Imperial Archive to unite all archives of the realm in a single building, including the prestigious Haus-, Hof- und Staatsarchiv. The vigorous minister of education, Count Leo Thun, established the Institute for Austrian Historical Research (1854) to foster the professionalization of research and the discovery of a more useable past for the modern neo-conservative state.

In this context, plans were undertaken to organize and expand the reach of traditional imperial patronage of high art through a new court museum. In a more modern gesture, a museum for art and industry was established by the state as a practical supplement. Everywhere the tendency in cultural organization was the same: to strengthen the old dynastic principle with the étatist one wherever possible, and, in the process, to fortify traditional inheritance with modern practice.

In Alexander Bach's wide cultural program, the shape and character of the capital city was an ever more pressing concern. To give it definition, Bach and his fellow bureaucrats reached out to the middle class. They drew its professional intellectuals—architects, historians, art historians—into the governmental councils as consultants. Mindful of the pressure for space on the still-closed glacis to accommodate new housing, Bach also drew municipal representatives into the planning process. Still the initiative remained firmly in the hands of the imperial authorities. It is important to understand, in view of our tendency today to see the Ringstrasse as a product of resurgent liberalism, how much its development was the work of neo-absolutist reformers. Their motive was to enhance the power of the state.

Through most of the 1850s, the contest over the modernization of the capital in terms of its representational functions in the politics of culture was spatially centered on the Hofburg. In view of the army's continuing resistance to building on the glacis, only occasional efforts were made to acquire sites for cultural buildings there. Instead, as the projects of renewal and expansion of the scepter's sway by means of culture increased, competing insider interest groups clamored for a site in the Hofburg area. Court officials pressed for new residential and visitors' quarters; the military, for new buildings for the Emperor's guard regiment and a new headquarters for the commandantura of Vienna. The Ministry of the Interior pressed for an Imperial Archive and an Imperial Geological Institute. In general, Bach's policy was to establish a whole range of state institutions of art and science that would ultimately outdistance and absorb the dynastic ones.[7]

The spatial focus of all these claims in the 1850s was the Äussere Burgplatz (Heldenplatz), between the old Hofburg and the Burgtor. Most plans for the cultural buildings, including both opera house and Burgtheater, envisaged expansion to the east and west of the Äussere Burgplatz. The Obersthofmeister, Carl Freiherr zu Liechtenstein, promoted the placement of the opera and the theater on either flank of the Burgtor. Both buildings were to be connected with the Hofburg by an arcade—a fitting expression of the primacy of the representational arts in Austrian court culture.[8] This plan failed of acceptance, but its shadow may be reflected in the final siting of opera and Burgtheater: although detached from the immediate Hofburg area, the two buildings were placed closer to it than any other major buildings on the inner side of the Ring.

The more insistent the demands for a vigorous expansion of neo-absolutism's cultural building program became, the less adequate the idea of centering the new capital on the Hofburg space proved to be. The multiple content was simply too great for the confined space. Piecemeal planning was reduced to political maneuvering in what became a futile game of musical chairs. To fulfill the multiple requirements of state policy, the confining Hofburg square had to yield to the larger circle of the glacis; the contained space of tradition, to the fluid space of the modern city. An absolute prerequisite for this was, of course, the removal of the sword that barred the way.

At the end of the year 1857, the civilian ministers, after careful political preparation, won the emperor's support for the inauguration of comprehensive planning of the new capital, with the glacis as its site. Juridically, the imperial rescript announcing this course was written still in the spirit of neo-absolutism, its language analogous to the imposed constitution of 1849. Where the draft prepared for Francis Joseph spoke only of the regulation of the city, the final draft substituted for the word *city* the more imperious phrase, at once dynastic and étatist, *meine Residenz- und Reichshauptstadt.*[9] But the basic fact remained: the emperor had finally ordered that the walls and bastions be razed, and the land opened. The liberal *Neue Freie Presse* hailed the imperial command as a fairy-tale liberation, which broke the cincture of stone that for many centuries had kept Vienna's noble limbs imprisoned in its evil spell.[10] The scepter had compelled the sheathing of the sword. Out of the empty glacis could soon rise the glory of the Ring, with the great monumental buildings disposed along its course.

THE RESCRIPT of 1857 has always been regarded—and rightly—as a crucial turning point in the history of the planning of the capital. Once the primacy of the military in determining the use and function of the glacis was broken, the thinking about the capital's spatial form changed. The area began to be thought of not merely as a space in which single public buildings might be located, but as a socio-spatial whole, an ideal city-within-a-city. This process took place slowly, in phases that were conditioned by political changes. I should like to delineate those phases, indicating how each affected the museum and its meaning in the urban constellation.

The first phase was still distinctly imperial or, to stay with the metaphor of my title, the phase of the scepter. The second phase, that of ascendant liberalism, began with the positing of a spatial counterweight to the Hofburg in the Rathaus area, and ended in the compromise of the Ring. The Maria Theresien Platz with its museums can be seen as the spatial keystone of that compromise.

In 1860, two years after the emperor's rescript, the first official plan for the Ringstrasse development was released (Figure 7.2). Its visual presen-

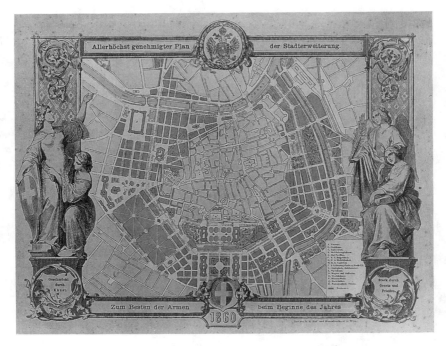

Figure 7.2. Official Announcement of Ringstrasse Plan, 1860.

tation reveals in several ways the persistence of monarchical primacy in defining the capital space. The plan is turned out of the normal orientation of the compass to create a vertical axis of Hofburg space from the Residenz to the Imperial Stables. The Heldenplatz is flanked by two proposed court buildings; the present site of the museums, by two guard and command buildings. Together, the four buildings define a Hofburg axis that in effect bisects the Ring, and serves as the salient center of the whole plan, as though drawing life to itself from the Ring on either side. That the plan showed only domestic buildings for the area adjacent to the Hofburg axis could only increase the latter's monumental impact on the whole. As for the museum, it is relegated to an area insulated by residences to the southwest. The Votivkirche is the nearest monument to the north, beyond the huge parade ground still reserved to the military. Thus the space is court space, the place for the sword is in it, and the scepter has clear primacy over the Ringstrasse, which appears only as an artery of communication, not as an organizing principle for the buildings along its course.

In the very year of the promulgation of this imperio-centric plan, 1860, the neo-absolutist politics upon which it was based was severely shaken. Against a background of defeat in Italy, the emperor had to introduce constitutional reforms which accorded new powers to the liberal élite, not only in the state but in the capital city. In the City Expansion Commission (*Stadterweiterungskommission*), the remarkable mixed commission that administered the development process, the liberal wind blew strong. The military presence in prime capital space was challenged once more. In 1864, Minister Count Schmerling reclaimed from the army the space allocated in the 1860 plan for its buildings on the present Maria Theresien Platz. By the time Francis Joseph opened the Ring formally in 1865, pressure to replace the military buildings with the museums had won the day. The interior minister and other elements in the City Expansion Commission argued for beautiful museums as opposed to utilitiarian military buildings as the fitting occupants of this most prestigious capital space. Although a plan by the influential architect, Ludwig Förster, for a single block-shaped building for all museums, both court and state, on the site, failed of approval, it won the support of the Vienna City Council. Art historian Rudolf von Eitelberger, through Count Schmerling, submitted a radical proposal for a comprehensive, nondynastic Oesterreichisches Museum or Reichsmuseum to include history, art, and science. The basic decision was soon taken: though the art and natural history museums should be court museums still, the imperial presence should manifest itself in the new capital space beyond the Burgtor not through arms, but through art.[11]

The competition for the design of the museums in 1866 was legendary for its bitterness, and not unaffected by the liberals' support of Theophil Hansen and Heinrich Ferstel against the more conservative championing of Moritz Löhr and Carl Hasenauer.[12] Hansen and Ferstel both projected the museum area as an enclosed square across the Ringstrasse, thus independent of the Hofburg area, which would be terminated at the Ringstrasse. In short, the cultural buildings would have won spatial autonomy from the court. Semper and Hasenauer, by contrast, with the backing of the court bureaucracy, incorporated the museums as flanking buildings in a vastly expanded Hofburg area to form a unified Kaiserforum (Figure 7.3). In short, culture was presented as an extension of the imperial power. From the point of view of contested space, Gottfried Semper also neutralized the Ringstrasse by unifying the court and museum areas with his proposed triumphal arches that would span the Ring, thus achieving

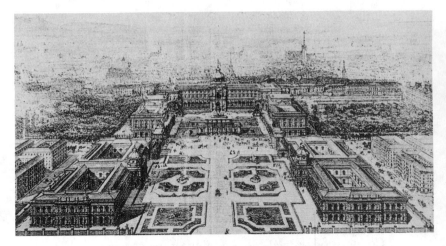

Figure 7.3. Kaiserforum, G. Semper, 1869.

the representation of full symbolic dominance of the imperial principle over the capital's civic space—and this at the very moment when constitutional liberalism achieved ascendancy.

PARALLEL to the expanded Kaiserforum project and almost synchronous with its final phase in the last years of the 1860s, there began a countervailing building project to incarnate the constitutional and cultural values of newly ascendant liberalism in comparable monumental splendor.

Once more a political shift lay behind a turn in Vienna's urban planning. This time it was the defeat at Sadowa that brought a new advance of the liberal forces in both the state and the city in 1867. These pressed the claims of three institutions quintessentially associated with liberalism: the Parliament, the Rathaus, and the University. Appropriate monumental buildings for each could have been located in separate spaces anywhere in the Ringstrasse area, and during the mid-1860s much discussion and maneuvering were devoted to their separate and independent placement. It was the city government of Vienna which in 1870, after three years of pressure, won the emperor's approval for a solution which, in a single stroke, brought all three citadels of bourgeois law and rational culture together on a single site. That the site should be the parade ground, the last major parcel of glacis land in the hands of the army, lent a kind of political poignancy to the solution.

Of the three institutions most prized by the liberals, the University is the one whose history in the search for a home since 1848 most vividly illustrates the problem of politically contested space. During the decade of neo-absolutism the University dwelt under the shadow of the major role it had played in the Revolution. The Academic Legion had been the heart of insurgent Vienna's fighting force. The imperial army could neither forgive nor forget its own ignominious withdrawal in the face of the intelligentsia-in-arms. With the suppression of the Revolution, the military occupied the old University (today the Academy of Sciences) and forced the dispersion of its functions all over the city.

The minister of religion and instruction under neo-absolutism, Count Leo Thun, had, to be sure, championed the University's quest for a restoration of its autonomy. As a conservative reformer, Thun sought to domesticate the University by using the traditional English college model and by linking it more closely to the church. Accordingly, from 1853 to 1868, he and his collaborators worked to create a university quarter around the Votivkirche. Its buildings, in Gothic style, would be clustered about the church like chicks around a mother hen. The army and the emperor resisted any centralized university. As late as 1868, Count Thun's plan was reactivated, with Heinrich Ferstel authorized to draft plans for it on the Votivkirche site. The eyes of the University's own building committee, however, had strayed elsewhere: in 1867, it had already suggested the parade ground as the proper site, one large enough for a single massive building to house the whole University. It would also remove the University from the shadow of the church (although I have no evidence that the professors of the building committee said so). When at last the parade ground was freed, Ferstel was asked to design the building not in Count Thun's favored Gothic, but in the Renaissance style that symbolized to the liberal professorate the emergence of modern secular culture.[13]

A similar tale, though shorter, might be told for the political buildings that, with the University, would constitute the new quarter of bourgeois *Recht und Kultur*: the Parliament and the Rathaus. For our purposes, it must suffice to say that the satisfaction of all three claims came quickly and together, in those brief years of liberalism's political high-water mark, 1867–1873. The most persistent and determined agent in producing the result was the Vienna City Council. In 1867, it had pressed the University's claim to a parade ground site, but the War Ministry rejected it. In 1868, thanks to a large offer from a bank, an imperial decision released the parcel, but without specifying its uses. Public agitation be-

gan for placing the Rathaus, previously slated for a location on the south-
ern part of the Ring, on the site.

At this point the Liberal mayor of Vienna, Kajetan Felder, produced
his master stroke, one which tells us something about the prestige that
the leading architects had acquired in the exciting years of building the
new capital. Felder asked Friedrich Schmidt, the master of medieval civic
architecture, to head a planning group for the parade ground area.
Schmidt enjoyed the favor of the arch-conservative Cardinal Rauscher,
for whom he had executed many church projects, but also that of the
liberals for his secular Gothic architecture.[14] Schmidt's two collaborators
were equally eminent architects who had been defeated in the museum
competition. Theophil Hansen roughed out the Parliament building in
the Classical style so prized by the liberals. Heinrich Ferstel, long experienced in the frustrating University project, returned to it in a final victorious assault. Mayor Felder, with the enthusiastic support of the City
Council, presented to the emperor their proposal for the Rathaus quarter, a triumph of historical eclecticism and the most eloquent spatial expression of bourgeois power in the new capital. On April 10, 1870, the
emperor agreed to turn over the parade ground for development.[15]

As the Rescript of 1859 had opened the way for the centering of the
new capital on the expanded Hofburg axis, so his decision of 1870 created in the Rathaus quarter a countervailing spatial center of civic gravity
that severely weakened the scepter's spatial primacy.

The generative element in this process of redefinition of Vienna's
monumental area can be thought of as two rectangles: the Kaiserforum
and the Rathaus quadrilateral. In 1870, thanks to the five years of quar-
reling among the planners of the Hofburg expansion, the Semper-Hase-
nauer Kaiserforum had only just been accepted. Truly this design would
have assured, at the very moment of liberal ascendency, the emperor's
long-cherished conceptual integration of Residenzstadt and Reichshauptstadt, symbolically defining the second in terms of the first. The Rathaus
quadrilateral, however, although certainly not conceived as in open competition with the Kaiserforum, created near it a powerful center for an
alternative cluster of political and cultural values belonging to the liberal-
rational sector of society. In effect if not in clear intention, it projected a
Bürgerforum (Citizens' forum) to correspond to the Kaiserforum (Emperor's forum). A plan drafted by the Vienna Municipal Building Office
(*Stadtbauamt*) envisaged that Rathaus and University would face each
other across a square, as the museums were to do, with the Parliament in

the center-rear where the Rathaus stands today (Figure 7.4).[16] This plan would have dramatized the interrelatedness of the values and functions of the several buildings. It would also have heightened the autonomy of the whole and freed it from the fluid magnetism of the Ringstrasse.[17]

This bold plan was not pursued. With the decision that each building should face the Ringstrasse, the collective, stable gravity of the square yielded its primacy to the street (Figure 7.5). Historical style differentiation reenforced further the autonomy that each building acquired as it turned its face from its neighbors to the street. The Greek of Hansen's Parliament, the Gothic of Schmidt's Rathaus, the Renaissance of Ferstel's University, the early Barocue of Semper's Burgtheater: in each case, the style chosen suited by association the function to which the monument was dedicated. This was indeed *Vergangenheitsbewältigung* (mastering the past) in nineteenth-century style, cultural self-definition as modern through the ingestion of a plural past. The visual pluralism of these four monuments certainly could compete for attention with the Hofburg complex, but at the price of surrendering some of its magnetic energy to the street. Thus it was that the Ring, the only tie between the individuated monuments, became the real forum of the imperial capital in its final form.

THE tension between Kaiserforum and Bürgerforum, and the form of its resolution, had its effect on the spatial signification of the Kunsthistorisches Museum. The abandonment of the arches that were to span the Ringstrasse to close the Kaiserforum weakened the museum's tie to the Hofburg. Yet the museum kept a certain independence from the Ring, for it did not face the street whose power was so strongly reenforced by the great liberal buildings to the north. Tied to neither complex, the museum thus occupied a mediating position between the monumental buildings of the dynasty and those of the liberals. This position accorded well with the museum's social function: to provide, through the traditional artistic culture it displayed, a crucial bonding element between the monarch and the new élite.

In the museum area, the most visible symbol of the political compromise that underlay this function is the statue of the Empress Maria Theresa that stands in the center of the square (Figure 7.6). The Empress's caring, motherly figure contrasts strongly with the two military

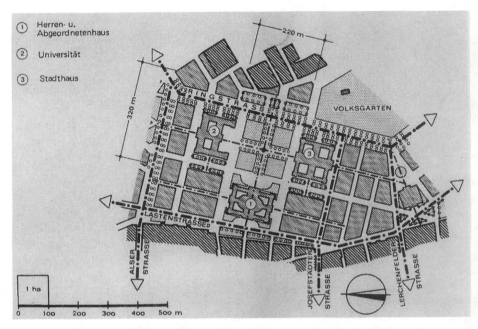

Legend:
1. Herren- u. Abgeordnetenhaus
2. Universität
3. Stadthaus

RINGSTRASSE

VOLKSGARTEN

LASTENSTRASSE

ALSER STRASSE

JOSEFSTÄDTER STRASSE

LERCHENFELDER STRASSE

220 m

320 m

1 ha

0   100   200   300   400   500 m

Figure 7.4. Civic Buildings Oriented to Each Other: A Civic Forum.

Figure 7.5. Civic Buildings Oriented to Ringstrasse: Parliament, Rathaus, University, Burgtheater.

Figure 7.6. Maria Theresa Monument.

heroes whom Francis Joseph had chosen in the 1850s as focal statues of the Heldenplatz across the Ring. She stands in contrast, as well, to the figure whom the liberals chose to place before their Parliament: Pallas Athena. Lacking any heroes of their own in Austrian history, the liberals had turned to classical culture for an appropriate symbol.[18]

Between the military heroes of the monarch and the rational goddess of the liberal élite, Maria Theresa occupies a middle ground. The emperor himself chose her for the spot, but a liberal historian, Alfred von Arneth, developed the complex program for her monument. A former 48er, Arneth's years of imperial service as director of the State Archive had given his liberalism a conservative cast. Through a celebrated ten-volume biography of Maria Theresa, he had contributed to the rehabilitation of her very Catholic majesty for a bourgeois liberal culture that had long held her in low esteem compared to the enlightened Emperor Joseph II, who were their favorite Habsburg ruler.[19]

Arneth's monument project called for the empress to be represented not alone but surrounded by the outstanding men of the realm who welded ruler and élite into the kind of partnership the liberals had come to prize with Francis Joseph. The monument pictures generals and great diplomats, yes; but also Enlightenment administrative and legal reformers: Joseph Sonnenfels, who abolished torture; Gerard van Swieten, who modernized the University. Great artists graced the pedestal, too: Gluck, Haydn, and the boy Mozart. In its contextualization of the empress in her society and culture, the rich iconography contrasts radically with previous statues of Habsburg rulers in Vienna, statues that portray them as self-contained figures of strength.

Arneth made one bold suggestion for his monument that failed of acceptance. He proposed that the empress carry no scepter in her hand, but rather a scroll containing the Pragmatic Sanction, the agreement that confirmed her, though a woman, as ruler. It symbolized legality, so prized by liberals, as the basis of royal power. That went beyond the tolerances of the court. Maria Theresa faces the Ring today with her scepter in her hand; it only rests on the Pragmatic Sanction's scroll beneath it.[20] The responsible committee had found the characteristic resolution of the conflict between traditional imperial and modern liberal values that, in the end, the whole Ring represents: synthesis in symbolism, compromise in fact.

By the time the Kunsthistorisches Museum opened its doors, the Ring had reached its mature character as one of Europe's most harmonious urban spaces, a magnificent fluid forum for a solid élite secure in its values and expressing them in the polysemic vocabulary of historical style architecture. The citizens and persons of culture could pursue their varied concerns without a sense of hierarchy among the different buildings of politics and culture.

In its neutrality and its equalizing power, the Ring leaves little to remind us of the history of contested space from which it had emerged. For only in troubled phases, in response to changes in social and political power, had the new capital taken form. In the fifties, the determinative, privileged element was the sword. Containment of the sword was the prerequisite to building a new capital on the glacis at all. After 1857, the scepter, even as it freed the glacis, projected an expanded Hofburg-centered order to dominate the capital. A decade later the ascendant liberals generated in the Rathaus quarter their own countervailing space on the Ring. The failure to realize either the Kaiserforum or the Bürgerforum in their fullness as independent spatial entities can be read as an index of the liberalization of monarchical rule and the turning of the liberals to the monarch as the guarantor of their new-won social and cultural power.

To this bonding of tradition and modernity in cultural politics, the Museum and Maria Theresa in the square give eloquent expression. They are in a way the keystone of the completed Ringstrasse, where imperial power expresses itself in aesthetic culture, and the liberal élite, redefining Maria Theresa, honors the Baroque dynastic tradition. The sword is sheathed, the scepter shows itself in gifts of art, and the Ring absorbs conflicting claims to political primacy into the circular flow of pluralistic compromise.

NOTES

1. See Carl E. Schorske, *Fin-de-Siècle Vienna: Politics and Culture* (New York, 1980), 34–62.

2. W. Wagner, "Die Stellungnahme der Mitiärbehörden zur Wiener Stadterweiterung in den Jahren 1848–1857," in *Jahrbuch des Vereines für Geschichte der Stadt Wien* 17/18 (1961–1962), 215–85.

3. R. Lorenz, "Politische Geschichte der Wiener Ringstrasse," in *Drei Jahrhunderte Jahre Volk, Staat und Reich* (Vienna, 1944), 487.

4. See the well-founded analysis in G. Kapner, "Ringstrassendenkmäler. Zur Geschichte der Ringstrassendenkmäler," in R. Wagner-Rieger, ed., *Die Wiener Ringstrasse, Bild einer Epoche* 9.1 (Vienna, Cologne, Graz, etc., 1969 et seq.), 9–14.

5. Lorenz, "Politische Geschichte," 489.

6. E. Springer, "Geschichte und Kulturleben der Wiener Ringstrasse," in Wagner-Rieger, ed., *Wiener Ringstrasse*, 2:85.

7. The most comprehensive account of the complex maneuvers of the 1850s is provided by Springer, ibid., chap. 5, passim; 310–11.

8. Ibid., 82–83, 135–39.

9. Ibid., 89, 94.

10. *Neue Freie Presse*, December 2, 1873.

11. Springer, "Geschichte und Kulturleben," 305–12.

12. The classic account of the architectural and conceptual contest over the museums is A. Lhotsky, *Die Baugeschichte der Museen und der Neuen Burg* (Vienna, 1941), especially pp. 36–92. Springer gives a condensed but often more historically insightful account of the competition in "Geschichte," 305–36. See also K. Mollig, H. Reining, and R. Wurzer, "Planung und Verwirklichung der Wiener

Ringstrassenzone," in Wagner-Rieger, ed., *Wiener Ringstrasse*, 3, Textband, 215–26.

13. N. Wibiral and R. Mikula, "Heinrich von Ferstel," in Wagner-Rieger, ed., *Wiener Ringstrasse* 8.3 (Wiesbaden, 1974), 44–47; also illustration 29. See also Schorske, *Fin-de-Siècle Vienna* 38–40 and notes.

14. A. Fenzel, "Kardinal Rauscher und Friedrich Schmidt," in Historisches Museum der Stadt Wien, *Friedrich von Schmidt . . . Ein gotischer Rationalist* (Vienna, 1991), 34–39. For Schmidt's sketch of the whole complex, see ibid., 118, cat. no. 2.41.

15. Mollig, Reining, and Wurzer, "Planung," 211–15.

16. Ibid., 248 ff. There is no evidence that any of the major architects wished the buildings to face each other. Schmidt assigned his Rathaus the central position occupied by the Parliament in the Building Office plan. Hansen definitely wished his Parliament to face the Ringstrasse.

17. I have not included the Burgtheater in this survey because it was not included in this phase of the planning. Had it been so, it would only have increased the weight of the Rathaus quadrilateral as an independent if not countervailing spatial power to the Kaiserforum.

18. Schorske, *Fin-de-Siècle Vienna*, 43.

19. "A. von Arneth," *Neue Österreichische Biographie ab 1815*, vol. 10 (Zurich, Leipzig, and Vienna, 1957), 46–60.

20. Kapner, "Ringstrasendenkmäler," 18–21.

PART TWO

Clio Eclipsed:
Toward Modernism
in Vienna

EIGHT

Grace and the Word:
Austria's Two Cultures and
Their Modern Fate

No ONE WHO has investigated the high culture of Vienna in the era of liberal ascendancy can fail to be impressed by the sturdy integration of its components. Not only were political, scientific, and aesthetic culture closely related to each other in principle and in practice but the very social life and cultural forms of the elite sustained the synthesis achieved. Yet by the end of the nineteenth century, this complex was breaking apart, with aesthetic culture often going its separate way from the liberal-rationalist political and academic culture with which it had been linked. The character of this union and its break-up will provide my theme.

In addressing the problem of Austria's two cultures, I work in the light provided by Robert Kann. In his search for the intellectual origins of the nineteenth century, he drew with masterful security of line the contrasting characters of Baroque and Enlightenment cultures at their height in the seventeenth and eighteenth centuries. He gave these cultures concreteness in two full-length portraits, one of a Baroque court preacher, Abraham a Santa Clara, the other of an Enlightenment professorial reformer, Josef Sonnenfels. Hence the German title of Kann's book: *Kanzel und Katheder*, pulpit and university chair,[1] in which the attempt of the rationalistic professor to overcome the legacy of the religious preacher is chronicled. The victory, as Professor Kann knew well, was far from complete, for the legacy of the Counter-Reformation kept reappearing in new forms.

If one starts with the 1860s, when the liberal bourgeoisie acquired power and began to transform the institutions of state and society in its own image, one can readily distinguish two clusters of values that reach back to the Enlightenment and the Baroque: one is moral, political, and scientific; the other is religious and aesthetic. The first, a rational culture of law and the word, claimed the primary allegiance of the bourgeois; but the second, a plastic and sensuous culture of grace deriving from the Counter-Reformation, exercised a continuing vitality, not overtly as religion, but subliminally as art. The interaction of the two will be my concern. To chart their changing interplay, I shall use as foci two institutions—the university and the theater.

THE moral and scientific culture of the liberal middle classes resembled that prevailing in the same social stratum everywhere in Europe in the nineteenth century. Morally, it was secure, righteous, and repressive; politically, it was concerned for the rule of law, under which both individual rights and social order were subsumed; intellectually, it was committed to the great metaphysical assumption of the Enlightenment, that a rational structure inheres in all things, despite the chaos of the surface. The liberal credo in the broadest sense demanded of its devotees the commitment of heart, mind, and will to a world ordered by rational, regulative principles. Whatever the creativity of the middle class in economic life, it drew its political leaders largely from the fields of law and science. Small wonder that in university education, the study of law—*Jura*—became for Austria's liberal elite what the study of classics was for the promising young man of the English governing class: the key to a solid public career.[2]

Yet for all the stress on the values of reason and law that produced as ideal social types a solid *homo juridicus* and a reasonable *homo sapiens*, the educated Austrian bourgeois cultivated an aesthetic culture of a kind and degree that distinguished him from his contemporaries elsewhere in Europe. Here he dwelt under the spell of a still-vital pre-Enlightenment Austrian tradition, that of the Counter-Reformation. Protestant and bourgeois culture saw the world as a terrain to be mastered by imposing order upon it under divine law. Austrian Catholicism viewed the world rather as an emanation of God's plenitude and grace, to be glorified in art. The Counter-Reformation conceived the cosmos as a spiritual-material continuum, in which God's spirit, through His grace, penetrated nature, spiritualized it. Accordingly, prerevolutionary Austria's intellectual achievements lay not in abstract philosophy and the art of the written word, literature, as in the Protestant north, but in the applied and performing arts: architecture, the theater, and music, wherein the spirit was concretely manifested. Austria's Counter-Reformation religion, intensely sacramental, centered religious devotion in ritual, in the ever-reenacted drama of the mass with its union of spirit and flesh; similarly, its secular culture, fostered by church and court, was theatrical and metaphoric. Truth and value were expressed in visible concretizations in sensuous form, pointing toward a divine order that was present but too ineffable to be finally grasped in thought.

Thus it was that theater, from the lowly folk-comedy to the lofty court stage, became the primary cultural form through which the Viennese of every class made meaning of their world. Theater became central also in the education of the aristocrats. In Jesuit and Benedictine colleges, students were prepared through acting in the school theater to play their roles in the theater of the world in the service of God and the emperor. Grace, gesture, adaptability, and the capacity to play his part were the marks of the Austrian cavalier—attributes very different from the stern moral and military virtues of the Prussian Junker. Hofmannsthal's Marschallin in *Der Rosenkavalier* expresses well the actor's ethos of her aristocratic class: "Und in dem *wie*, da liegt der ganze Unterschied" ("And *how* one acts makes all the difference").

Deep into the liberal era, when the religious and political-authoritarian content of the old Catholic aristocratic order was widely rejected, the sensuous mode associated with it continued to perpetuate itself in the structures of feeling and expression. In Austria as nowhere else in Europe, the middle class prized aesthetic culture as a mark of personal completeness and social status. Under the impact of a changing social situation, its aesthetic cultivation made that class peculiarly sensitive to psychological states, permeating its moralistic culture with an amoral *Gefühlskultur* (culture of feeling).

The university as rebuilt in the 1750s offers a fitting point of entry into the changing relations between the two components of Austrian high culture. Here, within the framework of the Baroque old regime, the stoutly Catholic Empress Maria Theresa launched the effort to introduce into a Jesuit university modern training in law and medicine. To create a professional cadre of public servants in accordance with new rationalistic and empirical scientific standards, she took as models the Protestant universities of Leyden and Hanover. True, she left the theological and philosophical faculties in the hands of the Jesuits. But she gave the Enlightenment culture of law and science its foothold in Austria.

A splendid ceiling painting in the ceremonial hall of the old univer-

sity—today it houses the Austrian Academy of Sciences—expresses met-
aphorically the relation of the realm of grace and the realm of the word
as Maria Theresa and her advisers conceived it. Pietro Metastasio, court
poet of the empress, drafted the program for the painting; another Italian, Gregorio Guglielmi, executed it. At the top of each of the room's
four walls as they pass into the ceiling are placed allegories of the four
faculties, rising into the heavenly space above in a grand trompe-l'oeil. In
the crown of the ceiling is a medallion bearing the features of the imperial couple, the presumed source of light that radiates and illuminates the
scholarly figures of the faculty. According to Metastasio, the design
would show that from the empress at the center "derive the beneficial
influences that illuminate and foster the fine arts and the sciences."[3] Here
is effective grace in action, not directly from God, but mediated through
the imperial patroness of the world of learning and the word. Although
the program of the painting manifests the secularization process in sub-
stituting for a religiously defined source of life the person of the empress,
the imagery still expresses the primacy of grace in the rational culture of
the word.

The bureaucrats and physicians who issued from Maria Theresa's reformed university, however, became the social spearhead of the culture of
law and, later, the creative leaders of the bourgeoisie. In the first half of
the nineteenth century, the withering of the reform impulse from the
crown brought on the second occasion in which the University of Vienna
served as a stage of history: the Revolution of 1848. This time it was not
the monarch who triggered the action from above, but the students from
below. On March 12, 1848, the students of the university met in the
same building and formulated for Austria the first comprehensive set of
demands for a society linking law not only with administrative order but
also with political and cultural freedom: popular representation, academic freedom, freedom of the press, etc. Among those students were
many young leaders-to-be of the later constitutional state, almost all
from the faculties of jurisprudence and medicine. (They could hardly
have been mindful of the monarch-centered late Baroque representation
of the university on the ceiling of the ceremonial hall above them as, in a
stormy session, they hammered out their program to make the rational
principles of the university the basis of principles for a reformed imperial
polity.)

Meanwhile in another part of the city in 1848, at the Burgtheater,
Austria's aesthetic culture was also confronting the value claims of the

liberal revolution. Because of the traditional importance of theater, control of the Burgtheater and its playbill became, in and after 1848, almost as important politically as control of the press or broadcasting houses have been in twentieth-century revolutions. Here again, an institution re-created from above by an enlightened monarch to advance the rational culture of the word was adapted from below to challenge the old order.

It was a North German, Heinrich Laube, who in 1848 came to the fore in Vienna and remade the Burgtheater into a center of bourgeois *Bildung* (education), where liberal values in ethics and political freedom were presented in the theatrical medium of aristocratic tradition. With a sensational play, *Die Karlsschüler*, glorifying the young Friedrich Schiller, literary hero of all liberals, Laube won the favor of the liberal revolutionaries. But with his defense of the Burgtheater's traditions against popular pressure he also earned the support of the court. Through tact and moderation, Laube succeeded in gaining and holding the support of both the court and the liberal elite for two decades. He shaped the Burgtheater into a vehicle of reconciliation of past and present, of aristocratic artform and liberal-rational substance.

Political defeat in the Revolution of 1848 slowed but did not stop the liberal bourgeoisie from extending its dominion over the economic and cultural life of the empire. By the 1860s, constitutional government was established at last. The liberals celebrated their triumph architecturally in the great urban complex of the Ringstrasse. In a portion of it were concentrated four great buildings to house the principal institutions of liberal *Recht und Kultur*. Two of these were the major centers of constitutional government: Parliament and Rathaus; the other two, the major centers of liberal high culture: the Burgtheater and the University.

Of these four buildings only one was free of serious political troubles in the last quarter of the nineteenth century: the Burgtheater. The Burgtheater did not become what Laube had dreamed of in 1848—a mirror of a Greater German national community that would weld all classes together. Yet its social importance was great. It became a major institution for bonding through culture the educated bourgeoisie and the liberal aristocracy into what was called the "second society," the real elite of the constitutional era.

We can get some idea of both the social function and the cultural substance of the Burgtheater in its heyday from the painting of young Gustav Klimt. In 1887, the Vienna City Council commissioned him to paint from the stage of the Old Burgtheater a vast group portrait of the Viennese elite assembled as audience. He included more than a hundred individual portraits, including such prominent personages as the emperor's friend, actress Katherina Schratt; the eminent surgeon, Dr. Billroth; and the future mayor, Karl Lueger. Klimt's partner Franz Matsch recalled how the persons chosen for the painting clamored for special sittings. It meant much to one's social status to be immortalized as a Burgtheater patron. The picture also showed how, in the theater as in salons, the intellectual, artistic, financial, and political elite consorted with each other in a single social life.

Klimt was also called upon to decorate the grand stairway of the new Burgtheater with ceiling paintings. They show us chapters in the history of drama, from the festival of Dionysus to modern times. But more: each mural celebrated the unity of theater and society, the players and their public, as in his painting of a performance of *Romeo and Juliet* in the Globe Theater.

The high value attached to aesthetic Bildung was of course passed on by the new elite to its children. Especially those born after 1860 received a second, out-of-school education in the theaters, concert halls, and museums of the capital. The artistic culture that was prized by the parents as a badge of status and an intellectual accomplishment often developed in the children a hypertrophied sensibility that made them turn to the arts as a source of meaning when their inherited expectations of a more rational world were undermined by events.

Indeed, the undermining of liberal bourgeois rule and its culture of law and the word came all too soon. Beginning about 1870, discontent with liberalism arose in four different areas: ethnic frustration, social injustice, economic depression, and political corruption. Aside from the new mass movements that pressed them from below, the liberals found themselves challenged in politics and culture by their own children. Aesthetic culture became a refuge from an uncongenial social reality. In 1900, the critic Karl Kraus could with some justice identify the widened interest in literature as a political product "of recent years, which have [seen] the sphere of action of Viennese liberalism confined to the parquets of theaters on opening night."[4]

It was not in the Burgtheater, however, but in the university across the

Ringstrasse that the crisis first showed itself as an intra-bourgeois affair, a crisis of sons against fathers. The university had survived years of exile from its old building, while the liberals had fought against their military and other foes for the right to a single new building and land on which to build it. Now, even before this new edifice was opened in 1883, an anti-liberal politics began to spread within the student body. Fired by the national and social shortcomings of liberalism, a new generation of youth sought not only a new politics in the 1870s and 1880s but also new philosophic and cultural premises to replace the juridical rationalism of their fathers. A militant, communitarian populism ran through the student population like the radical wildfire of our 1960s.

Whereas in 1848 the university had been the center of the revolt against aristocratic authority in the name of a culture of law, after 1880 it became the center of the revolt against bourgeois authority in the name of a culture of communitarian feeling. What Schiller was to the liberal militants of the mid-century, Richard Wagner became to the militant populist intellectuals of the 1880s. Aesthetic culture, once more detached from the rationalist tradition, acquired new importance as a source of values. For in their critique of the modern rational state and the scientific spirit, both Wagner and Nietzsche exalted theater—especially Greek drama—as an inspirational model for the regeneration of German society. Wagner added to the glorification of the polis the special allure of Germanic myth, thus enriching his archaic communitarian vision with a national-populist appeal for young German militants. In 1883, a massive Wagner celebration where Vienna's students fêted their hero generated a major conflict between young and old.

Most important for the culture of the fin-de-siècle generation was the depth-psychological thrust of Wagner and Nietzsche, their vindication of the claims of instinct against "bourgeois" reason and the analytic spirit. Instinct began to play the same intellectually empowering role as divine grace had played in Baroque culture. Activated in the public sphere, instinct seemed to create a new fraternal bonding that could transform a state based on competition and rationalized egotism into a true folk community. Liberated in the individual sphere, instinct would restore the life of feeling to a psyche suffering from what was felt to be an excess of intellect and rational desiccation. The new culture of instinct thus had both a political-communitarian aspect and a depth-psychological one. Both elements challenged and eroded the authority of liberalism as a socio-cultural value system.

THE purely political aspect of the new culture lost its grip on many well-educated young intellectuals when, in the 1880s, the populist movement turned militantly anti-Semitic. But the tendency for the aesthetic culture of feeling to assert its autonomy from the ethical-scientific strand in bourgeois culture continued to grow, spreading to literature. It was fed positively by the intensive aesthetic education and passion of the young, and negatively by the withering away of civic optimism under the pressure of mass politics. In the literary generation known as Jung-Wien, an autumnal pessimism and a narcissistic self-cultivation appeared together. The Jung-Wien writers explored the sensuous life, now artistic, now erotic. Their characters, like themselves, suffered from a seismographic consciousness, assailed now by the forces of instinct within, now by the inchoate powers of the world without.

In 1897, the new generation, Die Jungen, announced themselves in yet a third domain, that of the fine and applied arts. Their movement was called "the Secession." Its initial ideology and rhetoric still resonated with tones from the radical political culture of the university of the previous decades. Its declaration of war against the commercial spirit and corruption, its calls for a regeneration of Austrian culture through art recall the Wagnerite students of the early 1880s. But in the vigorous artistic activity unfolded by the Secession, these aims of the political Jungen play virtually no role. It is rather the preoccupations of the Jung-Wien writers that emerge: on the one hand, psychological explorations of the instinctual life, especially that of eros and the dissolution of boundaries between the I and the world, between thought and feeling; on the other, creation of a new, ahistorical beauty, in the applied as well as the fine arts, to satisfy the sensitive souls of the aesthetically cultivated. Both of these tendencies, grounded as they were in the culture of feeling and grace, encountered resistance from the guardians of the culture of law and the word.

∽

IN 1900, the university came once again to exemplify a crisis of Austrian society. This time not politics, but the culture of the liberal university itself was at issue, the culture of law and the word. The focus of the conflict was a series of ceiling paintings executed by Gustav Klimt in the ceremonial hall (*Festsaal*) of the university.

The new university building on the Ringstrasse itself represented the final triumph of the liberals over their most powerful and stubborn foe, the army, which in 1848 had evicted the university forever from the building provided for it by Maria Theresa. Although the university had opened its new building, symbol of its resurrection in 1883, a glorious Festsaal such as the one it had lost with the old university building was still incomplete. That hall, like the earlier one, was to be crowned with a ceiling painting representing the four faculties, this time expressing a modern conception of the liberal university.

Maria Theresa had had the program for her university ceiling painting drafted by her court poet, Pietro Metastasio. In 1894, in the modern bureaucratic state, it was no poet who developed the program, but the minister of culture (*Cultus und Unterricht*) in consultation with university professors. To the artist Gustav Klimt went the commission for the painting.

Between the time when, on the basis of his Ringstrasse paintings, Klimt was given the university commission in 1894 and the completion of the first paintings in 1898 and 1900, he had undergone a great sea change. As the Secession's leader, he had espoused a new *Weltanschauung* and a new *Gefühlskultur* (culture of feeling).

The new ceiling's central panel was to show the victorious struggle of light over darkness. This Enlightenment *agon* took the place occupied in the old university ceiling of 1757 by the medallion of the empress whose radiant beneficence was such that no struggle need be shown. The panel was executed by Klimt's partner, Franz Matsch.

Klimt's first completed painting, "Philosophy," conveyed no such Enlightenment confidence. Klimt showed himself still a child of theatrical culture, presenting the cosmos to us as if we were viewing it from the pit, a Baroque *theatrum mundi*. But the theatrum mundi was no longer vertically ordered, as in Guglielmi's painting, connecting the earth to heaven. In Klimt's theater, the earth is gone, dissolved into a darkly infinite cosmos that seems to fuse the vastness of heaven and the vaporous atmosphere of hell. Only the face of a figure at the base of the picture suggests a knowing mind—Klimt called her *Das Wissen* (Knowledge). She is placed in the rays of invisible footlights, like a prompter turned around, as though to clue us, the audience, into the cosmic drama.

The painfully psychologized world image that Klimt here projected is grounded in the philosophies of Schopenhauer and Nietzsche. It is a world of Will, blind energy in an endless round of parturience, love, and death. Like Nietzsche's drunken poetess in *Zarathustra*, Klimt's mantic

Wissen calls on us to affirm life in its mysterious totality, its unfathomable commingling of eros and thanatos. As in the Baroque, spirit and matter are joined, but this time, they are of one diffuse substance.

Klimt's "Philosophy" provoked outrage in the faculty in 1900. Eighty-seven of its members signed a petition to the Ministry of Culture to reject the work. The university's rector supported the professors with a critique that went to the heart of the controversy: in an age when philosophy sought truth in the exact sciences, he said, it did not deserve to be represented as a nebulous, fantastic construct. The professorial ideal of mastery of nature through scientific work, it was suggested, should have been represented by something akin to Raphael's "School of Athens" in the Vatican's Stanza della Signatura.

In the faculty battle over the Klimt paintings, the leader of the offensive was Professor Friedrich Jodl, a utilitarian philosopher famous for his *History of Ethics* in which he celebrated the emergence of rational ethics out of religious illusion and dogma. Cofounder of the Vienna Ethical Society, Jodl exemplified the culture of the word in its late liberal form. He championed all the Enlightenment causes of the day: adult education, women's rights, civil liberties, etc. The very nature of his rationalism prevented him from accepting into the university "a dark, obscure symbolism which could be comprehended only by the few."[5] His hostility to religion and his hostility to the new culture of feeling grounded in man's questionable position in a world of flux were of the same order in his mind. But because the anti-Klimt forces included Jodl's ancient foes, the censorious clericals and anti-Semites, he shifted the focus of his attack from philosophic substance to aesthetic quality. "We struggle not against nude art or free art, but against ugly art," Jodl declared.[6]

Franz Wickhof, a professor of art history, took up Klimt's cause against Jodl in what became a famous lecture entitled "What is Ugly?" In so doing, he developed for his own time a theory about the problems of modern aesthetic culture and the breakdown of the liberal cultural synthesis that has been our concern. "Beauty" and "ugliness," Wickhof argued, were matters of historically conditioned perception. The wider educated public, led by the learned, had come to identify beauty with history. The modern artist, by contrast, recognized that the present has its own life of feeling, and that artists give it its appropriate poetic form. A gulf had thus opened between past-oriented public and present-oriented artist. Those who, like the professors, see modern art as "ugly," Wickhof implied, are those who cannot face modern truth.

As for Klimt, he lashed back at his critics not in words but in paint. In his third ceiling panel, representing Jurisprudence, he made a frontal assault on the culture of law. In it, the pretensions of the law are exposed and subverted. The reality of the law lies not in the day-world of rational principles, allegorized in the top part of the picture, but in a space beneath, where justice is being executed: a hapless man is shown being devoured by an octopuslike polyp. There is no crime recorded here, only punishment. The punishment is psychologized, an erotic nightmare in a clammy hell. By stressing the suffering of the condemned, Klimt has laid bare the primacy of the instinctual that underpins the law itself. Undermined too was the idea of jurisprudence proclaimed so simply in the legend of the Guglielmi fresco of Maria Theresa's university: "Justi et injusti scientia."

Among those who joined the attack on Klimt in 1900 was the critic Karl Kraus. At one level, Kraus simply shared the views of Friedrich Jodl: "An unphilosophic artist may paint [philosophy]," he wrote, "[but] he should allegorize it [only] as it appears to the philosophic minds of his age."[7] At another level, Kraus had a deeper concern: namely, to rescue *Geist* (mind) and ethics from the sensuousness and the aestheticism with which, in his view, his own generation was corrupting them.

Kraus in journalism and literature, and his ally Adolf Loos in architecture and applied arts, are in some sense the last puritans of Austria, prophets of the culture of law and the word against those who would compromise it with hedonistic weakness and adventitious beauty. As the aesthetes of Jung-Wien and Secession broke the mid-century cultural synthesis by assigning primacy to cultivated feeling, the Krausians broke it by propounding the primacy of Geist. Kraus and Loos thus open a new chapter in the history of Austria's two cultures. They attacked first their fathers for hypocrisy, then their brothers for unprincipled aestheticism. They sundered what the liberal fathers put together when they assimilated gracious, theatrical culture into their own rationalist tradition, enhancing their social status and concealing their modern commercial identity behind historical screens, as in the Ringstrasse development. In this the last puritans were at one with the general disillusion of die Jungen of various persuasions. But where most turned toward the arts for their psychological truth, their redemptive power, their solace, or their capacity to produce through illusion a life of refined beauty, Kraus and Loos upheld and expanded instead what they saw as the masculine virtues of reason and language. Mordant in their critique of a society whose intel-

lectuals and spokesmen were *too* aestheticized, they left a place for the
truth of art essentially only in the sphere of private vision.

It was here that these conservatives of rational-ethical Geist became
protectors to artists of still another, younger new generation, the expressionists. Anti-aesthetes, these artists threw off the veil of sublimation to
express unmediated a raw and febrile existential truth that honored *no*
cultural convention. To this group belonged Kokoschka, the Schoenberg
of the middle years, the poet Trakl. The older partisans of Geist became
the patrons and allies of these new apostles of instinct, crushing the aesthetes between them.

WE STARTED in the university at the beginning of the liberal transformation of the Habsburg Empire. Let us close in the theater at its end.
Three major plays, completed after the disintegration of the empire, embody their authors' final visions of the function of aesthetic culture in
Austrian society: Hugo von Hofmannsthal's *Der Turm* (1926); Kraus's *Die
letzten Tage der Menschheit* (1926); and Arnold Schoenberg's *Moses und
Aron* (1932). Each play carries to its bitter end the strands of the tradition: Hofmannsthal's, the culture of grace; Kraus's, the culture of law and
the word; Schoenberg's, the attempted synthesis of the two.

Hugo von Hofmannsthal, reared in the temple of art to be the highest
exemplar of the aesthetic-aristocratic tradition, early broke out of a solip-
sistic lyricism to find in drama a way of knitting together the disparate
elements of his age. The poet, he said, would have to take into himself "a
wholly irrational mass of the non-homogeneous, which can become [his]
... torture."[8] The poet's trial would spur his task: to reveal the world of
relations [*Bezüge*] among the fragmentary elements, the hidden forms by
which the parts of life are bound to each other.

Hofmannsthal accepted the breakdown of language itself. Like a Baroque man, he affirmed a polylingual reality. In his plays, as in life, every
character has his own dialect. The problem is not to find and save the
single truth of pure language, but to adapt the voices, dialects all, to each
other, as, in letter writing, one tempers one's diction to the person addressed. The social potential of language was in its adaptability, its capacity to adjust to otherness, its plastic power for interpersonal bonding.

Hofmannsthal was drawn to the Baroque, and especially to the era of
Maria Theresa, as a culture of grace in which the deepest problems of

class relations were dealt with through a recognition of difference, yet with a faith in an unseen unity as the ground of reconciliation. The multiform and loose structure of Baroque language followed social and personal difference, and could produce a unity without uniformity.

In his play *The Tower*, on which he worked for twenty-five years, Hofmannsthal adapted a Counter-Reformation drama of Calderon, *La vida es sueño* (Life is a Dream), to the problems of his own time. The hero is a prince, imprisoned and brutalized by a father who justifies repression by the rationale of an order based on law. But the law excludes the masses from political participation, and rebellion ensues. The prince becomes a leader of the people and tries to redeem society with a dynamic form of social order by the nonaggressive paradigm of art. The poet-prince fails, outwitted by the manipulators of the masses. It is too late for a polity based, like the father's, on law alone; too soon for a renewed politics of grace that sublimates instinct in pluralistic harmonization as in the Baroque ideal. In the words of his dying hero, Hofmannsthal records the failure of his own mission as social poet-redeemer: "Bear witness that I was here," says Sigmund the prince, "although no one recognized me."[9]

The critic Karl Kraus, defender of the innate purity of language and the word, chose two principal roles in which to carry on his critique of culture: as journalist and as man of the theater. He exposed the lies of the press—and the society it served—by analyzing its writing. Similarly, as a lonely prophet in the theater, Kraus set himself up as savior of the dramatic art by reading plays to the public, thus removing them from the stage to the lectern. Since a debased theater yoked drama to the virtuosity of the performers, Kraus maintained, the text, the word, could recover its own truth-speaking power only by rescuing it from the corrupting incarnation of the stage. Lessing had once called the theater his pulpit; Kraus, with a not dissimilar moral conception of literature, made of his pulpit/lectern a theater, thus to save the word from the world, culture from society.

In his great apocalyptic satire, *Die letzten Tage der Menschheit* (The Last Days of Mankind), Kraus conflated his two chosen roles, those of reporter and of man of the theater. Of more than eight hundred pages of his work, a Baroquelike spectacle of Austria's self-destruction in World War I, about one-half consists of documentary material in loose collage—newspaper stories, speeches, decrees, poems, etc. Kraus is the exemplary journalist, the faithful reporter of the faithless abuse of language to disguise the hideous purposes of war. He places the abused language, the multiple dialects of social reality, in contexts in which what is said emerges as the negative of the ideality and the logical purity of thought that language itself contains. In utter contrast to Hofmannsthal, Kraus's language never reconciles or compromises; it only makes the truth visible by registering in pure overtones the opposite of its own fragmentation and debasement. The word remains transcendent; only the phrase (in the pejorative sense) prevails in the reality of war that is itself the horrifying consequence of the corruption of culture and society.

True to the decomposition of humanity that he wishes to portray through the degeneration of language, Kraus provides no plot line, only a vast series of episodes revealing relentlessly aspects of the end of mankind that is the last judgment. As he had read plays to save them from production, here Kraus wrote a play so vast as to appear unsuited for production. Of its characters, only a single, isolated commentator, the pessimistic curmudgeon, records the progress of dehumanization. He is in some sense the last *homo juridicus* whose sensitivity to corruption enables him to strike through society's masks of ideality and nobility, courage and aesthetic illusion, to the truth of bestiality into which the culture sinks in war. Although resembling a Baroque *Schauspiel* (drama) in its sprawling form, *Die letzten Tage* does not, in the Baroque manner, absorb the earthly tragedy into divine comedy. Instead the bitter earthly comedy is a divine tragedy. God has lost control of the world as bourgeois man destroys the Geist that is his birthright. It is a suicide of the culture of the word.

Where the last word in Hofmannsthal's Baroque drama is spoken by Prince Sigmund, the defeated hero of the culture of grace, the last word in Kraus's satirical *Trauerspiel* (tragedy) is spoken by God—a God of law whom Austrian society has rendered impotent: "I did not wish it"—"Ich habe es nicht gewollt."[10] God, so it is said, is repeating the words of Emperor Francis Joseph on the coming of the war.

Hofmannsthal and Kraus each memorialized in their dramas the failure of their own efforts to revitalize society through the cultures of grace and the word, respectively. It remained for Arnold Schoenberg to dramatize the failure of those two traditions in their relation to each other. This he did in his great opera *Moses und Aron*.

Schoenberg had been in his early years a participant in fin-de-siècle *Gefühlskultur*, expressing in his early music (*Verklärte Nacht*; *Gurrelieder*) its sensuous sense of flux and its aestheticized instinctualism. But he had come, with Kraus and especially Adolf Loos, to reject the cult of beauty in favor of Geist, asserted within his own acute alienation in a demoralized world.

In *Moses und Aron* Schoenberg dramatized truth and beauty, respectively, in the persons of Moses and Aron, joined in a fraternal alliance that failed. The two brothers stood between two great forces that they were ordained to connect: on the one side, God, the "unrepresentable," absolute spirit; on the other, the people, corruptible flesh, in need of redemption. The people cannot receive God's abstract truth directly; it must be given concreteness, be made accessible to the senses, through art. Moses, the prophet of God's word and law, can speak but does not sing: too pure for art, for the materialization of spirit, he cannot himself reach the people. Hence he commits to Aron the artist the communication of the word through the senses. Art's hull of sensuousness distorts the purity that is truth; the appetite of the people corrupts it further, debasing the sensuosity of art into the sensuality of the flesh. Thus the Golden Calf replaces the Decalogue. It was the highest irony that the composer's opera hero should be the anti-artist, incapable of song except in a fleeting moment when he calls on Aron to purify his thought. His most anguished moment of despair is at the failure of the word: "Das Wort, das Wort, das mir fehlt."

Within the opera's tragic impasse resonates a comprehensive rejection of all the major formative forces in the Austrian tradition: the Catholic culture of grace, wherein the word is incarnate and made manifest in the flesh; the secular adaptation of the culture of grace by the bourgeoisie to supplement and sublimate its own primary culture of law; and finally, the turning to art as itself the source of value, as religion-substitute in liberalism's crisis of the fin-de-siècle. The weight of all are felt in this Hebrew prophet's opera written against opera, the queen of Austria's theatrical arts.

Is art as a redemptive enterprise fully condemned then in *Moses und Aron*? Hardly. For without art, without Aron, the word could not and cannot reach the people. Put another way, one might say that Schoenberg implies that Hofmannsthal and Kraus need each other still. Without art and grace the word becomes impotent. Then the man of truth becomes a solitary, dwelling pure in the wilderness; solitary, far from the corrupting common lot. "In the wilderness," Schoenberg's Moses enjoins his people, "you are invincible and will achieve the goal: unity with God."[11] It is a victory of the word, but one that is de-socialized, removing the word from the world. It marks an end to the attempt of Austrian liberal culture to unify the two conflicting elements in Austrian cultural tradition, to build a rationalistic *theatrum mundi* with the help of art.

NOTES

1. Robert A. Kann, *Kanzel und Katheder. Studien zur österreichischen Geistesgeschichte vom Spätbarock zur Frühromantik* (Vienna, 1962).
2. Carl E. Schorske, *Fin-de-Siècle Vienna: Politics and Culture* (New York, 1980), pp. 5–8.
3. Metastasio's program of February 1755 is reproduced in Justus Schmidt, *Die Alte Universität und ihr Erbauer Jean Nicolas Jadot* (Vienna and Leipzig, 1929), 54–56.
4. *Die Fackel*, no. 1 (beginning of April [sic], 1899), 15.
5. *Neue Freie Presse*, March 28, 1900, cited in Hermann Bahr, *Gegen Klimt* (Vienna, 1903), 23.
6. Ibid. For a fuller account, on which the above is based, see Carl E. Schorske, *Fin-de-Siècle Vienna: Politics and Culture* (New York, 1980), 226–51.
7. *Die Fackel*, no. 36 (end of March [sic], 1900), 19.
8. Hugo von Hofmannsthal and Eberhard von Bodenhausen, *Briefe der Freundschaft* (Berlin, 1953), 97.
9. Hugo von Hofmannsthal, *Dramen, Gesammelte Werke in Einzelausgaben*, edited by Herbert Steiner (Frankfurt-am-Main, 1953), 4:207.
10. Karl Kraus, *Die letzen Tage der Menschheit* (Munich, 1957), 770.
11. Arnold Schoenberg, *Moses und Aron*, libretto, in Columbia Masterworks recording K3L241/KL520 (n.p., 1957), no pages; translation by author.

Generational Tension
and
Cultural Change

DOUBTLESS Greek myth-makers and modern psychoanalysts touched an eternal verity when they documented the troubles that beset the relations of fathers and sons. Eternal verities, however, do not express themselves uniformly in historical life. In Sophocles's Thebes, an Oedipal situation produced a political crisis; in Hamlet's state of Denmark, an Oedipal tension coincided with political rottenness. Among the intellectuals of Freud's Vienna, Oedipal tension first received reenforcement from a political crisis, then became generalized as a cultural phenomenon and finally was swept away by the Expressionist culturemakers of the early twentieth century.

The object of my concern here is not with the nature and validity of generational theory, but with the historical understanding of the emergence of modernist higher culture in Vienna. To what extent did those who hammered out a new set of cultural values identify themselves as a generation? When was generational self-definition connected with the substance of cultural innovation, when detached from it? The exploration of such questions, however tentative, may offer some clues to the stages by which the cultural innovators of the twentieth century asserted their independence both of the immediate past and, in a larger sense, of history as such. For a sense of distancing, a break from all that has preceded, characterized the consciousness of the Austrian "moderns" from their first appearance.

To connect this cultural change with that of generational identity, I shall follow the trail that the historical actors themselves marked out with a simple blaze: the term *Die Jungen* (the young ones). Whenever Die Jungen appear, we shall pause to investigate, to see whether new modes of meaning-making are issuing from the matrix of nineteenth-century culture under the sign of youth, of generational solidarity.

◦✐◦

AUSTRIAN liberal politics provided the context for the first appearance of Die Jungen. It was the unhappy fate of the Austro-German liberals in 1867 to establish constitutional government only as a consequence of national defeat. Prussia's victories, first over Austria in 1866, then over France in 1871, destroyed all possibility of a democratic Greater Germany with Austrian participation. With their long-cherished and juridical objectives largely realized in the constitutional reform of 1867, the classical liberals placed Austrian patriotism above German nationalism. The drama of Bismarck's unification of Germany, however, fanned the flames of national feeling, creating among many Austro-Germans bitter resentment against their government for its cosmopolitan indifferentism and its anti-Prussian posture.

In 1870, the parliamentary liberals divided on the national issue, with party cleavage taking the form of a generational one. "He who placed his Austrianism above his Germanism was 'old,'" the historian Richard Charmatz wrote. "He who felt that he had come into the world as a German . . . was 'young.'" At the polls, the Old Liberals prevailed, but in the universities, Die Jungen found powerful resonance. The universities became in the 1870s and 1880s the storm center of German nationalism, with student organizations and demonstrators engaging in almost constant conflict with university authorities. Old social divisions contained to some degree the spreading nationalist anger. The traditional, more aristocratic student formations—the so-called corps—remained loyal to the Austrian state. The more open *Burschenschaften*—nationalistic fraternities—and the newly founded German national clubs, whose members were middle-class and often Jewish, became the centers of nationalist political and cultural ferment.

Youthful indignation with the Old Liberals over the national question was compounded by the increasingly pressing social question. The so-called "Citizens' Ministry" of the liberals, while destroying the remnants of medieval craft organization in the name of economic freedom, took no measures to cope with the social suffering attendant on rapid industrial development. In 1870, socialist leaders of demonstrations for universal suffrage and the right to organize were tried for treason and sentenced to prison. The economic crash of 1873 occasioned new economic deprivation for which ascendant liberalism, both political and economic, was widely held responsible. It also led to the disclosure of scandals of speculation in which the liberal political elite was widely involved. Since civic rectitude and economic prosperity had been central to the liberals' claim to rule, corruption and depression struck to the heart of their legitimation.

The failures in four different areas, then—national unity, social justice, economic prosperity, and public morality—converged in the early seventies to produce a deep crisis of confidence in liberalism before it had had the chance to stabilize its newly won power. University youth, in anger and frustration at the comprehensiveness of liberalism's failure, sought not only a new politics but also new philosophic and cultural premises to replace the juridical rationalism of their fathers. The political side of this quest brought the student movement into alliance with the nationalistic new right. Its leader, the disaffected liberal Georg von Schönerer, found an intellectual foothold in the strongest Vienna student organization. The students found a cultural rationale for their new politics in Richard Wagner and the early Friedrich Nietzsche. Critical of the rational state and the scientific spirit, both thinkers exalted archaic Greek culture as models for the regeneration of German society. Wagner added to the glorification of the polis the special allure of Germanic myth, thus enriching his archaic communitarian vision with a national-populist appeal for the young German militants. Both thinkers affirmed instinct, vindicating its claims against "bourgeois" reason and the analytic spirit. Activated in the public sphere, instinct seemed to offer a new fraternal bonding that could transform a state based on competition and rationalized egotism into a true folk community. Liberated in the individual sphere, instinct would restore the life of feeling to a psyche suffering from an excess of intellect and rational desiccation. The new Dionysian culture, as William McGrath, the pioneering scholar of the subject, has called it,[1] thus had both a social-communitarian aspect and a depth-psychological one. Both elements challenged and eroded the authority of liberalism as a sociocultural system.

Biographical and literary evidence suggests that the emergence of the new Dionysian culture produced in its political phase both a sense of generational identity in university youth and a tension between fathers and sons. The critic Hermann Bahr recalls returning to his home in Linz from his freshman year at the University of Vienna and announcing to his father, "Liberalism is finished. A new age is dawning. Make way for us!" "What," asked his stunned father, "have they done with you in Vienna?" Soon, the son reports, it turned out that other fathers in Linz—"old liberals like him"—gathered with the elder Bahr to recount similar experiences with "sons who had brought [the word] from Vienna that liberalism was over. And the fathers sat together, unable to grasp it, to see all youth defecting."[2] McGrath has shown similar tensions invading the families of the Gymnasium students who were to provide the intellectual leadership of populist nationalism in the university.[3] Reflecting on his youthful experience in maturity, one of these erstwhile anti-liberals reminds us that youthful rebellion could be not only heady but traumatic: "Torn loose from everything existing around me, separated from my beloved father . . . , robbed of any support, I stood on a surface which shook volcanically. . . . Years passed in which I had the feeling of being a lost swimmer struggling against the waves of the ocean. Thus I had to experience within myself the entire dismemberment, the monstrous spiritual and moral distress and struggle of an individualistic time."[4]

From a purely historical perspective, the power of community formation exhibited by a peer group in times of socio-cultural crisis would seem to provide fortification and support to its participants. From a psychological perspective, however, the drastic reshuffling of the self required by the break from obsolescent inherited values perhaps generates the strong communal bonding associated with such movements—especially of students—as an answer to the individual's loss of familial anchorage and support. Certainly in the case of the crisis of fin-de-siècle Austria, Oedipal conflict surfaced as generational tension only in the context of the incapacity of the liberals in ascendancy to realize more than their constitutional goals. The quests for wholeness in the community and for instinctual gratification for the individual were ideologically cognate to the psychological needs of children of a legalistic culture caught in the dissolution of their own heritage.

The term *Die Jungen* did not long attend the radical national movement. With the establishment of a full-fledged German National party by Georg von Schönerer in 1885, the movement "grew up," and students lost their determining role in it. Although student nationalism continued as a strong political factor in Austria until 1914, it lost all autonomy. In contrast to the youth movement in Germany, which exploited the space allowed it by the social system but held aloof from politics, Austrian university nationalists were politicals, articulated into the radical right. The Wagnerian culture that the generational revolt had spawned sur-

vived among them only in flattened form as political ideology, while the
creative potentialities of that culture were developed in the nonpolitical
spheres of art and philosophy.

The critical factor in sundering the cultural impulse in Die Jungen
from the political one was the rise of anti-Semitism. A traditional current
in the conservative student organizations, anti-Semitism began at the end
of the 1870s to spread through the newer clubs that were the principal
carriers of the nationalist movement. Young Jews who had participated in
the crusade for German folkish "regeneration"—often in leading positions—found themselves extruded and excluded as the nationalism of the
new right showed its atavistic side. Theodor Herzl, Sigmund Freud,
Gustav Mahler, the later Socialist leader Victor Adler, and the historian
Henrich Friedjung were among those who underwent the traumatic experience of the corruption of their German cause and the blighting of
their hopes by anti-Semitism. As each perforce withdrew from German
folkish politics, he carried with him to the sphere of his life's work some
portion of the Dionysian culture. For all these men the rise of anti-
Semitism was not the first trauma, but the second of their short lives: as
the liberal culture of their fathers had failed them in the 1870s, so the
nationalist culture of their brothers turned against them in the 1880s.
Having quested for a new, holistic cultural community as Germans, they
found themselves threatened and abandoned to a new isolation as Jews.
Many gentile anti-racists shared their fate, and joined them as they
sought to make new meaning in a world that had eroded their social
faith.

⌾⌇

HAVING fallen into disuse during the 1880s, the term *Die Jungen* reappeared in the following decade on another terrain: that of the arts. The
literary movement which became known as *Jung-Wien* or *Jung-Oester-
reich* dissolved the linkage of culture with politics that had characterized
die Jungen of the seventies. German nationalism, the powerful catalyst of
cultural renewal in the seventies, gave place to a conscious cosmopolitanism and a deliberate outreach to the artistic models and movements of
other countries, especially France. Hermann Bahr, who more than any
other tried to define the movement's character, had in 1883 gone to Berlin in pursuit of his nationalist dreams. Soon disillusioned with Bismarck's Germany, he went on to Paris, where he passed from political

activism to aesthetic passivism. He returned to Vienna as a devotee of the French symbolists and decadents. Bahr's career represented concretely the wider evolution of the young bourgeois intelligentsia as it turned from a communitarian politics gone sour to aesthetic culture.

Jung-Wien had no formal organization, nor did it center upon a major figure in the manner of the school of the poet Stefan George in Germany. Not even a stylistic orientation gave coherence to the movement, for its writers ranged from the sociological naturalism of Arthur Schnitzler to the lyrical impressionism of young Hugo von Hofmannsthal. What gave the group its identity were two preoccupations: the nature of modernity and the life of the psyche.

The quest for "the modern" obviously implied a break from the past, but the young literati conceived this differently from the political Wagnerian culture makers of the seventies. The young Wagnerians had rejected the immediate past, in the form of liberalism, but sought attachment to the remote past, both Greek and Germanic, to regenerate society in the present and to build for the future. They still did their thinking with history. Jung-Wien espoused the "modern" (a word used only in deprecation by Wagnerians) as a form of existence and a sensibility different from all had gone before, one detached from history. Although they still used the repertorium of history as a source of images, they ceased to regard history as a meaningful succession of states from which the present derived its purpose and its place in human destiny. Modernity meant *das Gleitende*, said Hofmannsthal—the slipping or sliding away of the world. The literary figures who embodied the modern condition for these Jungen were playboys and/or aesthetes, men of sensuality or men of sensibility, socially functionless and existentially disengaged. In its psychological aspect, the modern malady was the dissolution of the ego. The seismographic consciousness of the fin-de-siècle character was assailed now by the forces of instinct within, now by the inchoate powers of the world without. The resultant condition portrayed in the literature was drift.[5] Ernst Mach's psychology, with its integration of stimulus and sensation into a single complex, provided the writers with an epistemological legitimation for their sense of loss of control. Mach's phrase, "the 'I' is unrescuable" became a virtual slogan for the literati.[6]

Jung-Wien showed little of the Wagnerians' anger at the culture of the fathers and their world—only sadness at the illusory nature of their elders' rational and moral premises. As Austrian society fell into the political impasse of national and social struggle in which none seemed able to

win and none to control, the Promethean temper of the younger generation yielded to an Orphic one. The autumnal mood of impotence and
pessimism, to be sure, only increased the sense of a break with the culture of the fathers. Generational identity focused now, however, not as in
the seventies on the failure of the fathers to realize the full promise of
the progressive liberal creed, but on the sons' incapacity to create community out of the pluralized elements into which the erstwhile social
whole had become fragmented.

What remained was for modern man to find his own voice, to learn
how to state his own truth independent of the dead hand of the past.
Hofmannsthal expressed the new distancing from the past in a lyric prologue to Schnitzler's *Anatol*. Though Schnitzler's play dealt with a modern sensualist, a role-player without social function or commitment,
Hofmannsthal set his prologue in a Rococo garden, to the modern Viennese a paradise lost of a gracious and well-ordered world. There the new
Young Ones could fleetingly erect the scaffolding to play "the commedia
of [their] spirit," the "agonies and episodes" of their precocious, sad existence. The ancient garden setting that gives meaning to the play-to-
come is historical: formal, geometrically ordered, and dead. The drama is
modern: an instinctual whirl. The traditional drama of society evoked in
the setting of the prologue is dissolved in Schnitzler's play itself into a
psychic scene of drifters.

In *The Road into the Open* (1907), the novel that he regarded as his
greatest achievement, Schnitzler painted a more comprehensive group
portrait of the young generation of educated Viennese trying to find a
way in Austria's social centrifuge. A large cast of young adults, many of
them Jews, illustrates the full range of options still open to them in post-
liberal politics and culture. Although the members of this generation
espouse conflicting positions—socialism, Zionism, the army, and so
forth—they form and sustain social and amorous relations with relative
ease across the intellectual and ideological barriers that divide them, as
though united by a tacit recognition of the partial and provisional character of all positions, all values, in their destructured world.

An Oedipal tension runs as a strong, subtly unifying subcurrent beneath the pluralized world of the young. Whatever the differences among
them, the youthful characters have all espoused outlooks that set them
off from their fathers. Yet Schnitzler treats the Oedipal tension, despite
its omnipresence, in terms of cultural difference between generations,
not as an eternal verity.

His older-generation figures are committed to work, individual responsibility, and humane understanding. They lack all insight into the historical condition that distorts the lives and commitments of the young. Their values are at once admirable and anachronistic. One character of the younger generation, the writer Heinrich Bermann, an evident spokesman for Schnitzler's own melancholy perceptions of the modern condition, also manifests father-hatred at its most drastic. Heinrich's father was a Jewish liberal whose parliamentary and legal career was destroyed by anti-Semitism. The son's existential wisdom is coupled with a bitter rejection of his father for his rationalistic illusions. He accepts the contradictory character of the new social reality and treats all the options his contemporaries embrace as having only a subjective validity. "I do not stand above the parties," he says, "but rather side with all of them or against all of them. I have no divine justice [like the father's], but a dialectic one."[7] Heinrich's too comprehensive vision reduces him both to political passivity and to ineffectiveness as a literary artist. His ultimate conviction is that all the "roads into the open"—the myriad philosophic or political alternative approaches to the problems of modern Austrian society—"lead into the self."[8] Schnitzler thus transmutes the social problem he so realistically describes into a psychological one. Where the fathers had lived by naive faith as the underpinning of social action, the sons, suffering from loss of control over life and destiny, can approach public life only as private option; hence they often withdraw to the life of art and instinct. Richard Beer-Hofmann expressed Jung-Wien's sense of the collapse of cohesion in modern culture and society in a phrase: "Keiner kann keinem Gefährte hier sein" (None can here be companion to another). The communitarian ethos of the political Jungen of the seventies, with its nationalism and its still-strong ties to history, had been swept away by the trauma of anti-Semitism, leaving only a sense of the incoherence of modern society and a turn inward in the search for meaning.

IN THE plastic arts, the cultural break from the past in the effort to define modernity came later than in letters, but was even more self-conscious. Within the Künstlergenossenschaft, Austria's principal artists' association, Die Jungen—the name was used once more—began in 1895 to organize against prevailing academic constraints in favor of an open, experimental attitude toward painting and the applied arts. Like Jung-Wien in literature, the young rebels in art looked to the more advanced countries for models of modernity: to French Impressionists and English Pre-Raphaelites, Belgian art nouveau and German Jugendstil. By 1897 the dissidents broke away to found a new organization called "the Secession."

No single aesthetic characterized the new movement. The artistic common ground of the participants was negative: their rejection of the classical and historical realist tradition of the mid-century in their search for "modern man's true face." Thus in its inception, the movement was as much a phenomenon of rupture and dissolution as of new construction.

The ideology and rhetoric of the Secession, however, was rich in resonances from the radical political culture of the 1880s. A spokesman explained that the Secession drew its inspiration from the Roman *secessio plebis*, when the plebs, defiantly rejecting the misrule of the patricians, withdrew from the Republic. At the same time, the Secession proclaimed a regenerative intent, calling its journal *Ver Sacrum* (Sacred Spring). This title was drawn from a Roman ritual of consecration of youth in times of national danger. Whereas in Rome the fathers pledged their young to a divine mission in order to save society, in Vienna the young pledged themselves to the redemption of art from the spirit of commerce and the dead hand of tradition that the fathers represented for them. The painter Gustav Klimt, spiritus rector of the Secession, expressed the Secession's aggressive accent on youth and its will to liberation in a poster for its first exhibition. He portrayed the figure of Theseus slaying the Minotaur to free the children of Athens.

On the new exhibition building of the Secession built in 1898, a veritable temple of the religion of art was blazoned another provocative profession of modernity: "To the time its art; to art its freedom." Klimt contributed to the first issue of *Ver Sacrum* an allegorical drawing linking youth and modern truth: *Nuda veritas*, in the form of a nubile waif, holds up the mirror to modern man. Thus the Secession combined in its initial rhetoric elements from both previous movements of Die Jungen: from the political-folkish Jungen of the seventies and eighties were drawn the themes of cultural regeneration and of revolt against corruption; from Jung-Wien of the early nineties, the anti-historical modernism. A tincture of Oedipal revolt suffused the whole.

Almost two decades separated the appearance of Die Jungen as protagonists of a new literary culture and the Secessionist rebellion in the quite different sphere of the visual arts in 1897. Can these be seen as parts of a single generational phenomenon? At the most literal level, that of the age cohort, there is clear commonality. In both Jung-Wien and Secession, most of the leading figures were born between 1860 and 1870.[9]

Although those most deeply engaged by the nationalist student movement were for the most part children of the 1850s,[10] those born in the early 1860s, like Gustav Mahler, Hermann Bahr, and Theodor Herzl, also participated as students in the peak of the movement's parapolitical Wagnerian intoxication in the early 1880s. It is not clear whether any of the artists of the Secession were involved in populist politics. But those who belatedly (in their thirties) became Die Jungen in the visual arts were certainly influenced by the cultural ideas associated with the earlier revolt. Two principal formulators of the Secession's aims were direct carriers. As literary advisors to *Ver Sacrum*,[11] Hermann Bahr and Max Burckhard injected the spirit and rhetoric of populist politics into the crusade for a new visual culture. Both had been active first in politics: Bahr, as we have seen, as student nationalist in 1882–1883; Burckhard, as an important progressive legal reformer who had set up a system of administrative courts to handle grievances against the decisions of bureaucrats. Whereas Bahr found political inspiration in Wagner, Burckhard was a Nietzschean as well. Both men had turned from politics to literature in the late 1880s. Bahr became a critical voice of Austrian modernism in Jung-Wien, while Burckhard in 1891 achieved one of the most prestigious positions in Austria, the directorship of the Burgtheater. In this post, Burckhard enlarged the classical historicism of the Burgtheater playbill with two new kinds of play: dialectic folk theater, and the works of modern, naturalistic dramatists such as Ibsen and Schnitzler. The first of these reflected Burckhard's populism, the second his commitment to the avant-garde. With Bahr, he brought to the Secession a politics of regeneration transposed into the cultural sphere, to give a civic significance to the new art. The two men assured that most of the layers in the history of Die Jungen were incorporated into the Secession's ideology. Only German nationalism was now noticeably missing from their ideology. In a spirit not specifically German, but cosmopolitan and modern, the Secession would open Vienna to the arts of all Europe in order to find forms appropriate to a modern, multinational Austria.

The burst of cultural communitarianism that gave a kind of parapolitical stamp to the Secession's "springtime of art" in 1897 and 1898 quickly evaporated. While folkish motifs appeared in some of the group's decorative arts—book illustration, art for children, textiles, and so on—their principal stylistic tendency was sophisticated and abstract. In painting, where the ideational content was strongest, Gustav Klimt set the tone, recapitulating in his own way the concerns of the literary men: the dissolution of the ego, the power and meaning of instinct—especially sexuality. In Klimt's drawings, one can see the energetic curvilinear style borrowed from the German Jugendstil dissolve into the short-fibered nervous contour of his tense and febrile female figures. His search for sexual liberation brought forth lubricious playgirls who were as threatening as they were seductive. (Nineteenth-century repressions died hard.) As previous generations of painters studied anatomy, Klimt attended lectures in psychopathology for inspiration.

Klimt's Orphic quest into the nether reaches of the psyche particularly shocked contemporaries, for he had firmly established himself as a master of what he now subverted: the solid historical naturalism that he had used with such success in decorating the great public buildings of the Ringstrasse. In the last of his major Ringstrasse commissions, a series of ceiling paintings for the University of Vienna, Klimt expressed the new generation's postpolitical sense of life. As we have seen in the preceding essay, these paintings, representing the faculties of philosophy, medicine, and jurisprudence, made the university a center of conflict over modern art as it had been over nationalist politics. Klimt used some of the same philosophical materials as the student radicals before him, but for pessimistic metapsychological purposes rather than militant political ones. Asked to produce pictures glorifying the victory of light over darkness, he projected instead a Nietzschean vision of philosophy in which Enlightenment rationality disappeared before the riddle of a universe of suffering, with only Zarathustra's midnight courage to transform chaos into beauty. Law is unmasked as instinctual vengeance; judgment, as in the words of Blake, is in the loins. In the storm of protest unleashed by the painting, liberal university professors and anti-Semitic politicians found themselves for once at one, condemning from their different perspectives Klimt's subversive modernist vision, so akin to Freud's.

By the years 1900–1903, the time of the public controversy over Klimt's university paintings, no one seems to have thought any longer in terms of generational conflict. The contestants defined what was at issue rather in moral and aesthetic terms. The pessimistic philosophic and psychological truths which Klimt purveyed had strong defenders, but not strong enough to make them acceptable in the public sphere. After a first defense, both Klimt and the Secession retreated, transferring their talents from formulating shocking truths to offering visions of sybaritic beauty. The Klimt group after 1904 turned increasingly to applied arts and portraiture, catering to the private patronage of the "advanced" elite. The regeneration of Austria through culture—the original aim they had so vigorously formulated—shrank to the definition of modern high style for the aestheticized life of the haut monde.

❧

As VIENNA's fin-de-siècle pioneers of twentieth-century higher culture came to the end of their creative thrust, a new generation of innovators arose to proclaim harsher truths and values. Like their predecessors the first "moderns," the Expressionists—for under this label they may loosely be grouped—found each other across the barriers that separate the cultural specialties. The painters Kokoschka and Schiele, the poet Trakl and the novelist Musil, the composers Zemlinsky, Schoenberg, and Berg, the architect Loos, the philosopher Wittgenstein, if they did not all know each other personally, supported the same periodicals and eagerly consumed one another's intellectual products, as the Wagnerians, Jung-Wien, and the Secession had done before them. There was, then, a sense of kinship as a generation. Yet they did not, as far as I can discover, call themselves *Die Jungen*. Nor did they revolt in any specific way against the fathers and their works.

The Expressionists were, I should suggest, too free of specific social loyalties to define themselves in relation to history, to cultural structure and function in temporal sequence. Not even "modern" had much utility as a concept for them, for the modern must derive its meaning in negative relation to that which, as history, precedes it. The Expressionists had taken up the task of overcoming history where the fin-de-siècle explorers had left it, and pressed forward on the *voyage intérieur* to the realm of raw, existential anxiety or anger, where all previous structures seemed phenomenological sham. Not the past, not modern life was the object of their apocalyptic vision, but human existence as such. They felt neither Austrian nor German, but human. When one of their magazines, *Der Ruf*, called for pulling down the boundary posts between Austria and Germany, it was not to reunite or "save" the Germanies, but to remove a meaningless symbol of statehood.

"Loneliness," wrote Oscar Kokoschka, "compels every man, like a primitive, to invent the [very] idea of society. But the knowledge that every society must remain a utopia forces one to take flight into loneliness." "Let us understand Expressionism as the living voice of man, who is to re-create his own universe." Ex nihilo: a large task! The only such order one could make was a heuristic one, posited by the individual in the face of tough enduring chaos. To discover the inherent destructiveness of that reality was the ground for affirming man's creative—if ultimately fated—power. Where the fin de siècle recovered the sexual instinct, eros, the Expressionists recovered the death instinct, thanatos. The metaphysical wrath of the Expressionists was perhaps too large to find focus in Oedipal revolt or generational resentment. Indeed, they often held their forebears in love and respect: Schoenberg worshiped Mahler; Schiele idolized Klimt. Loos had highest praise for Otto Wagner. They could perhaps accept their elders as role models because it was the elders who had dissolved the previous cultural inheritance, while the young began with modernity as premise to complete the elders' trajectory of alienation. Given the content of their ideas, generational resentment had little place. Robert Musil, in a legend for a future autobiography, suggests the distance of his peer group culture from an Oedipal self-definition. It reads: "My father was younger than I."

Where Musil and the Expressionist generation totally dismissed the Oedipal problem by subsuming it under a historical reality proclaimed dead, Freud proceeded in the opposite direction. He placed the Oedipal conflict at the center of all social existence. Freud's theory, the most widely diffused and visible legacy of the Viennese socio-cultural upheaval to modern thought, occupies a special place in its own historical context. Out of his personal response to his experience as young revolté, Freud avoided self-identification with "the modern," even while, more like the Expressionists than the fin-de-siècle culture makers, he confronted the chaos of history with the order of archetypes.

Freud worked out his theory of primal conflict between father and son in his extensive self-analysis between 1895 and 1899. In those years, the "increasing effects of anti-Semitism upon our emotional life," as Freud made clear in *The Interpretation of Dreams,* surfaced both in his dreams and in his waking recollections of his earlier deep commitments to politics, both as child and as university student. As one born in 1856, Freud had undergone all the experiences of political hope and frustration that shaped the generation of German-Jewish communitarian populists: from the glorious victory of liberalism in 1867 through the crisis of liberalism's national and social failure in the 1870s, the intoxication of the participation in the radical student movement, and the sudden transformation of its meaning by the rise of anti-Semitism. Like Schnitzler, Mahler, Klimt, and others, Freud pressed the experience of political defeat into the service of psychological exploration. But when all the others defined their predicament through the distinction between "historical" and "modern," Freud dissolved the whole cultural sphere into metahistory. Unlike the others, he kept much of the faith of his father—its self-conscious ethnic (though not its religious) Judaism, its principled liberalism, and its rationalism. Where his peers defined their tension with their fathers out of their demand for a new culture, Freud defined his paternal conflict not in revolt against the values his father professed, but in criticism of his failure to live by them fully. In recalling and recounting in the 1890s his dreams and memories of childhood, Freud indicts his father for lack of courage as a Jew and for failure to encourage his child in intellectual pursuits. When Freud finally made peace with his father in a dream crucial to the formulation of his Oedipal theory, he pictured his father as successful political leader and himself as servant through medical science. Integrating his conflict with his father with his own hostility to political authority, Freud coped with the second by establishing the primacy of the first. He thus elevated personal history, determined in the family, over general history, determined in the culture as a whole.[12] Oedipus for him carried all the dimensions of family relations and identity, but lost his character as *rex*. That is, Freud omitted the public significance of the myth in favor of its purely psychological significance.

Seen in terms of the experience of his intellectual peer group, Freud shared their trauma of dissolving liberalism, but subsumed the uniqueness of that experience under the eternal verity of father-son relations, rather than interpreting it as a historical crisis of rationalist culture. He found a form of thought for confronting the modern situation which eliminated the need for that *special* determination of the nature of modernism to which Schnitzler, Klimt, and his other peers devoted themselves. In so doing, he shared more with both the confident rationalism of the orthodox liberal fathers and the existential, archetypal worldview of the Expressionist sons than with his brothers, the ambiguity-ridden culture makers of his own generation who negotiated the difficult passage from historical to ahistorical culture.

———

In the years 1866–1867, when both Austrian and North German liberalism were facing the crisis of redefining their relationship to state, nation, and society, the philosopher-historian Wilhelm Dilthey raised the theoretical question of the role of generations in cultural change. He was then studying an earlier deep crisis of the German bourgeoisie, that of the French Revolution, which gave birth to German Romanticism. Dilthey discovered that many of the strongest creative individuals among the Romantics—Schlegel, Schleiermacher, Hegel, Hölderlin, Novalis, Tieck—were born within a single decade. Well aware that he was concerned with a small subgroup, Dilthey avoided a definition of generation applicable to the whole society. "[A] generation," he wrote, "is constituted of a restricted circle of individuals who are bound together into a homogeneous whole by their dependence on the same great events and transformations that appeared in their age of [maximum] receptivity, despite the variety of other subsequent factors."[3]

In the case of Vienna, the pioneers of twentieth-century high culture conform well to Dilthey's definition. The generational center of gravity of our culture makers falls in the early 1860s; their formative context, the failure of Austrian liberalism in the era of German unification and depression, in the 1870s. That the university became the center of political frustration for the scions of liberal families endowed the rebellion of die Jungen with an initial sharpness of age-group definition and introduced Oedipal tension into the political antagonism. More significant for the future of liberalism as a value system was that Die Jungen developed the Dionysian, populist counterculture as a support for their political criticisms and aspirations. This counterculture lent itself to anti-Semitism, in the same way that Jacobin rationalism spawned the reign of terror, with its grave intellectual consequences for Enlightenment culture. On the other hand, for those who recoiled in shock from the racist consequences of their nationalism, the Dionysian culture and the dissolution of the rationalist ego that accompanied it made possible the exploration of the psyche, the recovery of the nonrational dimension of man in all its richness and ambiguity. Thus the Jungen in literature in the nineties and the Jungen who broke open new vistas in the visual arts at the century's turn were the twice traumatized. The consciousness of the break from history and the search for the special nature of modernity belonged to the experience of depoliticization. The subordination of the social to the psychological as the arena where meaning was to be found was the special contribution of Vienna's generation of Jungen to late liberal culture.

In the light of this trajectory of cultural change, we should not be surprised that the new young ones, the Expressionists, however vigorous—even violent—in their rejection of society and culture, showed less sense of generational identity or Oedipal hostility than the culture makers of the fin de siècle. For this second wave of young revoltés only gave a final, drastic, archetypal formulation to the experience of social destructuring and psychological abandonment that their sensitive elders, in painful recoil from their own aborted regenerative crusade, had already proclaimed as the ground of being in their disintegrating liberal world.

NOTES

1. William J. McGrath, *Dionysian Art and Populist Politics in Austria* (New Haven, 1974).

2. Hermann Bahr, *Austriaca* (Berlin, 1911), 115.

3. McGrath, *Dionysian Art*, 17–32.

4. Max Gruber, quoted in McGrath, *Dionysian Art*, 20.

5. Carl E. Schorske, *Fin-de-Siècle Vienna: Politics and Culture* (New York, 1980), chap. 1.

6. Manfred Diersch, "Empiriokritizismus und Impressionismus," *Neue Beiträge zur Literaturwissenschaft* 36 (1973).

7. Arthur Schnitzler, *Der Weg ins Freie*, vol. 3 of *Gesammelte Werke* (Berlin, 1922), 420.

8. Ibid., 282.

9. *Jung-Wien*: Heinrich Schnitzler, 1862; Hermann Bahr, 1863; Richard Beer-Hofmann, 1866; Hugo von Hofmannstahl, 1873; Peter Altenberg, 1859. *Secession*: (1) painters: Gustav Klimt, 1862; Adolf Böhm, 1861; Wilhelm Bernatzik, 1853; Josef Engelhart, 1864; Carl Moll, 1861; Koloman Moser, 1868; Felizian Myrbach, 1853; Emil Orlik, 1870; and Alfred Roller, 1864; (2) architects: Otto Wagner, 1840; Josef Olbrich, 1867; and Josef Hoffmann, 1870.

10. Victor Adler was born in 1852; Heinrich Friedjung, 1851; Sigmund Freud, 1856; Theodor Herzl, 1860.

11. See *Ver Sacrum* 1:1 (January 1898), 1–3, 8–13.

12. Carl E. Schorske, *Fin-de-Siècle Vienna*, 186–200.

13. Wilhelm Dilthey, *Gesammelte Schriften*, vol. 5 (Leipzig, 1924), 37, as cited in Hans Jaeger, "Generationen in der Geschichte," *Geschichte und Gesellschaft*, 3:4 (1977), 432.

TEN

From Public Scene
to Private Space: Architecture
as Culture Criticism

THE RAPID, confused emergence of modernism in the late nineteeth century as a broad cultural movement self-conscious of its break from history drew architecture into its wake everywhere in Europe. But nowhere more than in Vienna. The reason is not far to seek. It lies in the city's great mid-nineteenth-century redevelopment, the Ringstrasse. There Austrian liberalism, as is the way of triumphant movements, built after 1860 its city on a hill, celebrating in stone its victorious values of rational ethical *Recht* and historical aesthetic *Kultur*. The Ringstrasse area was built into the old imperial capital like an Austrian Canberra or Brasilia into the wilderness. In a grand, homogeneous space was concentrated a complex of monumental public buildings—museums, theaters, the houses of constitutional politics, etc.—and palatial apartment buildings to house the elite. Conspicuously missing from this model city-within-a-city was any place for the industrial workers and work life on which the power of its builders largely rested.

Two features gave the Ringstrasse its importance for the origins of modernism in Austria: its power as a cultural symbol and its historicist style, in which buildings were constructed on Gothic, Renaissance, and neoclassical models. Such was the symbolic force of the new quarter that the Austrians named the whole era of liberal ascendancy for it: *die Ringstrassenära*, just as the English call the same era, after their queen, the Victorian Age. Whether evoking pride or arousing revulsion, the Ringstrasse made of architecture a major subject of public passion and controversy. Thus a contemporary liberal historian, Heinrich Friedjung, hailed the Ringstrasse development as a redeemed pledge of history, wherein the labors and sufferings of centuries of ordinary burghers, whose wealth and talent, long buried, were finally exhumed "like huge beds of coal" in the nineteenth century. "In the liberal epoch," Friedjung wrote, "power passed, at least in part, to the bourgeoisie; and in no area did this attain fuller and purer life than in the reconstruction of Vienna." The architect Adolf Loos, on the other hand, in one of his earliest and most arresting critical forays, branded Ringstrasse Vienna in 1898 with an epithet that stuck: "the Potemkin city." Its architecture he viewed not as the symbol of a fuller and purer life, but as a false front, screening with historicist façades the hollowness and corruption of Austrian society.

In the symbolic struggle over mid-century liberal culture, the so-called historical "style-architecture" in which the Ring was executed became an issue. For the builders and champions of the Ringstrasse, the multiplicity of historical styles, each usually associated with the function of the building it clothed, was itself a sign of the assimilation of the riches of the past by the new educated citizen. For the rebels and critics, on the other hand, the historical styles were signs that the bourgeois was concealing his identity under masks of the past; or—the other side of the coin—that he had failed to find an adequate stylistic expression for his own truth. In rejecting the legitimacy of historical style-architecture the makers of modernity in the late 1890s initially found common cause. If they had a common hell that brought them all together, namely, the moral short-comings of the Ring's historicism, it soon became clear that the critics had very different heavens. It tells us something about modernism and about Loos's place in it to discriminate among the critical tendencies.

ONE can distinguish four schools of architectural criticism of the Ring-strasse, each of which was embedded in a different idea of culture. Two of these had public and social standards, two had private or psychological ones. The public-social critics and the private-psychological ones be-longed to different generations. The two leading social critics, Otto Wagner and Camillo Sitte, were born in the early 1840s, and had lived their mature professional lives in the heyday of liberalism, during the three decades after 1860 when the Ringstrasse was built. Only late in life, in the 1890s, did both men, Wagner and Sitte, develop their critiques of the Ringstrasse.[1]

The psychological architect-critics belonged to the next generation, born in or about 1870. They matured in the 1890s when the great public construction program of the Ring was essentially completed, and com-missions for public buildings had largely dried up. Thus, regardless of political and cultural changes, the economic conditions of architecture alone effectively confined the professional opportunities of the younger generation to the private, largely residential sphere.

The two major critics of the older generation, Sitte and Wagner, saw in the Ringstrasse's design two traditionally recognized elements of architecture in tension: art and utility. Each advocated a different one of these values. Sitte set himself up as "an advocate of the artistic side" against what he saw as the cold, spatial planning of the Ringstrasse, which was adapted to the flow of traffic. Accepting historical style in architecture, with all its capacity for symbolic significance, he called also for the revival of historical design in urban space as well, with a stress on squares rather than on vehicle-dominated streets as in the Ringstrasse design. For him the wide circular street produced anomie and agoraphobia, both associated with the harsh individualism of modern life. Sitte's project was to restore the square in order to arrest the driving flow of men in motion in a space conducive to sociability and congregation. The square was for him the urban form that could generate and sustain community, could restore the sense of belonging to a polis that hectic modern commercial culture was killing.

Like Sitte, Otto Wagner criticized the Ringstrasse for the contradiction between its stylistic profession to tradition in architecture and its rational modernism in street layout and spatial design. But where Sitte demanded a greater fidelity to history, Wagner sought to overcome the antinomy from the other end. He championed the primacy of utility, of modern function. For his city expansion plan, Wagner chose a motto that would have chilled the heart of Sitte: "Artis solo domina necessitas" (Necessity is art's only mistress).

WAGNER had for two decades been a successful architect of Neo-Renaissance apartment buildings. Then he became involved with the design of Vienna's municipal railway system. His imagination caught fire with the possibilities opened for the city by new technology. He proclaimed the infinitely expansible modern city, the megalopolis. Architecture and urban planning must "adapt the city's image to modern man," a frankly economic man. Wagner saw him as energetic, rational, efficient, and urbane, a businesslike metropolitan, a bourgeois with little time, lots of money, and a taste for the monumental. In his innovative textbook, entitled *Modern Architecture*, Wagner called for the recognition of function (or, as he called it, *Zweck*, "purpose") as the determinant of form. During the nineteenth century, he said, the pace of social change had moved so swiftly that architects instead of developing styles suited to answer modern needs, had recourse to historical styles devised to answer the quite different requirements of earlier civilizations. The time had come to create an artistic style for the city consistent with new technologies and building materials, as had been done in the case of railway trains and bridges. "The function of art," Wagner proclaimed, "is to consecrate all that emerges, in the fulfillment of practical aims." Architects and city planners must "make visible our better, democratic, self-conscious and sharp-thinking essence, and do justice to the colossal technological achievements as well as to the fundamentally practical character of mankind."

Wagner showed the way by developing a radically simplified building style suitable to the vehicular perspective on great urban thoroughfares. Anomie held no terrors for this vigorous proponent of a busy megalopolis where the millions would be accommodated in large housing blocks. In these great blocks, Wagner believed, uniformity would be raised to a monumentality directly expressive of modern economic man, whom the builders of the Ringstrasse had hidden in the costumery of "style-architecture."

Sitte and Wagner, in opposite ways, thus attacked the Ringstrasse's historicist synthesis of art and utility, Sitte with the aim of restoring community, Wagner with the aim of creating a modern metropolis for modern commercial society. Both men were thoroughly committed to the public sphere, in which for them the individual acquired his meaning, and from which architecture acquired both its function and its form.

MEANWHILE a younger generation of Austrian intellectuals developed a more thoroughgoing rebellion against the cultural synthesis of the liberal fathers; first in politics, then in literature, and finally in art and architecture. The organizational expression of this revolt in art and architecture was the so-called Secession movement, founded in 1897. Its very name implied withdrawal from the culture of the elders. The motto inscribed on the Secession's exhibition hall proclaimed its break from the past: "To the time its art, to art its freedom." At first this commitment extended to public and private culture alike. The organization's periodical, *Ver Sacrum* ("Holy Spring"), proclaimed in its issues of 1898 the regeneration of

Austrian society through culture, indicting as corrupt and moribund the traditional historicist art of the mid-nineteenth century. It was Adolf Loos, later the most implacable foe of the Secession, who formulated for it the indictment of the Ringstrasse and its culture, under the title "The Potemkin City" (one of the essays later collected in his book *Spoken Into the Void*). The basic charge was hypocrisy. "Whatever the Italy of the Renaissance produced in the way of lordly palaces," he wrote, "was plundered in order to conjure up as if by magic a new Vienna for Her Majesty the plebs." The apartment houses of the Ring were occupied by "swindlers," parvenus who, however small their little room and bath within, presented themselves through the façades of their dwellings as feudal lords.

All Secessionists could agree on hypocrisy, on what was false in the pretentious world of bourgeois *Bildung* (culture) as expressed in the Ringstrasse. To restore its integrity, Sitte and Wagner had each espoused half the mid-century synthesis of historical style and modern urban space—Sitte the former, Wagner the latter. Loos and the Secession's moralistic-aesthetic critique rejected the whole synthesis in the name of honesty, of truth.

But what was modern truth? And what was the role of art in modern life? Here Die Jungen divided, in architecture as in other domains of higher culture, into two camps: the aesthetes and the ethicists. Both were concerned less with society than with the psyche, less with Wagner's and Sitte's communitarian and economic man than with the man of feeling. The artists of the Secession shared the preoccupations of contemporary Jung-Wien writers such as Schnitzler and Hofmannsthal: on the one hand, they explored the instinctual life, especially that of eros, and the dissolution of the boundaries between the "I" and the world, between thought and feeling; on the other, they tried to create a new, meta-historical beauty in architecture and the applied arts to satisfy the sensitive souls of the aesthetically cultivated. Inspired by the English arts and crafts movement, though not by its social theory, the Secession designers worked to transform the use-objects of daily life into works of art.

The presumed client, the new man of *Bildung*, in contrast to his predecessor who enriched his life with the works of acquired historical culture, was expected to define himself from within, to refine his own psyche into art. The forms of living—the house, its furnishings, its art—were to be personal expressions of each man's soul and beauty.

Under these circumstances, the architect became less the builder and more the artist. A new terminology reflected the change: the architect became a *Raumkünstler* (spatial artist); architecture was called *Raumpoesie*. (This in contrast to Otto Wagner, who changed the title of *Moderne Architektur* to *Moderne Baukunst*, the art of building, not poeticizing in space.)

Hermann Bahr, a writer who had his house designed for him by the architect of the Secession's building, Josef Olbrich, describes how, in principle, one should approach one's architect:

> I would first have to tell the architect about my inner beauty . . . through my favorite color, poem, song, my favorite hour of the day. . . . Then he would know me, could feel my essence. This essence he would then have to express through a line, to find the gesture of my essence. Above the gate a verse would be inscribed—the verse of my essence. And what this verse is in words, that same thing must be in every color and every line; and every chair, every wallpaper, every lamp, would be that same verse ever again. In such a house, I would everywhere be able to see my soul as in a mirror. This would be my house. *Hier könnte ich mir leben* [Here I could live of myself], looking at my own image, listening to my own music.

The soon fashionable personalist aesthetic did not often produce such narcissistic extremes, but some of the most important work of the Secession architects reflected its spirit. Especially prominent was the integral conception of exterior and interior, with common motifs serving to unify inner space and outer world. In the nursery of Olbrich's Villa Friedmann one can see not only the mottoes but the attempt to dissolve the walls symbolically, bringing nature into the interior by means of wall paintings consistent with the external scene. Pan-psychism and pan-naturism are fused in the organic forms of the specially designed furniture.

In the famous Palais Stoclet built by Josef Hoffmann, with Gustav Klimt and other Secession artists responsible for the decoration, the aim was to provide both a scene for and a symbol of the life beautiful. The exterior, with its molded bindings to contain the marble-clad blocks of which the house is composed, is a veritable jewel box for the precious and cultivated life it was to house. In consonance with the oft-cited aim of Oscar Wilde, to infuse all life with art, even the clothes of the Stoclet couple were designed to harmonize with the rich, uniformly stylized décor of their house. The portraits by Klimt that date from the time of the building of the Palais Stoclet (1904–1911) reveal the same hermetic encapsulation of the human figure in a luxurious interior whose symbols are largely without any historical reference.

᪥

IN THE face of this kind of glorification of art and its appropriation to the sybaritic life beautiful that soon dominated the Secession, Adolf Loos and his literary ally, Karl Kraus, opened a second front in the crusade for a purified culture. They dissolved the informal brother band that had revolted against the Ringstrasse fathers to launch fratricidal warfare, a warfare of ethicists versus aesthetes. Where the aesthetes of Jung-Wien and the Secession had broken the Ringstrasse synthesis of aesthetic and rational culture by assigning primacy to the aesthetic culture of feeling and the senses, Loos and Kraus took up the other half of the tradition, exalting *Geist*, Mind. The Secessionists turned to the arts for their re-demptive power, their solace and/or their capacity to produce a life of refined beauty, of poetry. Against them Loos and Kraus upheld and ex-panded what they saw as the masculine virtues of Reason, ethics, and the honest truths contained in ordinary language, whether in words or in things. By 1900, Kraus and Loos, doughty last puritans, found each other as champions of the virtues of truth against the corruptions of beauty, whether that beauty was historicist in conception, as with the fathers, or modernist, as with the brothers.

Kraus expressed the idea of the two-front warfare at once parricidal and fratricidal, which he and Loos unleashed:

> Adolf Loos and I—he in artifacts, I in words—have done no more than to demonstrate that there is a distinction between a vase and a chamberpot, and that culture has its running-room within this difference. The others, however, the men of "positive" outlook, are divided between those who treat the vase as a chamberpot [the historicists] and those who treat the chamber-pot as a vase [the modernists].

Kraus for his part chose two arenas of critical action: the press and the theater, the two most important verbal media of Viennese nineteenth-century liberal culture. The crime of the press was to deform the pure referential function of language in factual reporting with the personal coloration of the journalist. Art, or better, artfulness, in journalism was the means whereby the power elite and its journalistic servants manipu-lated the public. Kraus's method for redeeming the word from the aesthetic corruption of the press was close critical analysis of particular newspaper stories. He knew how to make the distorted language of reporting yield up its deeper factual and ethical truth that exposed the abuse to which it had been put. In his one-man journal, *Die Fackel* (The Torch), Kraus exposed like an angry prophet the corruption and hypocrisy prevailing in the public realm.

While demanding rigid moral standards in the public sphere of politics and law, Kraus championed sexual freedom and self-determination in the private sphere. In general, Kraus was a kind of anti-bourgeois bourgeois, upholding the traditional moral values of his class against the practices of his class. It was a hallmark of his cultural criticism that he saw art and the aesthetic as crucial instruments of corruption of the public, serving venality rather than veracity. Art, as expression of the affective life, had, in Kraus's view, best be confined to personal experience, isolated from the public world of power and promotion.

Even in the theater, Kraus hoped to restore purity by withdrawal to the private sphere. He believed that Vienna's theatrical public was corrupted by the excessive stress on the performance skills and popular cults of the actors at the expense of the texts. When Lessing in the eighteenth century created his German national theater for moral, social purposes, he announced that he was making the stage into a pulpit. Kraus, over a century later, went the opposite road: to save the text, the truth of the word, he removed the play from the public stage to the lectern. From it he gave private readings to select audiences. There the moral force of the word could be realized without the corrupting "art" of stagecraft.

In the same down-to-earth spirit that Kraus brought to cultural criticism through analyzing news stories, Adolf Loos tested the culture's state of health by exploring the simple use-objects of daily life—household utensils, furniture, clothing, luggage, plumbing, etc. His bête noire, like Kraus's, was art as it was injected into domains where practicality alone should rule. Not the artist but the craftsman should be our guide. Loos was not concerned with beauty except as it resulted naturally from finding a formal and material answer to a practical need. Again his first target was the historical style: "In the past two decades," Loos wrote, "we have gotten Renaissance, Baroque, and Rococo blisters on our hands because of door handles." He said that he made frequent pilgrimages to a new building because of a door handle. But would the reader not think himself fooled if he saw it? Its chief characteristic was—mere unobtrusiveness.

Simplicity, modesty, unobtrusiveness: such were the virtues that Loos linked to practicality and counterposed against the "stylistic" standards prevailing in the historical design culture of the mid-nineteenth century. It should be observed that all these virtues were ethical as well as aesthetic. Loos's criticisms of objects were at the same time criticisms of the culture that produced them. The early Loos was nothing if not a functionalist. That civilization was highest, he said, which accomplished the business of living in the most direct and economical way. The Greeks "created only that which was practical . . . without concerning themselves about any aesthetic imperative. When an object such as a vase was made so practical that it could not be made any more practical, then they called it beautiful." Are there any such civilized people in our age? Yes, answered Loos: "The English and the engineers are our Greeks. It is from them that we acquire our culture; from them it spreads over the entire globe."

The craftsman and the English gentleman: these two ideal types run through Loos's early criticism. In his Anglophilia, Loos simply shares an attitude fundamental to nineteenth-century Austrian liberalism. The gentleman represents for him the highest combination of bourgeois practicality and aristocratic grace, manifesting itself in a sense for the suitable, the appropriate. Clothing serves Loos as the vehicle for his argument. The German, he observes, asks whether a man is dressed "beautifully"; the Englishman asks only whether he is dressed "well," "correctly." For the gentleman seeks to be not outstanding but inconspicuous, *properly* attired for a given function, from bicycling to a formal occasion. Loos sees the same standard of fitness prevailing in English living culture, from railway cars to furniture. The English have liberated the craftsman from the artist-designer. The reform in our living environment would come, Loos maintained, never from above but from below. "And this below is the workshop."

The position thus far developed by Loos as a critic was a modernism consistent with Otto Wagner's in its stress on practicality. Wagner, however, thought on the grand scale of the res publica, as an urbanist committed to the commercial metropolis. He deliberately sought a new style that could *represent* modernity, an art to consecrate the practical. Loos thought on the small scale, of the multitude of practical objects of daily life. His practicality ignored the factory in favor of the artisan and craftsman who could be counted upon to avoid freighting his objects with adventitious decoration foreign to their purposes. Craft production for a specific purpose aspires to maximum efficiency and minimum cost—in labor, capital, and conception. Artists who add ornaments to give poetic status and meaning to useful objects violate the tendency to economy and rational function that is the mark of civilized man.

Loos thus sought not to find a new applied art, but to get art *out* of the crafts, just as Kraus tried to get literary art out of journalism. Art was not to "penetrate life," but, on the contrary, to be rolled back to the purely private, expressive sphere, where men and women could pursue freely their desires and their ways of making meaning, without dictation from the outer world—or even from the architect. The architect could help make their habitat, but could not and should not give "meaning" to their lives with his symbolic forms.

Loos's most polemical gesture against the Secessionist conception of the architect as space poet was to declare him not an artist at all but a craftsman. The architect's task was of the same order as that of the saddler or the tailor: to fill a practical need as economically as possible. Fantasy, so prized in the ideology of the Secessionists, properly belonged to the artist, but not to the architect. Loos distinguished the two from each other drastically, as follows:

> The work of art is the private affair of the artist. The house is not. . . . The work of art is answerable to no one; the house to everyone. The work of art wants to shake people out of their comfortableness [or complacency: *Bequemlichkeit*]. The house must serve comfort. The artwork is revolutionary, the house conservative.

With such a distinction, Loos placed himself at a polar remove from the Secession architects for whom the house was a projection of personal identity. It helps explain why Loos could, with Kraus, champion Kokoschka and other radical young Expressionists. The cool, geometric neutralism of a Loos house and the febrile psychologism of a Kokoschka or Schiele portrait repelled with equal but opposite force the aesthetic unity of the house beautiful and its symbolic function as private mirror and public expression of the owner's personality.

Loos CARRIED his effort to deprive the architect of his status as artist directly into his own practice. He presented himself, especially to residential clients, with a kind of assertive modesty as a counselor on living space, an advisor in interior renovation and furniture procurement. Even making an allowance for his ironical rhetoric, one must recognize that Loos eschewed in principle the aesthetic architects' attempt to design not only the house but all its furnishings. Loos's stated procedure, at least before World War I, was to urge clients to learn homemaking as they would learn fencing: by doing, by taking the rapier in hand. The architect would serve, like a fencing master, as teacher and consultant.

What issued in his practice from Loos's definition of the role of the architect was in fact a series of interiors, both in apartments and in his houses, furnished in the English manner, with paneling, cabinets, Sheraton and other traditional furnishings consonant with Loos's ideal of gentlemanly comfort and sobriety. This conservatism did not preclude the creation (on occasion) of an environment designed for love life. On the contrary. The principle of interior organization was freedom. Loos was himself a man of powerful sexual appetite. (Drawn to women under twenty, he married three such, had additional affairs, and, like his friend, the writer Peter Altenberg, tried to seduce children.)

The apartment he renovated and furnished for himself and his first wife, Lina, showed a combination of English sober comfort in the living room and frank sensuality in "*das Zimmer meiner Frau.*" Loos published photographs of both rooms in his short-lived periodical *Das Andere* (The Other), whose purpose was provocatively stated in its subtitle: *Ein Blatt zur Einführung abendländischer Kultur in Oesterreich* (A Paper for the Introduction of Western Culture into Austria). The living room with its exposed beams and cozy corner fireplace could have been designed by William Morris or Philip Webb; but the bedroom, with its ingenious integration of bed and floor through fur covering materials anticipates sexy Hollywood decor of the 1920s. What counts in the interior is *intimacy*, self-determination in privacy.

If we turn to the exterior of Loos's houses, we find a quite different character at work. An absolutely ascetic geometricity reigns. The exterior is faceless, or, better, deadpan. It conveys no messages of any kind, symbolizes nothing, represents nothing. It has the virtue of gentleman's clothing: it is *unauffallend*, not noticeable—literally, "not striking." "The house," Loos wrote, "does not have to tell anything to the exterior; instead, all the richness must be manifest in the interior." One can extrapolate from this a view of the public-private distinction in culture as follows: richness belongs not to the outside, the public domain, but to the inside, the private one. The exterior no more reflects the public realm than it expresses the private. It is a mere divider between public and private, proclaiming nothing, imposing nothing, receiving nothing from without, transmitting nothing to the life within but light. It is a wall and a mask that, because it represents nothing, misrepresents nothing. It does not join, but delimits.

◈

WE ARE at the point where the place of Loos in the trajectory of Viennese architecture-as-criticism can stand forth in all its singularity. The major issue which his ethical culture criticism led him to address in architecture was the relation between exterior and interior. This, not "art" and its proper function, contained the problem of modern man for Loos.

In the historical architecture of the Ringstrasse, which was his point of departure, the exterior was unashamedly false to the interior. What all the culture critics—Wagner and Sitte in the older generation, the aesthetes and the ethicists in the younger—saw as falsification can also be seen as aspiration. The Ringstrasse apartment house made a statement, through historical vocabulary, about the weight and worth of the resident. Behind the Renaissance façades people lived in flats decorated in a wide variety of styles—Biedermeier, Empire, high Victorian, not to mention décors inspired by the Secession itself. If the façade misrepresented the interior organization of space, it was in order to proclaim the better the status of its inhabitants as people of acquired high culture. The exterior fulfilled the function of representation; the public mask would be presumed to make the private man. In the dialectic of exterior and interior, the façade had priority; the private man was expected to live up to the historical values the public realm conveyed.

IN THE architecture that Wagner developed in consonance with his critique of the Ringstrasse on urbanist and utilitarian grounds, the interior began to assert itself over the exterior, but mainly through the methods of construction and the choice of materials. Wagner aspired to technological truth in his building form. His buildings, whether office buildings or apartment houses or subway stations, begin to be enclosed volumes rather than hollowed masses. But his exteriors remain public statements as well as expressions of new constructional truth. Architecture is conceived as an element in a larger urban whole, whose social functions and commercial and cultural values must govern its outer face. Wagner's economic man no longer hides his modernity behind historical screens, but is conceived of as a vigorous and convinced participant in the metropolitan public scene. Wagner was the architect whose criticism and building practice liberated the economic and technical realities that had earlier been repressed, buried under historical styles. His modernism is the modernism of a new public man, and his buildings were meant to be experienced as such, outside and inside.

The Secession architects built the house for another kind of modern man, the man of sensitivity and high aesthetic culture. With them, the primacy of the public sphere was subverted. The house became, as the critic Beatrice Colomina has shrewdly observed, a characterization of the owner by the architect. The distinction between exterior and interior is virtually liquidated—"liquified" would be a better word—as the symbolic themes and forms flow freely between outer wall and inner room as in Josef Olbrich's fin-de-siècle residences. As ego, id, and superego are melded in a single seismographic consciousness, the house becomes the mirror of the client. But it also presents him to the outer world. The public sphere has not been dissolved, nor the private encapsulated. For now the exterior gives expression to the personality of the private man, projects it into the public realm. The house serves both as private mirror and public image.

If Wagner transformed architecture within the public sphere, and the Secessionists established the primacy of the private by exhibiting it, Loos extended the logic of privatization by removing from architecture its representational function and its power of symbolic statement. A Loos house is a rational container, imperviously neutral. It cannot be read, for it says nothing; rather, it *does* something. Its exterior is a defense perimeter of the private man. It is fitting that the inveterate Anglophile Loos should have made the house a castle once again. But it is a castle in which the free private man no longer pays any obeisance to public duty, no longer wears a mark of civic identity. With the architect's help, he organizes and disposes of his inner space and inner life behind an outer wall that neither affirms public values, as did Wagner, Sitte, and the Ringstrasse architects, nor conveys private gestures in high aesthetic style, in the manner of Olbrich and Hoffmann. Out of his ethical impulses, his rejection of posing, his love of craft, and his hedonistic affirmation of the unsublimated world of desire, the cool Austrian gentleman Loos built us a dream house of reason, where personal choice could be preserved safe from the public sphere. In it, his relentless culture criticism revealed both its imaginative power and, almost insistently, its social irrelevance.

POSTMODERN architects such as Aldo Rossi and Peter Eisenman have been drawn to Loos as a pioneering forerunner. In his introduction to Adolf Loos's book, *Spoken into the Void*, Rossi pointed to an aspect of Loos's outlook that helps us to understand why: Loos was the enemy of the redemptive claims of modern architecture, which "mythified its relations with industry and reformist politics." Austere in its anti-symbolic facelessness, its deliberate aspiration to an inconspicuous nonsignification, Loos's puritan building style has indeed served those who have been transmuting the technological and social modernism of the first half of our century into the hedonistic formalism of the second.

After World War II, with the depoliticizing of our own intellectual culture under the banner of "anti-ideology," architectural interest has shifted—away from the French technological rationalism of Le Corbusier and the German social idealism of the Bauhaus to the Austrian aesthetic modernism of Adolf Loos. Our postmodernists can see him too as the master of architecture as a language that expresses essentially its own nature; as an architect whose cause is not some ideology external to itself, but the art of building *tout court*; indeed, as a purist who disentangled architecture from culture and society; finally, as a pioneer of that postmodernist form of *art pour l'art* in which architecture becomes self-referential, an architecture about architecture.

From the point of view of architectural form and style, the appropriation of Loos by the postmoderns is surely understandable. But if one looks at Loos in his own time, the relationship between Loos and his admirers today raises problems. For, as we have seen, Loos was above all a culture critic, merciless in his indictment of his society from an ethical point of view quite foreign to the essentially aesthetic concerns of most postmodernists. If Loos, as Rossi implies, did not tell men how to live, he told them in no uncertain terms how *not* to live. He told them not to define modern life through history and not to confuse art with life.

Still, there remains in Loos's critical and architectural utterance an affinity with the position of postmodernism. It lies in his vindication of the private, personal centering of life, posited against the claims of the public sphere, to be the source of human identity and meaning. Loos became the uncompromising champion of the self-defining person and his or her claim to a psychologically gratified life. For that kind of person, Loos, both as architect and critic, built shelters.

NOTE

1. For a full discussion of Sitte and Wagner, critics of the first generation, see Carl E. Schorske, *Fin-de-Siècle Vienna: Politics and Culture* (New York, 1980), 62–110.

ELEVEN

Gustav Mahler: Formation
and Transformation

IN 1897, GUSTAV MAHLER was named conductor and director of Vienna's Court Opera. In the Habsburg Empire, no career success in the arts could compare to that which the thirty-seven-year-old Mahler achieved with this appointment. That one of Jewish origin should be named master of Austria's most prestigious cultural institution seems even more remarkable, for the Opera was the artistic organization most closely bound to the Baroque tradition, the Catholic culture of the court. Moreover, 1897 was the year when the anti-Semitic Karl Lueger, leader of the Christian Social party, became mayor of Vienna.

That Mahler became a totally devoted servant of operatic culture in its lofty citadel not even his enemies denied. Even the critics in the anti-Semitic papers joined in the chorus of approval of Mahler's debut with *Lohengrin*.[1] Although no man of his stern, unbending nature could be the darling of his patrons or his public, Mahler won and retained respect and admiration among Vienna's opera-wise elite as a rigorous and inspired exponent of their traditional art. His success rested on total mastery of the European musical legacy that, in his career as conductor, he served with selfless zeal.

Mahler was prized by his contemporaries chiefly as a conductor. We cherish him as a composer. Mahler himself felt a tension between the two roles. Each called forth in him different attitudes toward music and its formal order as well as different ideas of society and how music could make meaning for it. At the center of the duality was Mahler's functional relation to the classical tradition. As conductor, his task was to preserve and invigorate it, a task in which he deeply believed. As composer, he aspired to construct a picture of the world true to his modern experience. In that function, Mahler followed a critical impulse, if not indeed a subversive one. Without any destructive or aggressive intent, he challenged the classical system of music.

Contemporary critics and public often judged Mahler's compositions to be, on the one hand, banal and vulgar in substance; on the other, loose and disorderly in form. The hearing of those contemporaries, even more than ours today, had been schooled in the classical tradition. Thus they were oriented toward a formal order that developed music abstractly and autonomously. That tradition was born in the world of Descartes. Descartes saw the physical universe, despite its surface heterogeneities, to be unified by rational principles immanent within it. Similarly, the classical system of music posited a rational universe of sound, a tonal order in which laws of harmonic motion could carry one through legitimated dissonance to reconfirm a stable state.

We usually think of the modernist revolution in music primarily as the subversion of the classical system's tonality, of the diatonic harmonic order. Richard Wagner decomposed it with chromaticism; Arnold Schoenberg reorganized its fragments, its equalized tonal units, into a new dodecaphonic system. Gustav Mahler took another road to a post-classical order, one that might be called sociological. He introduced musical materials from the world of everyday, which disrupted the purity and autonomy of the closed classical system: peasant dances and waltzes, Yiddish and Bohemian tunes, student songs, marches, trumpet calls. To be sure, earlier classical composers, from Haydn and Mozart to Wagner and Brahms, had long used vernacular materials, but they incorporated such musical elements of the common life into the musical logic of classical ideality, domesticated them to the conventions of classical structure. Mahler, on the other hand, restored its own voice to the vernacular music. He made the listener feel its autonomous character—the brassiness of marches, the sensuous swirl of waltzes, the heavy stomp of peasant dances—all that constituted their difference, crudeness, and otherness in the well-ordered house of classical music. This is why his contemporaries found it vulgar.

We must remember that classical music was—and still largely is—a class music, an art of the educated elite. By interjecting into the regulated movement of the lofty the dynamic of the lowly, Mahler produced a sense of shock, even of short circuit.[2] He expanded the social and existential content of the music of the educated, forcing upon them a wider awareness, one that would include the sound-world of the common people. Thus in the same era when his older contemporaries, Nietzsche and Freud, opened the intellectual and moral order of reason to the psychological claims of repressed instinct, Mahler opened the musical order of reason to the existential claims of the musics of the common man, past and present.

The expansion of abstract high-culture music with concrete vernacular substance was Mahler's first but not his only route to modernism. He also opened a second road that led away from the social into the self, to the depths of the life of feeling. In still a third phase, the composer gave musical form to the high aesthetic attitude toward life that marked the elite culture of Vienna in the fin de siècle. I should like to deal briefly with each of these three transformations in Mahler's creative work—the social, the psychological, and the aesthetic. I shall try to place each in the context of Mahler's encounters, as a person and a musician, with the changing society of fin-de-siècle Austria.

To UNDERSTAND how Mahler, child of disadvantaged Jewish parents, should have become such a masterful exponent of European high culture old and new, we must turn to his formative years. Mahler was born in 1860, the year that marked the beginning of a heady liberal "glasnost" and "perestroika"—it was called *die neue Zeit* (the new age)—in the Habsburg Empire. The government instituted constitutional and legal reforms that soon transformed Austria, even if incompletely, into a modern liberal state. None benefitted more dramatically from the change than the Jews. Truly this was the moment of emancipation. Out of conditions of often extreme civil disability, the Jews were suddenly vaulted into legal and educational equality, with the right at last to settle where they wished, to acquire property in all its forms, and to have equal access (if they were male) to higher education. Emancipation for the Jews was part and parcel of the program of the German bourgeoisie that had worked the change. There arose a strong social partnership between Jews and the liberal German elite. In social practice, "assimilation" meant entry for the Jews into the urban bourgeoisie, and the adoption of its secular values of *Bildung und Besitz* (culture and property), as the measure of man and the mark of status. Benefactor and beneficiary, gentile and Jew, embraced a shared cultural system with social mobility as its dynamic.

Bernhard Mahler, the composer's poor but ambitious father, took advantage of the new legal privileges to move his family from a small Czech hamlet to the German city of Iglau in Moravia. There he established a liquor business that, after some harsh vicissitudes, brought him a comfortable living. There he could readily find the opportunity to open the world of Austrian higher culture to his children.

Bernhard Mahler chose his city well. Nowhere was the heady atmosphere of the liberal perestroika of the 1860s and 1870s more palpable than in Iglau. A thriving industrial and administrative center of 20,000, it was a citadel of the German liberals. Through the changes of the sixties, they had won municipal self-government and new economic opportunity. For them too one could speak of "emancipation"—in this case from the yoke of neo-absolutism in politics and Catholic religious power in cultural life. The liberal gentiles could say with the Jews, "Bliss was it in that dawn to be alive."[3]

One can watch the construction of social rapprochment between the Jews and the gentile bourgeois elite in public ceremonials and their rhetoric. Thus in 1863, when the newly organized Jewish community dedicated its temple, city and state officials honored the occasion with their presence—a gesture of tribute unthinkable, as far as I know, throughout Austria's long past. The eminent rabbi Adolf Jellinek, chief preacher of the Jewish community of Vienna, gave the main address. He signaled a new function for the temple, for both the Jews and for mankind. Traditionally a refuge of the Jews from the hostility of the gentile, he said, the temple would now become a center whence Judaism's universal truths of justice and right would radiate to all peoples to a world transforming itself in harmony.[4]

As the Jews reached out in the euphoric 1860s, they were welcomed in. In the Iglau press one finds the evidences of Jewish participation in civic ceremonies, such as a visit from a royal personage at which the Jewish choral society sang. Or, closer to our subject there is a report of the celebration of the birthday of Friedrich Schiller, the principal culture hero of the German liberals. There the twelve-year-old Gustav Mahler performed Liszt's *Mendelssohn Variations*, evoking what an Iglau newspaper called "endless applause for the brilliant achievement of the already well-known young virtuoso."[5] A few years later, Mahler, who knew reams of Schiller poetry by heart, would write his major Gymnasium paper on Schiller's *Wallenstein*.

❧

I HAVE tried to find evidences of the emancipation outlook in the culture and behavior of the Mahler family. They are not easy to come by. We know that Bernhard Mahler proudly displayed his certificate of Iglau citizenship on the wall of his living room.[6] Yet he exercised his civic functions through the Jewish community's social organizations, which he served as an active committee member. On the other hand, the available family letters and the recollections of Gustav Mahler and his friends contain no reference to Jewish customs, obligations, or even turns of language. We do not even know whether Gustav and his brothers were bar mitzvah. The only solid evidences of the Mahler family's Jewish practices are two: a report card proving that Mahler took Jewish religious instruction in his public school;[7] and a loud complaint to Gustav by his sister Justine about the intrusive presence of a marriage broker in her adolescent life.[8] What is indubitable is that Mahler's intellectual culture and even his sense of cultural identity was simply not Jewish, however others might view him. In this, he was quite unlike Sigmund Freud, whose family underwent an historical experience similar to that of the Mahlers.

Mahler's parents were committed to furthering the progress of their children through German high cultural acquirement. Once he recognized Gustav's gifts, Bernhard Mahler supported the boy's musical training. But he wished his son to be more than a mere musician in the technical sense. In 1875, when a Bohemian patron sent Gustav off to the Vienna Conservatory for his vocational training, Mahler's father insisted that he finish his humanistic studies at the Gymnasium as well, to assure him the status and character of a man of *Bildung* (culture).

Mahler once asserted that "in artistic creation, almost none but those impressions received between the ages of four and eleven become decisive and ultimately fruitful."[9] He was acutely conscious of an element in his Iglau environment of which we have not spoken and which the liberal emancipation did not include: the Czech element. The Czechs were regarded by the Jews assimilating to the German Austrian bourgeoisie as the blacks were by the more prosperous European immigrants to America: as an indigenous underclass that could serve them as menial domestic labor. Mahler, like Freud, had a Czech nanny or household maid to whom he was attached; but more: he absorbed the rich country dance music of the Czech villages around Iglau, with its sharply contrasting instrumental sonorities—not unlike Klezmer music. "The Bohemian music of my childhood went into many of my works," Mahler wrote. In "its crudest basic characteristics, the national element in my music can be heard out of the piping of any Bohemian band."[10] The military band music of Iglau's garrison also stocked Mahler's capacious reservoir of vernacular musics upon which the composer could later draw in constructing his multicultural symphonic collages.

Mahler's induction into the world of elite music was well served in Iglau. The small city boasted a rich musical life, combining the strong amateur instrumental tradition of the Austrian bureaucrats with the challenging new choral culture of the German bourgeoisie. The municipal director of music, Heinrich Fischer, who pulled these strands together under the liberal regime in the 1860s, was, as luck would have it, a neighbor of the Mahlers. His son and Gustav Mahler formed a durable friendship in childhood. While Gustav studied piano with other teachers, Fischer became his general musical mentor, introducing him to the many domains in which he was himself actively involved: sacred music in two Catholic churches, the theater orchestra, amateur opera, the male chorus, and the municipal orchestra (*Stadtkapelle*). After Mahler went to study in Vienna, he would, on returning for his holidays to Iglau, perform and conduct in various local settings that his mentor opened to him.[11]

The raw materials for Mahler's later enlargement of elite music as a composer were provided by the popular functional musics of Iglau, both Czech and German. But, with the full thrust of the liberal emancipation toward the high-culture bonding of the Jews to the Germans—the Jews like the Mahlers reaching up, the gentiles like the Fischers reaching out to help them in—it was a vocation in the German classical tradition, musical and otherwise, that prevailed in Gustav's youthful formation. The activation of his informal treasury of Iglau vernacular as a component in his work as composer had to await his encounter with a new kind of intellectual culture. This he experienced as a student in Vienna.

※

IF THE solid and optimistic liberal culture of Iglau provided Mahler with the foundation for his career as a musician, his student years in Vienna after 1875 drew him into a counterculture that transformed his perspective. The context of this transformation was a crisis of the liberal culture in which he had been formed. In a series of failures and reverses—in nationality policy, economic prosperity, social welfare, and political ethics—liberalism in the late 1870s lost its promise and much of its support. As frequently happens when a society enters a crisis, as we know from our own 1960s, university students can play a leading role in the critique of the social order and the transformation of its value system.

In the years 1878–1881, Mahler became identified with such a student group, one composed of highly gifted individuals, several of whom became pioneers of Austrian modernism in politics and culture.[12] Beginning as devotees of Richard Wagner, the principal student culture hero, this group developed a critique of liberal, materialist society, espousing a combination of populist politics, social reformism, and anti-rationalist philosophy. This radical ideology affected Mahler deeply. He even had his moment of German nationalist enthusiasm. Think of him playing patriotic songs for a student group on the piano of Victor Adler, the future leader of Austrian Social Democracy! Yet the populism that Mahler adopted in his student years was not basically political or nationalistic, but multicultural. Like Berthold Brecht, he valued the arts of the people, whatever their nationality, for their concrete, raw, realistic expression of the ups and downs of human experience. In this cultural pluralism Mahler was not so much German as Austrian, a multinationalist. Here there was perhaps a Jewish element too. Hannah Arendt showed us that, whatever nationality they became acculturated to, the Austrian Jews were a state-people, loyal to the transcendent emperor and the central institutions that tried to keep at bay the centrifugal force of the nationalisms that threatened the Jews as well as the state.

From the student counterculture Mahler also imbibed the probing anti-rationalist philosophies of Schopenhauer and Nietzsche. Increasing his sensitivity to psychological states and to the power of the instinctual, these thinkers provided Mahler with a philosophical frame for his mission as composer. As populism enlarged his music socially, so the philosophers deepened it psychologically. They also fortified him to face directly and to accept the fragmented world of human experience in all its uncohesive and mutable vitality. It is perhaps not too much to say that these two conceptual legacies of his student culture—the populist and the psycho-philosophical—empowered Mahler as composer to break out of the established musical culture that he was to serve so faithfully as conductor.

Whatever the critical countercultural impulses of his student years, they did not restrain the driving ambition with which Mahler pursued his conducting career. In sixteen years, he climbed with steady, vigorous tread the ladder of prestige in which the opera houses of Central Europe were ranked, from provincial operas like Ljubljana and Cassel, through Leipzig, Budapest, and Hamburg to the very top in Vienna. Yet his career success never relieved Mahler of the sense of being an outsider. He never felt at home in the high society to which his growing eminence gave him access. Wherever he worked, he always returned when he could to Vienna to be with the close circle of friends of his student years—largely professionals and socialists, mostly Jewish.

Mahler's ethnic and lower-class origins left their mark in a self-image he formed early and never abandoned: that of a wanderer. In the figure of Ahasuerus, Mahler as a late adolescent conflated the image of wandering Jew with the romantic topos of the alienated artist.[13] In his first major song cycle (1884), Mahler chronicled his experience of an unrequited love. He used not an ethnic image—the Jew—to represent the rootless one he felt himself to be, but a social one, that of the artisan. Entitling this cycle *Songs of a Wandering Journeyman*, Mahler described it as rendering the experience "of a journeyman who . . . after a blow of fate, goes out into the world and now wanders aimlessly."[14] The social ambiguity of Mahler as populist and marginal intellectual is evident also in the character of the text: he wrote several of the verses himself, but he also incorporated into the cycle one poem from the folk anthology *Des Knaben Wunderhorn*, as if to complete his identification with the folk-substance.[15]

In his First Symphony, 1884–1888, Mahler's ambiguous cultural position emerges in both his selection of constituent materials and the way he relates them. Mahler used song themes from his "Wandering Journeyman" cycle as primary elements, appropriate to the existential idea that governed the project in his symphony: the experience of the world of a sensitive, anguished, and passionate hero. (Bruno Walter called the symphony Mahler's "Werther.")[16] The hero's sensitivity is that of the romantic; but the world he encounters and belongs to is that of the common man. Drawing themes and timbre from the vernacular, Mahler achieves a realism in the depiction of the world that is energetic, harsh, often grotesque. By placing in succession quotations from popular musics, well-defined and with strong emotional and social connotations, Mahler could link death and mockery, joy and fear, crudeness and gentleness in a shocking temporal juxtaposition that revealed the random, often ironic, vicissitudes of life. Thus in the third movement of the First Symphony, Mahler transforms the folk-round "Frère Jacques," with its theme of the little friar who does not rise on time to attend to his social duties, into a funeral march. The merry chiding of the lazy boy, set in major in the original folk version, is turned in Mahler's adaptation into a solemn dirge in minor. The childish failure thus becomes deadly serious. In its turn that earnest funeral march soon flows into raucous tunes from the Czech and Yiddish vernacular that, with brazen indifference, turn the march of death into a crude dance of life. How easily a heavy Ländler can be transformed into a fleeting, graceful waltz, tinctured with irony! In Mahler's picaresque procession of emotion-laden states, no mood tarries long. The listener is whipsawed between compassion and laughter, tenderness and terror, as the multihued spectacle of life unfolds.

"I feel very strange about these works when I conduct them," Mahler wrote of his early symphonies, after conducting his First in New York in 1909. "A searingly painful feeling crystallizes in me: what a world that is, that projects such sounds and shapes as its reflected image!"[17]

What a world indeed! In substance, Mahler's image of it consisted of a vast multitude of heterogeneous elements, a musical vocabulary drawn from different ethnic and social traditions, high and low. Mahler organized that vocabulary by a kind of serial association to form a continuous metamorphic flow, reflecting the unpredictable and erratic character of experience. The complex object "world" drew him to symphony as a comprehensive medium; the experiencing subject "I" led him to song. In the high culture of fin-de-siècle Austria, the relation between "I" and "world," mind and outer reality, had become problematical for the intelligentsia, causing subject and object to flow into each other. Mahler expressed that condition in music by blurring the boundary between symphony and song. By employing vernacular musical idioms, he achieved a musical realism richer—because more socially heterogeneous in its symbolic referents—than the classical tradition had allowed; yet he presented that uncohesive, pluralized reality as psychologically experienced, with the kind of personal intensity that belonged to the tradition of the art-song.

❧

"THE WUNDERHORN years": That is the term generally used to characterize Mahler's first creative period, down to his assumption of his Vienna post. The term derives from the collection of folk poetry, *Des Knaben Wunderhorn (The Youth's Magic Horn)*, that fed his musical imagination in the way Germanic mythology nurtured Richard Wagner's. The anthology had been made by two young intellectuals of an earlier student gen-

eration to inspire the German nation against Napoleon.[18] Mahler embraced it not for its nationalistic import, but for its existential realism, a
realism born out of the raw social experience of the people, much of it in
the Thirty Years War. It provided Mahler with poetic material bearing a
natural kinship to the vernacular musics of his Iglau childhood. Mahler
not only used the texts for songs but, once the songs were written, used
them in turn to enrich the social psychology of his symphonies.

In the Third and Fourth Symphonies, Mahler combined this vernacular realism with high-culture existential philosophy into a comprehensive
Weltbild, a picture of the world. In this socio-philosophical synthesis he
worked in the spirit of the Viennese student subculture to which he had
belonged.[19] The philosopher behind him was Friedrich Nietzsche. Mahler thought of calling the Third Symphony, "Meine fröliche Wissenschaft" (My Joyful Science), borrowing the title from a work of
Nietzsche. He spoke openly of his philosophical intentions for the work,
calling it "a musical poem comprehending in a step-by-step intensifica-
tion all the stages of evolution." Mahler's symphonic hierarchy of being
begins in "Pan's awakening," where the life force frees itself from inert
matter. He soon sweeps us into the crude, heavy vitality of Nietzsche's
Dionysian primordial world, as set forth in *The Birth of Tragedy*. Mahler
follows Nietzsche again in conjoining Dionysian intoxication with Ap-
pollonian dream, making possible the affirmation of life in all its joy and
pain. And at the very center of the Third Symphony, Mahler placed, as
the voice of human wisdom, Zarathustra's "Drunken Song of Midnight."
After Zarathustra's affirmation of Dionysian power in prophetic vision,
Mahler invokes the folk once more, this time in a new spirit of community joie de vivre, based on another *Wunderhorn* poem, a childlike vision
of Christian compassion.

The crown of this philosophic *theatrum mundi* is the Fourth Symphony. It develops a Biedermeier utopia in music, where folk fantasy
proclaims the victory of the pleasure principle and the affirmation of the
gratified life in a kind of infantile regression. "Was mir das Kind erzählt"
(What the child tells me): such was the programmatic idea under which
Mahler first conceived the childlike heaven of the Fourth Symphony.
The folk-paradise of another *Wunderhorn* poem served Mahler as vehicle
of this populist-Apollonian vision, the counterpart in the Fourth Symphony to the heavy vernacular music with which he projected his popu-
list-Dionysian vision in the Third.

In the Wunderhorn years, from the mid-eighties to the end of the century, Mahler thus expanded the mental and psychological universe of music with a variegated vernacular vocabulary that "absolute" classical music had expurgated or refined as European culture became class-differentiated and class-enclosed. He did so, however, not with the aim of either preserving or restoring some dying trans-class historical culture, but to achieve a comprehensive, archetypal sound-picture of life as a whole, beyond the cultural limits of the upper classes. In the Third and Fourth Symphonies, the greatest and final works of the Wunderhorn years, Mahler integrated his populist archaism with the existential philosophy of Will that he had absorbed with it in his Vienna student years as a radical intellectual.

IN 1900, shortly after completing his Fourth Symphony, Mahler entered a crisis that led to a reshuffling of his ideas as a composer and a deep transformation of his creative work. The precipitate of the crisis was Mahler's conducting. Not at the Opera: there he enjoyed support from both his bureaucratic superiors and the public. It was as conductor of the Vienna Philharmonic that he elicited a degree of hostile criticism that wounded him to the depths of his being.

Although Mahler's roles as conductor and composer had followed separate tracks, his ideas and interests as a composer certainly affected his interpretations of the works of others. As his compositions were in some sense collages or mosaics of clearly individuated elements, so his interpretations concentrated on clear differentiation of parts and on luminosity of detail. An otherwise friendly French critic complained in 1900: "A purpose is discovered in every note; . . . the structure is invested with so much complexity that the basic design is destroyed."[20] As in his own music, Mahler drastically widened the emotional range of the music he performed, stressing its contrasts and antinomies of feeling. To players and audiences used to a more architectural interpretive conception, a grand line, Mahler seemed a fragmenter. Here too Nietzsche's view of the multiform, pluralized universe had left its mark on Mahler, to the bewilderment of his still Cartesian public.

It was over Beethoven, the culture hero of both Mahler and musical Vienna, that the conflict about interpretation reached the breaking point. Mahler did not hesitate to retouch and reorchestrate Beethoven scores in order to achieve, with modern instruments and in a large modern hall, the sound that he thought the composer had intended for his own day. His anti-traditional procedures aroused opposition not just among critics and public but, worst of all, among the musicians who had elected him as conductor.[21] After a storm over Beethoven's Ninth, Mahler fought back. He designed a program that embraced three works devoted to titanic figures who had boldly defied authority and suffered for it: Beethoven's *Prometheus*, Schumann's *Manfred* and Mahler's own First Symphony that he had early named "The Titan." If Mahler had willed suffering and rejection, he could not have devised a stronger means to bring them upon himself than this bold self-identification with such revered composers as Schumann and Beethoven.

In the wake of the tumultuous reception of his own symphony by critics and public, Mahler lost his self-control. He made a bitter speech to his musicians charging them with faithlessness. "I acted," he said, "like a general abandoned by his troops." On April 1, 1901, Mahler resigned as conductor of the Philharmonic in frustration and defeat.

Against this dark background of rejection as composer and conductor, Mahler also suffered serious internal hemorrhaging in February 1901. Alarmed about his own condition and exhausted, Mahler withdrew for the summer to his retreat in the mountains. There, in a creative outburst of staggering dimensions, he produced in two months a series of compositions that shook up the ideational premises of his music.[22] It is perhaps not too much to say that in these works he killed off much of what had given him hope in humankind thus far: faith in the truth of the folk; and hope in the child. He reconsidered both under the sign of withdrawal and death.

In a final, stark song from *Des Knaben Wunderhorn*, "The Drummer Boy," a poor youth who has failed in his duty goes to his death. So too does Mahler's reliance on the great anthology from which he had drawn so much earthy philosophic sustenance. Mahler turned now from folk poetry to art poetry—to Friedrich Rückert, a romantic who spoke in the cultivated accent of personal introspection and alienation. Of the Rückert songs Mahler wrote that summer of 1901, the final one was called "Lost to the World." It poignantly expresses the state of the introvert. Having died to the struggles of the world where he has so long spent his substance, he lives resigned and apart in his heaven, his love, and his song. In giving musical expression to this idea, Mahler found a new lean, ascetic voice, in which time seems to stop.

In his *Kindertotenlieder* (Songs on the Death of Children), also by

Rückert, Mahler dealt a stunning blow to the ideal of the child and child utopia that had crowned the Weltbild of the Third and Fourth Symphonies. He places the child now in the shadow of death. Mahler seems thus to be consigning to the grave his own earlier musical re-creation of Biedermeier utopian innocence, and with it the vernacular child-fantasies of the *Wunderhorn*.

In that summer of 1901, Mahler also began his Fifth Symphony, completing its key movement, a scherzo. There Mahler shows popular music, folk dance, and bourgeois waltzes shattering, as powerful forces of chaos—or is it existential angst?—erupt in them. Mahler prophesied, somewhat contemptuously, that conductors of the future would make nonsense of this scherzo. And as for the public: "Oh heavens," he wrote, "what kind of a face will they make at this chaos that is forever giving birth to a new world, which in the next moment collapses, to these primordial-world-sounds, to this roaring, howling, tossing sea, to these dancing stars."[23]

We are a long way here from the great chain of being of the Third and Fourth Symphonies—and from their character as *fröhliche Wissenschaft* (joyful science). Conceiving worldly reality as painfully nonhomogeneous, Mahler seeks solace no longer in a folk utopia but in projecting a transcendent metaphysical peace. After his crisis of rejection by the musical traditionalists, his psychological introversion and his religious impulse fed upon each other, generating powerful new musical ideas for the three wordless symphonies he wrote between 1901 and 1905. The first of these, the Fifth Symphony, set the tone for all of them with its terrifyingly destructive scherzo on one hand and its serene, resigned adagietto on the other. Into the latter, Mahler fittingly wove the music of his Rückert song: "I am Lost to the World."

In all three symphonies, Mahler developed a new treatment of the orchestra as a reservoir of smaller, transient instrumental clusters whose timbre can express reaches of feeling not accessible through received orchestral form. It is to this expansion of the aural universe through sonority that Pierre Boulez and Luciano Berio look back in gratitude to Mahler, seeing him as a pioneer of their own expansion of music into uncharted galaxies of sound.

WITHIN months of the painful yet fruitful summer of 1901, Mahler's personal life took a crucial turn, one that opened a new direction in his

social life, his ideas, and his art. He fell in love with the beautiful Alma
Schindler and, almost at once, married her.

The daughter of a painter, Alma brought her husband into a new and
powerful subculture of Vienna's cultivated elite, quite different from the
philosophical radicals who had remained his closest friends since student
years. Alma's friends were mostly artists, pioneers of Austrian modernism. Under the leadership of Gustav Klimt, they had founded the Secession, a movement of revolt against tradition in the plastic arts. Mahler's
previous friends, largely Jewish, and progressive in outlook, had been
committed to restoring the social and cultural wholeness of society
through art and action. His new associates, largely gentile (though close
to their Jewish patrons), embraced art as a kind of surrogate religion and
a way of life. They labored to create a modern life beautiful for those
who could appreciate and afford it. Mahler first joined the Secessionists
by contributing to one of their most important cultural events: a show
glorifying Beethoven as the sainted hero of their religion of art. Mahler
arranged for wind choir Beethoven's setting of one of the most mystical
verses of the Ninth Symphony's "Ode to Joy."[24]

Among his new associates Mahler found one who became his partner
at the Opera: the painter-designer, Alfred Roller. Together they transformed operatic productions for the twentieth century, with Roller's art-
deco sets and brilliant use of lighting and color reinforcing Mahler's
drive to tense, simplified dramatic structure. In the partnership, Mahler
seems to have found a new sense of mission as opera director.[25]

Mahler's involvement with the aestheticism of Vienna's elite soon made
itself felt in his composing too. First in affirmation, in the Eighth Symphony of 1906; then in critical distantiation, in *Das Lied von der Erde* of
1908. The first of these works is a monumental celebration of the creative spirit; the second, a spare, ascetic threnody on the vanity of the
cultivated life beautiful.

While the aesthetic hedonism of the Viennese *moderne* could not alter
his essential philosophic seriousness, in the Eighth Symphony Mahler
came close to the glorification of art that prevailed as the highest value in
the Secession. Once again Mahler united symphony and song, as he had
done before the crisis of 1901 that had destroyed his social realism and
folkish utopianism. In the earlier phase, his poetic materials had been
secular and vernacular;[26] in the Eighth, they were Catholic and Baroque.
The symphony begins with a medieval invocation of the Holy Spirit,
"Veni creator spiritus." It is the hymn used to open papal conclaves,
though Mahler adapts it to an urgent cry, such as an artist might utter,

for creative inspiration. In the second half of the work, Mahler set a text revered in German Bildung: Goethe's Baroque-like apotheosis of Faust. Through the inspiration of ideal womanhood, represented in the different personae of Mary, striving man achieves eternal blessedness. "It is the greatest [thing] I have ever done," Mahler wrote to the Dutch conductor Willen Mengelberg. "Imagine the whole universe beginning to ring and resound."[27] Or again: "My other works are all tragic and subjective. This one is a great dispenser of joy."[28]

Sometimes called "The Symphony of a Thousand" because of its huge choruses and massive orchestral resources, the Eighth was Mahler's one instant and overwhelming success with the public. It is Haydn's *Creation* and Beethoven's Ninth rolled into one. Here Mahler the composer comes closest to Mahler the operatic conductor, producing a musical spectacular in the Baroque tradition. As a celebration of *homo creator*, the work expressed the powerful commitment to art as a source of life that late liberal Viennese culture prized as perhaps no other culture had done before it.

The mood of glory did not hold. In Mahler's very next work, *The Song of the Earth*, the bright heavens of the Eighth are darkened. Choosing aristocratic Chinese poetry for his symphonic song, Mahler plunges us into an Ecclesiastes mood, a profound musical realization of the vanity of vanities. The exotic setting in refined and stylized Chinese culture seems a metaphor for the high aesthetic lifestyle and cultivated hedonism of the Secession and its patrons. Botticelli-like maidens and vigorous young ephebes on white stallions disport themselves in a stylized, Chinese garden setting. Mahler's *Lied* exposes the ephemerality and hollowness of the aestheticized life; his singer, the disillusioned one, prepares not, like Faust in the Eighth, for redemption, but for the final farewell and the return to the beautiful but indifferent earth.

From a magnificat of high art in the grand Baroque manner to a kind of moral-existential indictment of the aestheticized life: Mahler's change of direction was swift indeed. He swung from Catholic sensuous mysticism, associated with *mater gloriosa* and with Alma, to the opposite realm of his religious sensibility: that of the Old Testament, where his earliest roots lay buried beneath the rich Chinese literary surface. Surely Mahler's capacious consciousness embraced both, though neither in a fideistic form.

Das Lied von der Erde, along with the *Kindertotenlieder*, made Mahler the culture hero of a quite different social subgroup than the aesthetes.

They were ethical modernists, followers of the rationalist critic Karl Kraus. With Kraus, the young musical intellectuals among them— Schoenberg, Berg, and their circle—rejected the Secession and the whole cult of art and beauty so widespread in the Viennese elite. "The artist," wrote Schoenberg, "has no need of beauty. For him truthfulness is enough."[29] Mahler, with his intense economy of musical means, his newfound *Klangaskese* (asceticism of sonority) became the incarnation of that truthfulness: it was anti-sensuous, ruthless in its direct psychological statement of existential pain. To the young modernists of what soon became the Second Vienna school, the liberators of dissonance, Mahler thus became the revered idol that Richard Wagner had been to his own generation.

A HISTORIAN cannot fail to be struck by Mahler's capacity to be deeply admired by and to speak in his music to both the advocates of the beautified life, inheritors of the culture of Grace, and the expressionist, ethicist avant-garde, children of the culture of the Word. Those two groups had divided between them the unified liberal Bildung in which art and ethics, beauty and truth had served each other in the mid-nineteenth century. But had it not always been the special genius of Mahler to take into himself and his own psyche the great polarities that Austrian culture generated, and to unify them in dynamic tension and dialectic interaction? In every major phase of his life he had integrated the dissociated, the contradictory, or the contrasting. In Iglau, from his Jewish lower-class base, he entered fully into German gentile elite culture. As a student, he absorbed the student populist radicalism and the Nietzschean psycho-philosophical critique of bourgeois culture, using both to expand and enrich, not just to erode and destroy, the elite musical tradition. That was the achievement of the musical Weltbild of his Wunderhorn years.

Let us think of Mahler's creative phases as an hourglass, with the Wunderhorn years (1888–1899) as its top, the crisis years (1900–1902) as its waist, and the two-cultures conflict as its bottom. At the waist, in his conflict with his Philharmonic musicians, Mahler had pressed the union of his social roles too far, allowing his function as conductor-guardian of the classical tradition to be governed by his modern consciousness as composer. Forced into the interiority of the self by his rejection, Mahler cut his allegiance to both the populist and the Nietzschean visions of the

Wunderhorn years. When he reentered the social world, it was as high-culture artist only. Yet again he embraced a duality, the one into which Viennese elite culture split after 1900. Identifying with both aesthetes and ethicists, he committed himself fully to neither, drawing strength from both as conductor and composer. Mahler's rich associative genius pulled together in the metamorphic logic of his music what history had put asunder: vernacular and elite culture, tradition and modernity, the iridescent life of art and the stern dictates of existential truth in Vienna's high culture in its last creative outburst. That Mahler, child of Iglau in *die neue Zeit* of generous emancipation, was a completely acculturated Austrian gave him the capaciousness of vision to embrace the contradictions of the Austro-European world and its cultures. Through all his career success, he remained somehow the wandering journeyman. That he was, as he said, "thrice homeless, as a native of Bohemia among Austrians, as an Austrian among Germans and as a Jew throughout the world,"[30] gave him, perhaps, the hard clarity of vision to perceive the world in its daunting contradictions, and the warm will to make those contradictions, for the sake of life, cohere.

NOTES

1. Henry Louis de la Grange, *Gustav Mahler*, enlarged edition, 3 vols. (Paris, 1979–1984), 1:655, 666.

2. Robert P. Morgan, "Ives and Mahler: Mutual Responses at the End of an Era," *19th Century Music*, 2:1 (July 1978), 72–81.

3. For a revealing official chronicle of Iglau in the liberal era, see anon., *Die Gemeinde Iglau und ihr Wirken in den Jahren* 1865–1889 (Iglau, 1890). The Czech historian Jan Havránek generously provided me with this invaluable source.

4. Adolf Jellinek, *Rede zur Einweihung des israelitschen Tempels in Iglau* (Vienna, 1863). For a fine analysis of Jellinek's synthesis of Jewish "truths" and secular liberal universalism, see Marsha L. Rozenblit, "Jewish Identity and the Modern Rabbi," *Leo Baeck Institute Year Book* 35 (1990), 110–18.

5. *Der Vermittler* (Iglau), November 11, 1872.

6. De la Grange, *Gustav Mahler*, 1:22.

7. *Gymnasialzeugnis* no. 27 (Iglau, 1870), copy in de la Grange dossier, "Enfance, Kalisch-Iglau," Bibliothèque Gustav Mahler, Paris.

8. Knud Martner, ed., *Selected Letters of Gustav Mahler* (New York, 1979), 379.

9. Quoted in Vladimir Karbusicky, *Gustav Mahler und seine Umwelt* (Darmstadt, 1978), 22.

10. Ibid., 26. See chap. 2, passim, for a comprehensive formal analysis of Mahler's vernacular music heritage and his use thereof.

11. Theodor Fischer, "Aus Gustav Mahlers Jugendzeit," *Die Heimat* 7 (1931), 264–68.

12. The classic study of the Vienna student counter-culture, including its impact on Mahler, is William J McGrath, *Dionysian Art and Populist Politics in Austria* (New Haven, 1974).

13. Henry A. Lea, *Gustav Mahler: Man on the Margin* (Bonn, 1985), 44–45; Martner, ed., *Letters*, 56.

14. Letter to Friedrich Löhr, April 1, 1885, in Alma Mahler, ed., *Gustav Mahler Briefe* (Berlin, Vienna, and Leipzig, 1925). 34.

15. See the discussion of the *Wunderhorn* ingredient in the early cycle in Donald Mitchell, *Gustav Mahler, The Wunderhorn Years* (Berkeley and Los Angeles, 1980), 117–19. The fact that the romantic compilers of *Des Knaben Wunderhorn* were especially attracted to the wandering element in the population (*der Fahrende*)—soldiers, players, musicians, artisans, beggars—suggests a special affinity of Mahler for this anthology. The life of the road—*die deutsche Landstrasse*—combined the value of personal freedom from philistine or bourgeois restraint with an intense sense of collective experience. Cf. H. A. Korff, *Geist de Goethezeit*, 5 vols. (Leipzig, 1953), 4:166–67.

16. Wolfgang Schreiber, *Gustav Mahler* (Rheinbeck bei Hamburg, 1971), 137.

17. "*Was ist das für eine Welt, welche solche Klänge und Gestalten als Widerbild auswirft!*" Letter to Bruno Walter, n.d. (December 1909), in Mahler, ed., *Gustav Mahler Briefe*, 419.

18. Korff, *Geist der Goethezeit*, 4:161–70.

19. I follow here the findings of McGrath, *Dionysian Art*, chap. 5.

20. Quoted in Kurt Blaukopf, *Gustav Mahler* (New York, 1973), 158.

21. The Vienna Philharmonic was constituted as a self-governing, autonomous association by the musicians of the Court Opera. While in the Opera the members of the orchestra, as employees of the state, were under Mahler's authority as director, in the Philharmonic the same musicians elected him as conductor and held him responsible to them.

22. For a rich psychoanalytic treatment of Mahler's crisis and two of the Rückert songs that followed it, see Stuart Feder, "Gustav Mahler um Mitternaht," *International Review of Psychoanalysis* 7 (1980), 11–26.

23. Quoted in Karbusicky, *Gustav Mahler und seine Umwelt*, 1.

24. For the Beethoven show considered within a comparative trajectory of the lives and work of Mahler and Klimt, see Carl E. Schorske, "Mahler and Klimt: Social Experience and Artistic Evolution," *Daedalus*, Fall 1978, 111–12.

25. See the assessment of Mahler's partnership with Roller in Blaukopf, *Mahler*, 168–75.

26. An exception must be made for the Second Symphony, which dealt with the Christian theme of resurrection using the art-poetry of Klopstock. On the relation of the Second to Mahler's cultural identity problem, see the theoretical reflections of Michael Steinberg, "Jewish Identity and Intellectuality in Fin-de-Siècle Austria: Suggestions for a Historical Discourse," *New German Critique*, Spring 1988, 23–28.

27. Martner, ed., *Letters*, 294.

28. Quoted by Donald Mitchell in notes to Mahler's *Symphony No.* 8, Pro Arte CD.

29. Quoted from Arnold Schoenberg, *Harmonielehre* in *Die Reihe*, English edition (Bryn Mawr, Pa., 1958), 2:6.

30. Reported by Alma Mahler in *Gustav Mahler, Memories and Letters* (Seattle and London, 1971), 109.

To the Egyptian Dig:
Freud's Psycho-Archeology
of Cultures

In March of 1933, a new patient came to Freud. She was an American poet, Hilda Doolittle—better known to us by her pen name, H.D. The clouds of Nazism hung heavy over Europe that spring. H.D., severely traumatized by World War I, was frightened. She came to Freud, as she tells us, "in order to fortify and equip myself to face war when it came." "With the death-head swastika chalked on the pavement leading to the professor's door," she wrote in her brilliant *Tribute to Freud*, "I must calm as best I could . . . my own personal little dragon of war-terror."[1]

Freud also was possessed by the menace to civilization in Europe. Spurred by Hitler's rise to power, he was engaged at a new level of intensity with defining the nature of Jewishness, and the place of the Jews in the making of Western culture.

The transaction that ensued between the poet-patient and the professor must have been unique in the annals of psychoanalysis. Because both suffered acutely from the sense of an historical ending in modern Europe, their dialogue—even to the suggestive articulation of their powerful transferences—took the form of cultural discourse about antiquity, its symbols, and their meanings. We have but one side of the discussion—H.D.'s; but her report makes us consider anew Freud's lifelong attempt to build, in effect, a meaningful interpretation of Western civilization, and to find his own place in it.

Freud had a large collection of archeological artifacts, in which H.D. evinced an immediate interest. A group of religious figurines stood arrayed on his desk, "like a high altar," she observed, in his study. From the assembled divinities, Freud chose a tiny Athena and showed it to his new patient, almost as if it were a flower. "'*This* is my favorite,' he said . . . 'She is perfect . . . *only she has lost her spear.*'" H.D. felt the power of the gesture, and allowed it to resonate in her mind. "He knew that I loved Greece. . . . 'She has lost her spear,'" H.D. continues.[2] She does not explore the sexual implication of the loss of the spear for the androgynous goddess, nor its relevance to H.D.'s own bisexual proclivities. Nor does Freud, although he had done some revealing digging into Athena's nature.

Athena and Hellas provided a common ground of culture between the Jewish professor and the Christian poetess. It was a point of departure for a psycho-archeological quest which soon led them to Egypt, first together, in the analysis; later, each on his own. There, Freud and H.D. sought to decipher the origins of human culture in ways that would fortify both in defining their own natures amidst the terrors of the modern world. H.D. recorded the yield of her dig in the long poem, *Helen in Egypt*; Freud, in the work that will concern us here, *Moses and Monotheism*.

That Athena should have been Freud's favorite among his archeological artifacts can come as no surprise. To anyone socialized in Austrian liberal culture in the mid-nineteenth century, as Freud had been, Athens served as a comprehensive symbol of all that his culture held dear. After the Austrian liberals finally achieved a constitutional state in the 1860s, they placed a great statue of Athena before their new Greek-style Parliament building. Protectrix of the free polis, she was also goddess of wisdom, a symbol well-suited to a liberal elite that believed in the liberating power of science and reason.

What was true of the symbolism of Athena for politics acquired even greater force in the substance of Austrian education. Classical culture was the foundation on which Austria's highly effective reformed elite education was built. Greek and Roman civilization provided a religiously neutral ground for constructing a secular liberal culture. For no social group did this have more decisive meaning than for the newly emancipated Jews. Jewish children could join their Christian school fellows in acquiring a common gentile culture, the religion of which was dead and hence no threat to their own. The classics and ancient history opened for the Jews a road to a deep cultural assimilation into the gentile world without implying either heresy or apostasy.

At home and in separate religious instruction, young Sigmund Freud imbibed Hebrew and Jewish culture. Of particular interest to him was the part of the Bible story that told of the Jews in Egypt and their response to life in an alien gentile world. In the public realm, at school,

Freud became a Greek. Austrian liberalism's cosmopolitan secularism allowed him to find in the myths and ideas of both Greeks and Hebrews the materials to construct his identity, his values, and his stance in a culturally and politically divided modern society.

To use past cultures thus, as reservoirs of human models and symbols, is not the same as exploring cultures as historically specific collective constructions. In his youth Freud shared the deep interest in history characteristic of his time, and in his readings he explored in close detail the histories of both ancient and modern cultures to which he was particularly drawn. In his mature work, however, despite his enormous historical and cultural erudition, Freud interested himself principally in the exploration of the universal nature and dynamics of the individual psyche, from whatever culture it may have sprung. Only once, at the end of his life, did he attempt in his writings to come to grips systematically with the character and construction of a particular culture, as historians and anthropologists do. This task Freud undertook with considerable hesitation in *Moses and Monotheism*, where he tried to get at the nature of Judaism. Although deeply attached and indebted to Greece and Rome, he never considered analyzing either as a whole culture. The arc traced over the course of Freud's life by his changing relationship to different historical cultures sheds light on the connection between his deepest personal values and the shifting focus of his intellectual concerns.

ONCE Freud had defined his scientific mission as the exploration of the buried reaches of the human psyche, he drew an analogy between his work in depth psychology and that of the archeologist in exhuming and decoding buried cultures. It was only natural for this child of nineteenth-century Europe to assign priority to those ancient cultures that were regarded as progenitors of his own: Greek and Roman, Hebrew and Egyptian. Modern European cultures, by contrast, interested him little in his mature years. Yet as a young man Freud was drawn to two contemporary civilizations that meant much to his intellectual formation: those of Protestant England and Catholic France. His descriptions of them betray the underlying influence exerted on him by the two cultural traditions that continued to contend for dominance in the Austria of his time: the rational Enlightenment culture of the Word and the sensuous Catholic culture of Grace (see Essay Eight above). Freud's fascination with these traditions as they found expression in the more modern context of Western European history and culture set a tone of duality that lasted all his life. It also prefigured the gender dimension in his later approaches, both psychoanalytical and historical, to culture.

Like many another Austrian liberal, Freud was a passionate Anglophile from his youth. His family experience confirmed his political prejudice. When the Freud family fortunes sustained reverses in the late 1850s, Sigmund's older half-brothers emigrated to build successful careers in Manchester, while father Jacob removed the rest of his family from Freiberg in Moravia to a life of economic hardship in Vienna. After graduation from Gymnasium in 1875, Freud made his first visit to his relatives in England, a visit which left an indelible impression on him. In 1882, newly engaged but deeply frustrated about his career, England surfaced in his consciousness as a land of hope. In a letter to his fiancée, Martha Bernays, Freud gave passionate voice to a longing to escape from Vienna and the shadow of "that abominable tower of St. Stephen"—symbol of Catholic reaction. "I am aching for independence," he wrote, "so as to follow my own wishes. The thought of England surges up before me, with its sober industriousness, its generous devotion to the public weal, the stubbornness and sensitive feeling for justice of its inhabitants, the running fire of general interest that can strike sparks in the newspapers; all the ineffaceable impressions of my journey seven years ago, one that had a decisive influence on my whole life, have been awakened in their full vividness."[3]

The "decisive influence" of his early visit to England, if we are to believe a letter Freud wrote to his closest friend immediately on his return in 1875, embraced both professional and intellectual values. England, as the land of "practical works," inclined him away from pure science toward medical practice. "If I wanted to influence many people rather than a small number of readers and co-scientists, then England would be the right country." At the same time, the young freshman bore witness to the impact of English scientific thought: "The acquaintance which I have made with English scientific books will always keep me, in my studies, on the side of the English for whom I have an extremely favorable prejudice: Tyndall, Huxley, Lyle, Darwin, Thomson, Lockyer and others."[4]

In 1882, in his mood of discouragement, Freud fanned the smoldering embers of Anglophilism that remained from his visit with reading of a wider kind. "I am taking up again," he reported to his Martha, "the history of the island, the works of the men who were my real teachers—all of them English or Scotch; and I am recalling again what is for me the most interesting historical period, the reign of the Puritans and Oliver Cromwell." One might have expected that the future liberator of sexuality would have defined his interest in the Puritans negatively. Not at all, for his eye was seeking civic virtue.

"Must we stay here, Martha?" Freud wrote of Vienna. "If we possibly can, let us seek a home where human worth is more respected. A grave in the Centralfriedhof (the municipal cemetery) is the most distressing idea I can imagine."[5] Although he seems often to have entertained the idea of emigrating to England in the 1880s, Freud could not shake off his attachment to hated Vienna as the scene of his professional self-realization. It was only Hitler that caused him finally to leave for London, in the end to be buried there rather than in the Centralfriedhof.

In his devotion to England as an ideal society, Freud shared an attitude widespread in the Austrian liberal bourgeoisie before World War I. Indeed, when the Great War broke, Freud, who would soon give "all my libido . . . to Austria-Hungary," hesitated in his allegiance. As he wrote to Karl Abraham, "I should be with it [Austria-Hungary] with all my heart, if only I could think England would not be on the wrong side."[6]

Within the larger whole, however, there were different kinds of Anglophilism. Most of Freud's contemporaries among the intellectuals admired England for producing a human type who fused bourgeois practicality with aristocratic grace, business, and high style. The writer Arthur Schnitzler portrayed in a novel an Austrian Jew who, making a new life in England, embodied the typical Englishman as Austrians of the fin de siècle saw him: cool and gray-eyed, courteous and self-possessed. The poet Hugo von Hofmannsthal and his friends in the higher bureaucracy wanted to establish a public school on the English model in Austria to breed such personalities. Theodor Herzl's Jewish state too would cultivate such aristocratic realists à la anglais. Adolf Loos, architect and critic of Austria's visual culture, when he founded a journal called *Das Andere* (The Other) "to introduce Western culture into Austria," exalted the gentlemanly values of sobriety and practicality reflected in English clothing, interior decor, and use-objects.

Freud's Anglophilism showed none of these aristocratic-aesthetic features. He drew his image of England from an older, more militant mid-century liberalism, hostile to aristocracy and to the Catholicism associated with it in Austria. Parliamentarism was what they prized in English

politics; philosophic radicalism was their lodestar in culture. Freud studied philosophy under Franz Brentano, a leading protagonist of English
positivism in Austria. Under the editorial guidance of Theodor Gom-
perz, a classicist who, following George Grote, embraced the Sophists
and radical democrats as the finest flowers of Athens, Freud worked on
the German edition of the complete works of John Stuart Mill. (He
translated "On the Subjection of Women," "Socialism," "The Labor
Movement," and "Plato.") Though he does not speak of a debt to Bentham, Freud's early theory of instincts, with its duality of pleasure principle and reality principle, resonates with echoes of Bentham's hedonistic
system. From the seventeenth to the nineteenth century, those whom
Freud claimed as his "real teachers—all of them English or Scotch,"
were the protagonists of libidinal repression and the advocates of post-
poned gratification—whether as Puritan foes of aristocratic squandering
and the Church of Rome or as secularized utilitarian moralists. They
were builders, stern and rational, of the liberal ego which, for Freud,
made of England the classic land of ethical rectitude, manly self-control,
and the rule of law.

Freud named all his children after his teachers or their wives—except
one. Oliver, his second son, he named for Cromwell. Thus the great sex
theorist paid tribute to the public virtues of private repression and the
special achievement of English political culture.

IT HAS become a commonplace of Freud scholarship to identify Paris
with the impact of Jean Martin Charcot, the great theorist and clinician
of hysteria, on Freud's intellectual development. Justly so. Freud went on
a fellowship to the Salpetrière Hospital for Women in 1885 as a neurologist exploring the organic basis of nervous disorders. Charcot turned him
in a new direction, toward the study of hysteria, especially hysterical
paralysis, as a disease which behaved "as if there were no anatomy of
the brain."[7] He also opened Freud's mind, even if only in informal discourse, to *la chose génitale*, the sexual component in the etiology of hysteria. When Freud returned to Vienna to open his own practice, it was
as a neurologist still, but one with a special interest in "nervous cases"
that others found tiresome: patients who did not suffer from organic
lesions of the nervous system.[8] Thus returning from Paris with a pro-
nounced predilection for what we would now call neurotics, Freud set
out for the first time, boldly if only half aware, on the *via regia* to the
unconscious.

Freud's letters to his fiancée during his half-year in Paris make it clear that the city itself, or more accurately, his encounter with it, both prepared and reinforced the impact of Charcot

England was good order, morality, and liberal rationality, appealing to Freud as a possible refuge from the social inequities and professional frustrations of Austria. Paris was the very opposite: a city of danger, of the questionable, of the irrational. Freud accepted, but richly elaborated, the stereotype of Paris as wanton, the female temptress; he approached it in a spirit of adventure at once thrilling and terrifying.

Until he went to Paris in 1885, there is, as far as I could find, no reference to the city in his writings, either as fact or as symbol. More than a decade later, however, in *The Interpretation of Dreams*, he tells the reader cryptically that "Paris . . . had for many long years been the goal of my longings; and the blissful feelings with which I first set foot on its pavement seemed to me a guarantee that others of my wishes would be fulfilled as well."⁹ What wishes? Freud does not say. In the beautiful letters he wrote to his fiancée and her sister during his Paris *Lehrjahr*, however, the intense and impressionable young Freud seems to have opened himself to the whole world of forbidden *fleurs du mal* that Freud the Anglophile and liberal Jew had until then rejected or avoided: the Roman Catholic Church, the bewitching power of the female, and the power of the masses. As London was the city of the ego, where the whole culture supported one's independence and control, Paris was the city of the id, where instincts erotic and thanatal reigned.

Two months after his arrival in Paris, Freud could still write of it, "I am under the full impact of Paris, and, waxing very poetical, could compare it to a vast overdressed Sphinx who gobbles up every foreigner unable to solve her riddles."¹⁰ Freud chose his image well, for the Sphinx united beauty and the beast, defying natural law with her composite being and challenging rationality with her fateful riddle that only brilliant, perverse Oedipus could solve.

Mindful of the bitter lifelong disgust and mistrust in which Freud held Catholicism, recalling his yearning to escape from the shadow of "that abominable tower of St. Stephen" to England in 1882, we are stunned to watch his reaction to Notre Dame. "My first impression was a sensation I have never had before: 'This is a church.' . . . I have never seen anything so movingly serious and somber, quite unadorned and very narrow." What Freud reported of the companion with whom he paid his first visit to Notre Dame must have been true of himself: "There he stood, deeply lost in wonder."¹¹

Freud associated himself not only with the beauty of the cathedral but with its beastly side as well. He later recalled that the platform of Notre Dame was his "favorite resort" in Paris. "Every free afternoon, I used to clamber about there on the towers of the church between the monsters and the devils." When Freud, in a dream of omnipotence, identified himself with Hercules, he discovered behind the dream Rabelais's Gargantua, avenging himself on the Parisians by turning a stream of urine on them from the top of Notre Dame.[12]

As for the people of Paris, they simply frightened Freud. They struck him as "uncanny." To be sure, political turbulence marked the months of Freud's stay, a period of governmental instability (the so-called *valse des ministères*) following the fall of Jules Ferry, stormy elections, and the rise of a proto-fascist movement, Boulangisme. Freud rarely identified the objectives of political demonstrators; what he saw was mob behavior as such, something that to become all too familiar again in Vienna a decade later: "The people seem to me of a different species from ourselves; I feel they are possessed of a thousand demons. . . . I hear them yelling 'à la lanterne' and 'à bas' this man and that. I don't think they know the meaning of shame or fear. . . . They are people given to psychical epidemics, historical mass convulsions, and they haven't changed since Victor Hugo wrote *Notre-Dame*."[13]

To the awe of the Church and the fear of the feverish crowd one must add one more perspective to triangulate Freud's Paris: the theater, and especially its women. Freud went to theater first in hopes of improving his French, found he understood little, but returned ever again for other reasons. Freud devoted one of the longest of his long letters to a scene-by-scene account of Sarah Bernhardt's performance in Victorien Sardou's melodrama, *Theodora*.[14] He was utterly bewitched by her portrayal of the Byzantine heroine, a prostitute become Empress: "Her caressing and pleading, the postures she assumes, the way she wraps herself around a man, the way she acts with every limb, every joint—it's incredible. A remarkable creature, and I can imagine she is no different in life from what she is on the stage."

"For the sake of historical truth," Freud continues, "let us add that I again had to pay for this pleasure with an attack of migraine." The tensions of the Paris experience, his new receptivity, sensual as well as intellectual, to the realm of instinct were doubtless related to Freud's long separation from his Martha. He cheerfully admitted to her his frequent recourse to cocaine to keep his tensions down or his spirits up. While he surely concealed no actions from her, he revealed one fantasy—that he might marry the attractive daughter of Dr. Charcot and thus in one

stroke solve his problems of power—professional, social, and sexual—
that evidently evoked a nettled response from Martha, who could not
take it as lightly as Freud tried to present it.[15] One suspects that the
decorous Freud could not and did not reveal the full extent of his newfound feelings. They are perhaps better expressed in a joke he delighted
to record at a later time, when he had discovered that jokes contain the
expression of repressed wishes: a married couple is discussing the future.
The man says to his wife: "If one of us should die, I shall go to Paris."[16]

In one of Freud's remarkable Paris letters, the very imagery he used
seems to bring all the dimensions of his Paris experience into relation to
the impact of Jean Martin Charcot: "I think I am changing a great
deal. . . . Charcot, who is one of the greatest of physicians, and a man
whose common sense borders on genius, is simply wrecking all my aims
and opinions. I sometimes come out of his lectures as from out of Notre
Dame," our militant anti-Catholic continues "with an entirely new idea
of perfection. . . . It is three whole days since I have done any work, and I
have no feelings of guilt," the erstwhile Puritan adds. "My brain is sated
as after an evening in the theater. Whether the seed will ever bear fruit, I
don't know; but I do know that no other human being has ever affected
me in the same way. . . . Or am I under the influence of this magically
attractive and repulsive city?"[17]

Surely it was both. Paris, and Freud's quasi-stereotypical perception of
it, provided the ideal setting to receive from Charcot conceptions of
mental disorder that opened the way to that questionable province of the
psyche where neither body nor conscious mind seemed in control.

The historical interests Freud cultivated while he was in Paris confirm
the ambivalent feelings of attraction and repulsion toward French Catholic culture found in his letters. In an extensive series of publications,
Charcot and his followers had advanced the view that many of the phenomena associated with the religious outlook of medieval Catholicism,
such as belief in miracles, saints, witchcraft, and demonic possession,
could actually be explained as misunderstood instances of hysterical disorders. Freud enthusiastically embraced this idea, and over the following
decade made use of it frequently in his early publications on the subject
of hysteria. Employing such an analytic framework allowed Freud the
satisfaction of using modern science to refute Catholic religious notions,
but his writings also betray a strong sense of fascination—sometimes
bordering on approval—with the way the specific characteristics of these
phenomena had been accurately described by monks and priests even
while their underlying causes had been misunderstood. Freud's historical

studies of medieval Catholic culture provided an invaluable road map to his understanding of the hysterical symptoms observed in the patients who came to him in the 1890s.[18]

Before Freud left Paris for home he cemented his relations with Charcot by volunteering as translator of a volume of his *Leçons sur les maladies du système nerveux*, including his lectures on hysteria. Thus Freud's tribute to English thought in his translation of John Stuart Mill's essay on the subjection of women found an appropriate French equivalent. Freud carried the symmetry into his family too: he named his first-born son Jean Martin for Charcot, as he would soon, in tribute to Puritan England, name his second son Oliver, after Cromwell. Thus Freud's personal exemplars of English ego and Parisian id each had their namesakes among his children.

When Freud returned to Vienna he entered practice as a doctor of nervous diseases. He chose Easter Sunday to publish this good news in the *Neue Freie Presse*. Thus the Jewish admirer of Notre Dame combined an announcement of his own resurrection and new life with a defiance of Catholic sensibilities worthy of a Puritan prophet. Such were the extreme polarities which entered into the genesis of psychoanalysis.

ONE cannot fail to be struck by the radical contrast between Freud's characterization of English and French cultures. He not only kept their identities separate and antithetical but sought in neither any trace of the features he saw in the other. The Puritan-rationalist spectacles he wore when he looked at England allowed him to see there nothing of the cathedrals, crowds, or women that so caught his eye in France; nor did he remark the gracious, aristocratic side of English life and manners. In France, on the other hand, the image of the female and the Sphinx so dominated his perception that the positivist, rationalist, masculine side of French bourgeois society scarcely entered his field of vision. Finally, Freud made no attempt to establish any relationship between the contrasting values that attracted him in English and French culture. This he was to accomplish only indirectly in his encounter with Rome, where male and female, ethics and aesthetics—in short, the ego-world of London and the id-world of Paris converged in bewildering conflation.

ROME had engaged Freud's fancy on and off since childhood. Not until the 1890s, when he was in his forties, while at work on *The Interpretation of Dreams*, did he conceive a truly passionate interest in the Eternal City. As in the early 1880s, when he had contemplated escape to the refuge of England, he entered in the mid-1890s another, deeper professional crisis. Where the impasse of the 1880s applied only to his career opportunities, the new one involved, by virtue of the very depth of his frustration, Freud's personal identity and intellectual direction as well.

I have elsewhere tried to show how the seething crisis of Austrian society, in which liberalism lacked the power to sustain itself against the rising tide of the Catholic and nationalist anti-Semitic movements, affected Freud.[19] It drove him into social withdrawal as a Jew, into intellectual isolation as a scientist, and into introspection as a thinker. The more his outer life was mired, however, the more winged his ideas became. In his fundamental work, *The Interpretation of Dreams*, Freud transformed the poison of social frustration as Jew and as scientist into the elixir of psychological illumination. Essential to his procedure was to plumb the depths of his own personal history, thus to find a universal psychological structure, a key to human destiny that would transcend the collective history that until then had seemed to shape man's fate. Where he had once been tempted to withdraw to England, he now turned inward into himself, to face and overcome the conflicts between his wishes and his hostile environment by means of psychoanalysis as theory. As he did so, he also resolved, by means of psychoanalysis as therapy, the conflicts between his wishes and his values.

It was in the context of working through this intellectual and personal crisis that Freud's interest in antiquity and in Rome arose. It was then that he hit upon the analogy between his own procedure of digging into his own buried past as depth-psychologist and the work of the archeologist. Soon his mild interest developed into an insatiable passion. He eagerly read the biography of Heinrich Schliemann, who claimed to have fulfilled a childhood wish by his discovery of Troy. He began the collection of ancient artifacts that soon graced his office in the Berggasse. And, especially rare in those days of his social withdrawal, Freud made a new friend: Emanuel Löwy, a professor of archeology. "He keeps me up until three o'clock in the morning," Freud wrote to his dearest friend; "he tells me about Rome."[20]

In the years 1895–1900, when Freud struggled toward the intellectual breakthrough embodied in *The Interpretation of Dreams*, Rome, mother of cities, came to occupy a crucial place in his life. Then a strange problem arose. He developed what he called his "Rome neurosis."[21] Freud, the avid traveler, could not get to Rome, though the city haunted his dreams. To do so, he had to dig up the Rome in himself, by analyzing his dreams.

I shall not deal here with Freud's Rome neurosis and the way he resolved it psychoanalytically.[22] What concerns me is rather his cultural perspective. Unlike his approach to either England or Paris, his perspective on Rome is Jewish, that of the outsider, but it is a double one. On the one hand, Rome is masculine, the citadel of Catholic power, and his dream-wish, as a liberal and a Jew, is to conquer it. On the other hand, other of his wishes show Rome as feminine: Holy Mother Church, promising gratification, is to be entered in love. His powers were too weak for the project of conquest, his conscience too strong for the opposite possibility, to embrace the Church in conversion. Hence the neurotic impasse. Freud found the roots of these antithetical wishes in his psyche: in his childhood relations to his Jewish father and to a beloved Catholic nanny. But Rome had brought into conjunction the feelings attached to masculine England and feminine Paris, tangled together. While Freud resolved the problems presented by Rome in his self-analysis by reducing them to family relations, the cultural problems of the Jew in a gentile world troubled him more than ever.

Once more Freud was drawn to the classical era for emotional comfort. This became clear when he overcame his Rome neurosis through self-analysis and, in 1901, was able to enter the city at last. Medieval and Baroque Rome evoked his hatred of Catholicism once more: "I found almost intolerable the lie of salvation which rears its head so proudly to heaven." But beneath Catholic Rome was the city he really cherished: classicial Rome, in which he became "totally and undisturbedly absorbed." His feelings for it as the foundation of European civilization welled up as did Gibbon's when he surveyed the ruined forum from the Capitoline. The focus of Freud's pathos was, not surprisingly, Athena, in her Roman persona, Minerva. He wrote to his friend Wilhelm Fliess, "I could have worshiped the humble and mutilated remnant of the Temple of Minerva."[23]

Was Freud's Roman Athena the same as the one that the liberals of Vienna had chosen as their symbol of rational wisdom and justice? One suspects that she was, for she filled him still with serenity and a sense of intellectual security. But not for long.

Shortly before he described to Fliess his reaction to Rome, Freud had written him to announce his next big psychological study. It would be called "Bisexuality in Man."[24] Athena could well symbolize this more ambiguous and ambitious psychoanalytic enterprise, lying far beyond her orthodox nineteenth-century signification as goddess of rational order. For Athena, as Freud would soon explain, was an androgynous goddess. In her rational cool and ascetic bisexuality Athena unified the ethical civic spirit that had so attracted him to manly England, and the questionable feminine beauty and irrational religious power that had so stirred him in seductive Paris. After his conquest of Rome, the pursuit of these related opposites led Freud to new cultural sites, to strata lying deeper both in history and in his psyche than Greece and Rome, namely, to Israel and Egypt.

❧

BEFORE we follow Freud on his explorations in these more remote cultures, let us pause with him in the middle of the journey on the acropolis of Athens. Freud visited it in 1904. In sharp contrast to his golden moment in the flats of Rome, where he had "worshipped the . . . remnant of Minerva's temple," Freud felt on the heights of Athens an unsettling malaise. He later analyzed that experience in an essay, "A Disturbance of Memory on the Acropolis,' concluding that his joy had been undermined by guilt.[25] His whole acquired classical culture, which had served as a solid, secular common ground between Christian and Jew, now appeared to him under the aspect of his own detachment from the Jewish tradition to which his father had resolutely clung. Thenceforth, the road to Israel beckoned.

A few years later, returning to Rome, Freud felt again a flash of the apostate's guilt. This time it was in confronting Michelangelo's statue of "Moses." Freud at first identified himself with the mob of backsliders to the golden calf upon whom the angry prophet's eye is turned, "the mob which has neither faith nor patience, and which rejoices when it has regained its illusory idols."[26] But then Freud detached himself from this guilt as a Jew. Michelangelo's Moses, he argues in his famous essay of that name, is not the "historical figure," the tablet-breaking angry prophet of the Bible. He is rather an exemplar of masculine moral control over the instincts, who governs his rage for the sake of his cause.[27] Most Freud biographers agree in seeing this Moses experience as connected with Freud's tension with his followers over his effort to make a gentile, C. G. Jung, his successor as head of the psychoanalytic organization so that psychoanalysis might not be a purely Jewish science. Freud found in Moses a model from which to draw strength as the embattled, patriarchal leader of his movement. Far from assaulting the father—that is, Moses—in identification with the backsliding mob of sons, Freud was hardening himself into being a powerful father himself, as he confronted his fractious followers.

The second road that led away from Athens ran in an almost opposite direction, to Egypt. At one level, this would seem a logical counterpart to Freud's renewed preoccupation with his Jewishness. Israel, and especially the two biblical figures that most engaged Freud from childhood on, Joseph and Moses, were fundamentally defined in relation to Egypt.[28] For the Jews, Egypt was the archetypal land of gentile high-cultural opportunity and also of cruel, absolutist oppression, not unlike Germany in Freud's life span. In his *Autobiography* Freud indicates that his deep interest in the Bible story as a child strongly affected the direction of his later interests. The family Bible which he read, the Philippson Bible, included an extensive commentary drawing on a rich array of Enlightenment insights into psychology, anthropology, and philosophy to reinforce and explain to a more modern time the traditional elements of religious faith. Particularly in its description of the Egyptian culture that so strongly influenced the Jews from the time of Joseph to that of Moses, Philippson's commentary came alive to the young Freud as a source of ideas and images (provided in part by the Bible's extensive illustrations) that stimulated his thoughts and feelings.[29]

Yet after 1900 Egypt nurtured in Freud interests that were in drastic contradiction to the faith of his fathers and even to the male orientation of psychoanalysis—interests closer to his new project of 1901: "Bisexuality in Man." For Egypt was a land of the primal mothers, and even as a child Freud seems to have shown some awareness of this aspect of Egyptian culture. The one dream of his childhood that he later recorded and analyzed in *The Interpretation of Dreams*, the Dream of the Bird Beaked Figures, drew its imagery from the illustrations of Philippson's Bible. Freud indicates that the bird-beaked figures in the dream were derived from Philippson's drawings of Egyptian deities, and analysis of the dream connects it to Freud's anxiety concerning his "two mothers," his actual mother and the Czech Catholic nursemaid who played such an important maternal role in his early life. Freud's analysis of this early dream offers no clues to whether his interest was drawn to the religiously expressed bisexuality associated with many of the Egyptian deities. This subject touched ultimate and even dangerous questions of the psyche to which Freud devoted scant attention before he fell under Egypt's spell in the decade following publcation of *The Interpretation of Dreams*.[30]

EVER since the Renaissance, Egyptomania had periodically seized the European imagination. That mysterious land promised access to the womb of culture and the tomb of time, to the original and the hidden, the voiceless (*infans*) childhood of humanity. In the fin de siècle it was the finds of archeologists that aroused anew the desire to decipher the culture of the Nile, as the philologists had done a century before. The archeologists' work swept the educated public in its wake.

Freud caught the fever. By 1906 at latest, his intoxication with things Egyptian far exceeded his earlier infatuation with Rome. He began to build a substantial library on Egypt. The most tangible evidence of his passion was in his expanding collection of artifacts, today preserved in the Freud Museum in London. In it Egyptian culture was the most strongly represented. There were no fewer than six figurines of Egypt's polytheistic holy family: Isis, Osiris, and Horus. Egypt soon dominated Freud's consulting room, with photos and stone reliefs of Osiris and his family at the doorway to his study. Freud meditated upon—virtually communed with—these ancient images, not only at the desk where H.D. had noticed them and where he worked under their gaze, but even at the dinner table.[31]

Another index of the strength of his addiction is Freud's behavior on a week's visit to his beloved London in 1908, his first since 1875. This time it was not the virtuous character of English culture that captured him. Though he did some sight-seeing, his biographer Ernest Jones reports, "What meant most to him [in London] was the collection of antiquities, particularly the Egyptian ones, in the British Museum. He did not go to any theater, because the evenings were given up to reading in preparation for the next day's visit to the museum."[32]

As early as 1907, Freud turned the attention of a prized new disciple, Karl Abraham, toward Egypt. On Abraham's first visit to Vienna, Freud not only gave him his "first Egyptological lessons," but even put two little Egyptian figurines in his guest's briefcase as a surprise farewell gift.[33] The lesson took; five years later, Abraham in turn surprised Freud, presenting him with a brilliant psychoanalytic study of Amenhotep IV, the pharaoh who was later to be the central figure in Freud's *Moses and Monotheism*. Freud wrote his friend in delight and gratitude: "Amenhotep IV in psychoanalytic illumination! That is certainly a big step in 'orienta-

tion'"—the pun in German implies, as it would in English, turning toward the East.[34]

In 1910, the consequences of Freud's interest in Egypt appeared for
the first time in his published work. As his road to Jewish culture had
passed through the Renaissance via the art of Michelangelo, so the road
to Egypt lay through the art of Leonardo da Vinci. In Moses, the problem Freud addressed was patriarchal control; in Leonardo, it was homosexuality.[35] Freud analyzed a childhood memory of Leonardo's, in which
he is visited in his cradle by a vulture that strikes his mouth with its tail.
Freud sees Leonardo's homosexuality in this infantile fantasy: the vulture
represents a new figure on the psychoanalytic scene: the phallic mother.
Freud grounds his analysis of Leonardo's fantasy on the vulture-headed
Egyptian mother goddess, Mut. She is one of Egypt's original her-
maphroditic divinities who survive alongside later gods that are sexually
more differentiated. Freud analogizes the symbolic culture of Egypt, in
the childhood of the race, to the infantile fantasy of the pre-Oedipal
individual. He sees the androgynous gods of Egypt as "expressions of the
idea that only a combination of male and female elements can give a
worthy representation of divine perfection."[36]

Suddenly, in this connection, Athena reappears in the text on Leonardo. Locating her origins in Egypt, Freud describes her now as a
Greek descendant of an Egyptian phallic mother goddess, Neith of Sais.[37]
From this line of inquiry into bipolar unities also stemmed Freud's later
interpretations of the Gorgon Medusa, the snakes on whose head are
penises threatening castration. It was the Gorgon's fierce face that adorned
the breast and shield of Athena to keep her male antagonists at bay.

In 1910, Freud published another fruit of his Egyptian explorations,
this time concerning language. The article, "The Antithetical Meaning
of Primal Words," took the form of a review of a book published almost
three decades earlier. Its author, the philologist Karl Abel, had demonstrated that, in the primal language of Egypt, a single word denoted both
an idea and its opposite; e.g., both strong and weak, both light and dark.
Freud noted that this linguistic finding about primal language was the
same as his own view of dreams. "Dreams feel themselves at liberty . . . to
represent any element by its wishful contrary."[38] Primal words thus have
the same character as the primal bisexual divinities of Egypt; they constitute a unity of opposites. Only later are they split into autonomous antithetical, or complementary, terms.

Some of Freud's boldest later inquests into female psychology, bisex-

uality and the pre-Oedipal mother (e.g., "Female Sexuality" [1931];
"Contributions to the Psychology of Love" [1918]) might be traced back
to the study of Egyptian culture that so fired his imagination in the prewar years. They yielded new psychoanalytic concepts that could break
through the essentially male confines of most of Freud's cultural theory,
especially *Totem and Tabu*. But the advent of Hitler and the problem of
saving the Jews led Freud back to Moses and away from the new veins he
had opened in his first Egyptian dig.

Moses and Monotheism, written in the 1930s, explores as history the
problem Freud had explored in his own psyche in analyzing his Rome
neurosis: the relation of Jew and gentile. The work is both Jewish history
and Egyptian history. As Jewish history it centers on two sensational,
anti-traditional ideas. The first is that Moses was not a foundling Jew but
a high-born Egyptian. The second is that, after the Exodus, Moses was
killed by the more primitive of the Jews who could not abide the severity
of his law.

Both of these startling historical theses link the Jews, as Freud explicitly aims to show, to the world of the gentiles: the first, culturally, to the
Egyptians; the second, by analogy with the crucifixion, to the Christians.
With these identifications of Jew and gentile through Moses, Freud ac-
complishes two things: First, he vindicates the Jewish people by defining
them as carriers of the highest mark of civilization—one first achieved by
Egypt. Second, in his myth of the killing of Moses, Freud gives the Jews
a basis for abandoning their exclusivist self-definition, which in his view
prevents them from realizing, as Christians do, their own universality.
For that, Freud says, the Jews must recognize as Christians do their own
patricidal crime, and assume its guilt as participants in the brotherhood
of man.

The particular Egypt that Freud provides as setting for his Moses story
in the 1930s is strikingly different from the land of bisexual religion and
primal mothers that claimed his attention before World War I. We
should see it as a second Egyptian dig. Freud concentrates now on a later
phase of Egyptian history, the reign of Amenhotep IV, who renamed
himself Akhenaten. That pharaoh of the eighteenth dynasty was the
nearest thing Egypt produced to a European enlightened despot of the
eighteenth century, like Joseph II of Austria. Akhenaten was a man after

Freud's heart, a rebel-reformer. Establishing a monotheistic cult of an abstract sun god, Aton, the pharaoh suppressed the polytheistic religion of Egypt. Akhenaten's monotheistic cult stressed not salvation but truth-fulness, ethics, and justice. His was an elitist creed developed "in deliber-ate hostility to the popular [religion]."³⁹ But when Akhenaten died, his victory over the superstition and darkness of Egyptian polytheism was swept away by a Counter-Reformation, much as the Emperor Joseph II's Enlightenment had been by Catholic reaction.

According to Freud, Moses, the Egyptian nobleman, member of Akhe-naten's intellectual elite, was caught in the Götterdämmerung of Egypt's Enlightenment. Moses was one who, as Freud put it, "lost his fatherland" when the values it stood for under his pharaoh were destroyed.⁴⁰ Like the enlightened anti-Nazi gentiles in Freud's time. Determined to rescue the pharaoh's cultural achievement from Egypt's Counter-Reformation, Moses chose as his vehicle the Jews, a poor alien people settled in a border province, who worshiped a primitive tribal God. In effect, Moses made Egyptians out of the Jews, so that they might preserve the highest culture that his country had achieved. He gave them three Egyptian gifts: monotheism, the ethical code of the Aton cult, and the practice of cir-cumcision. With these three gifts of Egyptian Enlightenment, Freud ar-gued, Moses created the most fundamental characteristic of Jewish cul-ture ever after: *Geistigkeit*. That term embraces both spirituality and intellectuality. It is the opposite of *Sinnlichkeit*, the realm of the senses. It is London as opposed to Paris. The eternal task of Geistigkeit is to con-trol Sinnlichkeit and the instincts that drive it. That is what civilization is all about.⁴¹ The Egyptians achieved it first among all peoples in Akhenaten's brief moment in history. Moses imparted its essentials to the Jews, to save it and cultivate it for the future.

It was a man's job. Not for nothing did Freud entitle his book in Ger-man, "*Der Mann Moses*." He did not say "*Der Mensch Moses*." *Mann* con-veys what Freud wanted: manliness, maleness, and its attributes: courage, force, principle, uprightness.⁴² One recalls his earlier political-cultural heroes, Hannibal and Oliver Cromwell. Moses, the able, masterful aristo-crat who, Freud fantasizes further, might have aspired to rule Egypt as Akhenaten's successor. In any case it fit his nature to plan for the Jews: "to found a new empire, to find a new people [*ein neues Reich zu gründen, ein neues Volk zu finden*]."⁴³ Freud associated Moses's imperial manliness of course with his Geistigkeit. Demanding of the Jews instinctual renuncia-tion, Moses liberated the Jews not so much from Egyptian bondage as from their own instinctual drives. A father to the childish people, Moses trans-

formed them into a father-people, exemplifying the victory of male abstraction, the central prerequisite of civilization, over female sensuality and
materiality. Thanks to their intellectual and ethical strength, the Jews as
Kulturvolk (cultural people) par excellence would always be attacked whenever repressed instinct broke loose in civilized society; thanks to the same
masculine virtues, they would have the power to endure in adversity.

The ideal historical base for Freud's final exploration in culture in
Moses and Monotheism, we must by now realize, is no longer Greece, but
Egypt. In the Egypt of his second dig, the Jews acquired an honored
place in gentile history such as neither Athens nor Rome nor the classicism of the Austrian Gymnasium could provide them. For in Egypt, the
Jews became the Kulturvolk that rescued the highest gentile civilization
from the unholy alliance of priests and ignorant people; just as, in modern times, the Jews and cultured gentiles were, through exodus and exile,
saving Europe's enlightened civilization from Hitler.

LET us look now at the Egyptian side of the equation. What has Freud
done with Egyptian history to sustain his image of Moses? And, in so
doing, what has he done to his previous excavations of Egypt for the
psychoanalytic understanding of culture?

In the first Egyptian dig, Freud's findings were related to bisexuality,
the phallic mother, the union of opposites in religion and even in language. In the second dig, undertaken in search of the origins of the Jews,
we find a different Egypt, one wholly oriented toward masculine cultural
achievements, with Geistigkeit and instinctual repression at the center.

In pursuit of this difference, I began to look at Freud's sources. The
trail led first, of all places, to Chicago. James Henry Breasted, founder of
Chicago's Oriental Institute, published in 1905 *The History of Egypt*, a
great classic of its time, and Freud's principal source. Breasted had written his doctoral thesis in Berlin on the hymns of Akhenaten's sun god,
Aton. There he showed the world's earliest monotheism in birth in poetry. Then, in his comprehensive history, Breasted charted Egyptian culture as it struggled out of chthonic darkness to the achievement of
rational enlightenment in the reign of his hero, Akhenaten. In the progressivist spirit of America's New History, which had a principal center
in Chicago, Breasted made of Egypt a paradigm for the whole history of
European civilization, at a time when Greeks and Hebrews were both
still in a primitive state.

As Freud was a secularized Jew seeking roots deeper and anterior to those of his faith, Breasted was a secularized Protestant Christian engaged in related quests: to deny to their respective traditions claims to be the divinely ordained founders of civilization by exalting Egypt as creator of the first Enlightenment culture. Even as Freud began work on *Moses and Monotheism*, Breasted was publishing a popular book on Egypt under the title, *The Dawn of Conscience* (1933)—what Freud could have called "the origins of the super-ego." Breasted included in its preface an explicit expression of concern about revived anti-Semitism in order to offset the fact that he was undermining the Judaeo-Christian claims to primacy in creating our civilization.

Freud's portrait of Akhenaten and his religious revolution is firmly grounded in Breasted's account: monotheism, rationalism, the construction of an ethical code, even circumcision are in it. But Breasted includes another aspect of Akhenaten's culture nowhere mentioned in Freud: a rich sensual element. No Egyptian nobleman could have escaped it.

If the god Aton was de-materialized, the earthly life and cultural forms of his cult were far from it. Breasted shows how the art of Akhenaten's reign broke the stiff, hieratic geometrical tradition of Egypt in favor of a sensuous, naturalistic plasticity worthy of art nouveau. Frescoes depicting Akhenaten and his beautiful queen Nefertiti in tender communion or playing lovingly with their daughters radiate the joy of Sinnlichkeit.

"To the sensitive soul of this Egyptian dreamer," Breasted says, "the whole animate world seems alive with the presence of Aton: . . . the lily-grown marshes, where the flowers are 'drunken' in the intoxicating radiance of Aton." "The deepest sources of power in this remarkable revolution," the Emersonian Breasted concludes, "lay in this appeal to nature, in this admonition to 'consider the lilies of the field.'"[44]

None of the sensual side of the Akhenaten culture described by Breasted appears in Freud's account. Freud selected from Breasted's *History* what connects the Egyptian Enlightenment to the Geistigkeit he sees in the Jews. In his own copy of Breasted's history, Freud marked only those passages that sustained this commonality. The rest—and the richer information on the sensuous culture of Akhenaten in *The Dawn of Conscience*—he ignored.

Another omission in Freud's book is even more astonishing. Neither in text nor footnotes is there any reference to the one major psychoanalytic study of Akhenaten and his cultural revolution: Karl Abraham's "Amenhotep IV." This was the long article with which, as I have mentioned,

Abraham, the faithful disciple, had surprised the master in 1912.[45] He wrote it under the stimulus of Freud's interest in bisexuality and its presence in the Leonardo analysis and Egyptian religious culture.

Abraham's psychoanalytic portrait of Akhenaten centers squarely on the pharaoh's androgynous nature. Reared by a powerful mother to whom he remained passionately attached, Akhenaten lived in a permanent state of anger against his strong father. Akhenaten's self-representation in art, no less than his behavior, showed striking androgynous characteristics. It was also marked by allusion to the most primitive styles. Identifying his god Aton with the earliest sun god, and claiming descent from him, Akhenaten outflanked his father, Amenhotep III, and replaced his cult. His archaism, Abraham argued, betrayed a well-known neurotic symptom: the fantasy of high parentage. Akhenaten made his god a god of love, a completely spiritualized ideal father. "He had sublimated his aggressive instinctual impulses to an extraordinary extent," Abraham maintains, "and had transformed them into an overflowing love for all beings, so that he did not use violence even against the enemies of his empire." Though Abraham saw Akhenaten as a predecessor of Moses as monotheist, "[his] conception of god has more in common with the Christian than with the Mosaic conception." A God of love.[46] Finally, Abraham stresses the tremendous influence of women—especially his wife, Nefertiti, and his mother, Tiys—on Akhenaten's court and cult. If ethical Geistigkeit was one aspect of the monotheistic god Aton, intense, aestheticized sensuosity was the other. Freud left this dual character out of his account.[47]

The project of vindicating the Jews as a masculine Kulturvolk led Freud in effect to ignore in his second Egyptian dig the conceptual treasures he had unearthed in his first. He abandoned the shafts he had himself opened into a possible bisexual theory of cultural development. He expurgated or repressed the knowledge of Breasted and Abraham, his best informants, with respect to the integration of Sinnlichkeit with Geistigkeit, female with male, in the culture of Akhenaten. Freud paid a price for his suppression of the truth about the androgynous pharaoh, a price not without its irony: in making of Moses an Egyptian, he had ended by making of Akhenaten a Jew.

⌇

OUR story has been one of a dualism that worked itself out again and again in Freud's explorations in culture: in the 1880s, there was puritan, manly England versus fascinating, feminine Paris; in the 1890s, anxiety-provoking Rome, with its menace of masculine papal power conflated with the temptation of the Church as Holy Mother; in the 1910s, virile Michelangelo contrasted with androgynous Leonardo; and finally, Egypt: the land of primal bisexual culture confronting the enlightened patriarchal despotism of Akhenaten/Moses.

What, in all this, has become of Athena, who had accompanied Freud throughout his cultural odyssey? After the experience on the acropolis in 1904 Freud left her with a sense of guilt about their relationship. In 1910, in the swamplands of the Nile, he found her in a primal form, a phallic mother goddess. How she would have shocked the good liberals of Vienna who had chosen her as the virginal symbol of their rational polity! In *Moses and Monotheism*, Athena appeared once more, though only in a footnote. There Freud speculated on the origin of Athena's Greek persona: a great earthquake, such as he thought might account for the tidal wave that swallowed the Egyptians in the Red Sea, had also sealed Athena's destiny as a mother goddess. Like the matriarchal goddess of Crete, Freud suggested, she had lost all credibility when her womanly powers failed to protect the Greeks against the volcanic eruptions of nature. Then male gods like "earth-shaking Zeus" took over. The mother goddess Pallas Athena, Freud tells us, "was demoted to a daughter, robbed of her own mother, and through the virginity imposed upon her, permanently excluded from motherhood."[48] Thus denatured by her father Zeus, she had henceforth to serve his patriarchal purposes as intellectual brain-child. We recall Freud's words on Athena to H.D.: "She is perfect . . . only she has lost her spear." In the light of Freud's suppression of bisexuality in his final work of cultural analysis, those words on Athena have a melancholy ring.

In May 1938, Freud fled Vienna for England, the land of civic virtue to which he had thought of emigrating over fifty years before. Taking the Orient Express westward to London, he stopped for a night at the other favored city of his youth, Paris. There he enjoyed the hospitality of a favorite disciple, his "dear Princess," Marie Bonaparte. "An energy devil," Freud had called her; "a quite outstanding, more than half masculine female."[49] As if to justify his characterization, the princess had boldly smuggled his favorite statuette, Athena, out of Vienna, when he feared his collection of artifacts might be lost.[50] Now she put it into the old man's hands.

Freud carried Athena on to London himself. It was his last voyage with that old androgynous companion from antiquity, whose changes had recorded so faithfully the changes in Freud's understanding of humankind. But as he left for London, it was not to Athena that Freud's thoughts turned to define his situation. "I compare myself," he wrote to his son Ernst, "with the old Jacob, whom in his old age his children brought to Egypt."[51]

For the sake of the Jews in Hitler's Götterdämmerung, Freud banished from his mind the promising insights into sexuality and culture he had found in Egypt, and abandoned them in *Moses and Monotheism*. Now he could go to England to die in freedom with his historical illusions, a Jewish patriarch in the enlightened gentile country of his youthful dreams.

NOTES

1. H.D., "Writing on the Wall," *Tribute to Freud* (New York, 1956), 93, 94.

2. Ibid., 68, 69.

3. Quoted in Ernest Jones, *The Life and Work of Sigmund Freud*, 3 vols. (New York, 1953–1957), 1:178–79.

4. Ronald M. Clark, *Freud: The Man and His Career* (New York, 1980), 38–40.

5. Jones, *Freud*, 1:179.

6. Ibid., 2:171.

7. Ibid., 1:233. For an able discussion of Freud's relation to Paris and Charcot somewhat at variance with mine, see Léon Chertok, "Freud in Paris (1885/86)," *Psyche* 5 (1973), 431–48.

8. Marthe Robert, *The Psychoanalytic Revolution*, translated by Kenneth Morgan, paperback edn. (New York, 1968), 72.

9. Sigmund Freud, *Works*, Standard Edition, edited by James Strachey et al., 24 vols. (London, 1966–1974), 4:195.

10. Sigmund Freud to Minna Bernays, December 3, 1885, in *The Letters of Sigmund Freud*, edited by Ernst L. Freud, translated by Tania and James Stern, paperback edn. (New York, Toronto, and London, 1964), 187.

11. Freud to Martha Bernays, November 19, 1885, in *Letters*, 183.

12. Freud, *Works*, 5:469.

13. Freud to Minna Bernays, December 3, 1885, in *Letters*, 187–88.

14. Freud to Martha Bernays, November 8, 1885, in *Letters*, 178–82.

15. "Now just suppose I were not in love already and were something of an adventurer; it would be a strong temptation to court her [Mlle. Charcot], for nothing is more dangerous than a young girl bearing the features of a man whom one admires." Freud to Martha Bernays, Paris, January 20, 1886, in *Letters*, 197–98; see also February 2, 1886, ibid., 201; February 10, 1886, ibid., 206–7.

16. Freud, *Works*, 5:485.

17. Freud to Martha Bernays, November 24, 1885, in *Letters*, 184–85.

18. William J. McGrath, *Freud's Discovery of Psychoanalysis: The Politics of Hysteria* (Ithaca and London, 1986), 156–59, 165–72.

19. Carl E. Schorske, *Fin-de-Siècle Vienna: Politics and Culture* (New York, 1980), chap. 4; idem, "Freud: The Psychoarchaeology of Civilizations," in *The Cambridge Companion to Freud*, edited by Jerome Neu (Cambridge, Eng., 1991), 16–23. Unless otherwise indicated, what follows is largely drawn from the materials presented there.

20. Freud to Wilhelm Fliess, November 5, 1897, in Sigmund Freud, *The Origins of Psychoanalysis: Letters, Drafts and Notes to Wilhelm Fliess, 1887–1902*, edited by Marie Bonaparte, Anna Freud, and Ernst Kris, translated by Eric Mosbacher and James Strachey, paperback edn. (Garden City, N.Y., 1957), 232.

21. Freud to Wilhelm Fliess, December 3, 1897, ibid., 239.

22. Schorske, *Fin-de-Siècle Vienna*, chap. 4.

23. *The Complete Letters of Sigmund Freud to Wilhelm Fliess, 1887–1904*, edited by Jeffrey Masson (Cambridge, Mass., 1985), 449.

24. Freud to Wilhelm Fliess, August 7, 1901, in Freud, *Origins*, 335–36.

25. Freud, *Works*, 22:239–48.

26. Freud, "The Moses of Michelangelo," ibid., 13:213.

27. Ibid., 233.

28. For the association of Egypt with both sibling rivalry and the death of the mother in Freud's childhood experience and his later dreams, see McGrath, *Freud's Discovery*, chap. 2.

29. Ibid., 26, 44–53.

30. An original and suggestive analysis of Freud's relation to Egyptian mythology and its implications for his theory is provided by Joan Rafael-Leff, "If Oedipus Was an Egyptian," *International Review of Psychoanalysis* 17 (1990), 309–35. Ms. Leff integrates the perspectives of psychoanalyist, Egyptologist, and feminist.

31. Ellen Handler Spitz, "Psychoanalysis and the Legacy of Antiquity," in *Sigmund Freud and Art*, edited by Lynn Gamwell and Richard Wells (Binghamton, N.Y., and London, 1989), 154–55.

32. Jones, *Freud*, 2:52.

33. Sigmund Freud and Karl Abraham, *Briefe, 1907–1926*, edited by Hilda C. Abraham and Ernst L. Freud (Frankfurt, 1965), 28.

34. Ibid., 115.

35. The Leonardo text also involved a new relationship between mythology and sexuality, bringing Freud closer to Jung but on the basis of misunderstanding. See George B. Hogenson, *Jung's Struggle with Freud* (Notre Dame, Ind., 1983), 26–40.

36. "Leonardo da Vinci and a Memory of Childhood," *Works*, 11:93–94. Freud conflates Mut with another mother goddess, Nut, who alone is identified with a vulture. See J. Harnik, "Aegyptologisches zu Leonardos Geierphantasie," *Internationale Zeitschrift für Psychoanalyse* 6 (1920), 362–63.

37. Freud, *Works*, 11:94. Freud had initially connected Egypt with Greece in the case of Leonardo's vulture, too: "It can be proven that Leonardo was acquainted with the vulture as symbol of motherliness through his reading of Greek

authors, who were thoroughly steeped in Egyptian culture." Presentation in *Minutes of the Vienna Psychoanalytic Society*, edited by H. Nunberg and E. Federn (New York, 1967), 2:342. Freud omitted this claim from the published version.

38. Freud, *Works*, 11:155.

39. Freud, "Moses and Monotheism," *Works*, 23:20–26.

40. Ibid., 28.

41. Ibid., 64; 86 n. 1; 111–23.

42. Bluma Goldstein, *Reinscribing Moses* (Cambridge, Mass., 1992), 102–3.

43. Ibid., 28. I have brought the translation closer to the original German.

44. James H. Breasted, *The Dawn of Conscience* (New York, 1933), 292–98; idem, *A History of Egypt* (New York, 1923), 376–78.

45. Karl Abraham, *Selected Papers*, 2 vols. (New York, 1955), 2:262–90; Leonard Shengold, "A Parapraxis of Freud's in Relation to Karl Abraham," *Imago* 92 (1972), 123–59.

46. Abraham, *Selected Papers*, 2:275, 287.

47. Breasted cites a source (a hymn?) calling Aton "the *father and mother* of all he has made" (*A History of Egypt*, 377), my italics. This dual character of the god recalls Freud's observations in his Leonardo essay that to the Egyptians "only a combination of male and female elements can give a worthy representation of divine perfection."

48. Freud, *Works*, 23:45 n. 2.

49. Quoted by Peter Gay, *Freud, a Life for Our Time* (New York, 1988), 541, 542.

50. Jones, *Freud*, 3:227–28.

51. Ibid., 3:225.

AFTERWORD

THIRTEEN

History and the Study
of Culture

HISTORY is one of the few disciplines to boast a muse, Clio, thanks to the academic intelligentsia of Alexandria who assigned her to our craft. The muses are, of course, female. If any among them has partaken more than others of the nature and destiny of woman in a man's world, it is Clio.

In 1988, a conference was held at Scripps College which dramatized the degree to which Clio's life has been dependent. The title of the symposium was "History and. . . ."[1] Participants of various nonhistorical disciplines were asked to examine their relations with history in a series of pairings or couplings: history and philosophy, history and anthropology, etc. They were to reflect on new interests in history emerging in postmodern academic culture. But notice that history, although at the center of the inquiry, does not pose the questions. The conference is foregathered to scrutinize Clio's value as a partner, present or future: is she a satisfactory helpmeet? Can she, does she, could she enrich the performance of her partners from other disciplines in the academic quadrille?

How should Clio deport herself in this dating game?

For good and for ill, the only thing she is really good at is dates. In both senses of the word: "date" as a measure and locus in time, and "date" as an exploratory erotic encounter that can lead to a gratifying relationship of indeterminate duration. Clio's fixation on dates in the first sense is deep and serious. The calendar is for her a kind of sacred book, but it has ill equipped her to establish an autonomous existence or a fullbodied faith. Every other discipline defines itself either by its subject matter, the terrain or objects of its study (like anthropology, literary criticism, biology), or by pursuing principles through rigorous internal mental procedures to create a world of meaning (philosophy, mathematics). Not so history. It has neither turf nor principles of its own. Historians may choose their subject matter from any domain of human experience. At times, we have had universal historians, who have aspired to make the whole world their oyster. In more modest moments, historians have made the oyster their world—as when they study a small episode: a diplomatic incident or, nowadays, a peasant festival or a single text. But always historians have been concerned with describing their objects of study under the aspect of change, under the ordinance of time. They may delineate a subject with the purest linear simplicity or with the densest textural complexity, but always they stick to the elemental conviction that the beginning of wisdom is to know whether something happened before or after something else. Thus a historian will not let a poem or a text stand alone as a literary analyst does, letting it illuminate its self-enclosed particularity, but seeks meaning by relativizing the poem to other objects in a time series. He or she will not listen to the angry cry of the poet Archibald MacLeish, "A poem should not mean, but be"[2]— a cry later echoed by the New Critics in literature and their intratextualist successors in every field of the arts, after years of bondage to the flattening effect of historicization on the arts. There is something partial and unreliable about the historian's fidelity to the object compared to that of the specialist in a discipline defined by subject matter. The historian pursues the analysis of the object's particularity (whether it be a poem, an institution, or a unit of culture) only to the extent that he or she can appropriate it as an element in weaving a plausible pattern of change.

If we turn from subject matter, the domains and objects of the historian, to the principles or concepts historians use in organizing them, we find again a certain limit to their commitment. A political scientist or philosopher strives to formulate concepts and to develop a series of mental operations to prove their validity. The historian is singularly unfertile in devising concepts. It is not too much to say that historians are conceptual dependents. Here is where the dating game begins.

Historians do not demonstrate the truth of the concepts they borrow, but only use them as a means, in order to give plausibility or cogency to the unfolding *Gestalten* in which they reconstitute a past. Thus, historians might use the Freudian concept of narcissism to explain the behavior of a historical actor, but they feel no obligation to prove that concept, let alone to subscribe fully to the psychoanalytic system that generated it. They adopt principles and concepts not to prove or even illustrate their truth, but to lend authority, explanatory force, and meaning to the convergences they are plaiting into a temporal process or configuration.

Confined to no single domain of human experience, historians move into any terrain in search of the materials that they will organize into a temporal pattern with the help of the concepts borrowed from those fields of learning that generate them. They reconstitute the past by relativizing the particulars to the concepts and the concepts to the particulars, doing full justice to neither, yet binding and bonding them into an integrated life as an account under the ordinance of time.[3] In the tapestry the historian weaves, diachronic dynamics are the warp, synchronic relations are the woof. Clio, in short, is on the distaff side. She spins her yarn partly from materials she has chosen and carded but not grown, partly from concepts she has adopted but has not created. Her special skill is to weave them together into a meaningful account on the loom of time—a loom that is truly her own. This skill makes Clio prized by others, sometimes to be wooed, sometimes to be enslaved. She herself necessarily wills her involvement in relationships with other branches of culture, for without them she would lose her power to realize her own identity. The problem, now more than ever, is to choose those relationships freely and to make them meaningful, fruitful.

⟨ornament⟩

GIVEN the core of history as a mode of knowing and being as I have described it, what has been the orientation of history toward the study of culture? I cannot avoid treating the problem historically; that is the only way for me, a self-reflexive modern like the rest of you, to get a fix on it. Thus I shall try, *en bon historien*, to address the kinds of intellectual relations that characterize history in the field of cultural study today by the special form of distancing that the past provides.

Let me not frighten you if I begin with Herodotus. He is not far from the problem of history and cultural study today. Arnaldo Momigliano correctly observed the "strange truth that Herodotus has really become the father of history only in modern times."[4] The reason for this is that Herodotus allowed culture (in the wide, anthropological sense) to play a critical role in his *Histories*. While the narrative core of his work was the Persian Wars, he treated the conflict between Greeks and barbarians as a clash of cultural systems. Herodotus's integrated historiography was unseated by the sharper but narrower political historiography of Thucydides. Thucydides too had what we would think of as interdisciplinary external relations—ties to sophistic philosophy, Hippocratic medicine, and Sophoclean dramaturgy. But with all his breadth, he shrank Herodo-

tean cultural analysis down to the dynamics of power within the framework of the Hellenic polis system. With Thucydides, politics became the
central concern of the historian, and its field was ethnocentrically defined. Herodotus's very breadth was held against him thereafter. The Al-
exandrians, to be sure, prized him as fabulist and artist—no mean status
in a culture that valued history as a branch of literature. They honored
him by attaching the name of a muse to each of the nine books of his
Histories. But Greco-Roman and Christian "universalism" produced a
kind of high-culture ethnocentricity that doomed Herodotus's multi-
faceted cultural approach to history to incomprehension for more than
two thousand years.

The reception of Herodotus's *Histories* gives access to the changes in
Clio's intellectual alliances and epistemological fashions perhaps better
than any text in our craft. I shall not pursue it here. But let me give you,
by means of an image of the historian's work (Figure 13.1), two bench-
marks in the story—one from 1716, the other from 1980. The engraving
shows how Herodotus—and with him, cultural history—was seen in the
beginning of the eighteenth century, when he began to be restored to
favor. An allegorical frontispiece to a Dutch edition of the *Histories*, it
pictures Herodotus being crowned by the muses. As befits their Dutch
patrons, these muses use a map, indicated on a great parchment unfurled
to memorialize Herodotus's work. On it are pictured the great movements of the barbarian hosts and the Greek defenders, the political and
military struggles that, in the eighteenth-century view, constituted Herodotus's central focus and claim to Clio's crown of laurel. Across the
shadowy portion of the picture on the left are scattered the symbols of
the non-Greek cultures described by Herodotus the ethnographer: the
Egyptian pyramids and the image of a scribe; the tripod—is it the golden
one that Croesus King of Lydia gave to Delphi?; a horse's head bridled in
the Scythian manner; a Persian sun symbol and winged lion; in the far
rear the city of Babylon with its tower. These cultural remains are presented in disorganized array, reminders of the ethnographer and myth-
ographer Herodotus, whose accounts could amuse the eighteenth-century public, but not instruct it as the political ones did. By 1716, the
connection of culture with the narrative of great events had long been
lost to the reader. It was lost even to Clio herself, as represented in the
engraving. She directs our gaze away from the symbols of culture as she
points insistently to the great parchment that validates the coronation of
Herodotus as a historian of great actions.

Figure 13.1. Herodotus Crowned by the Muses.

If some of our cultural historians were to prepare a similar tribute to Herodotus today, the subject matter on either side of the panel would be switched. Clio would point her approving finger at the parchment, but the map would be erased, and the white sheet would be labeled *écriture*. On it would be displayed the symbols of the non-Hellenic cultures taken from the lower half. (There might be some dispute among the muses as to whether the symbols should be organized systematically, in the manner of anthropologists, or disposed as random bricolage to be caught for a moment in a kaleidoscopic frame, in the manner of Theodore Zeldin or Eugen Weber.) Herodotus would win his laurels as historian for his services in constructing a synchronic representation of past culture, complete with burial rites, kinship systems, child-rearing customs. Meanwhile, consigned to the shadows in the left and lower half of the picture in our 1980s version would be the images of the great Persian and Greek hosts, reminders of Herodotus's interest in politics, warfare, and cataclysm that have largely lost their commanding position as subjects for historians.

The fact is that I found the engraving of 1716 in a recent work of anthropological and textual history, published in 1980.[5] Its author, François Hartog, has reproduced it as an emblem of the historiographical tradition he intends to overcome. Hartog has chosen a title for his excellent book that marks it clearly as on the cutting edge of cultural study in 1980: *Le Miroir d'Hérodote. Essai sur la représentation de l'autre* (The Mirror of Herodotus. An Essay on the Representation of the Other). The book focuses on one of the barbarian cultures that Herodotus found especially engrossing, the Scythian. Hartog, brushing aside the question of what Scythian culture could have been, shows how Herodotus constructed a picture of the Scyths that would serve as a kind of magic mirror for defining Hellenic identity, one that would reinforce the Greek cultural values that Herodotus shared. The "other" itself, Scythian culture, is swallowed in the Greek view of it; and the Greek view in turn is swallowed in Herodotus's mental and literary construct, the text. Hartog's study shows the characteristic fruits of Clio's new partnerships with literary criticism, linguistics, and anthropology: subtle and convincing textual analysis and the exploration of the mental organization of social perception. But some of the burning questions that Herodotus posed get lost: How did the Greeks and the barbarians come to fight? (In Herodotus's words, "What were the grounds of their feud?") What is the effect of war on the cultures of the belligerents? These problems of interlinked temporal transformation of power structure and cultural values recede in favor of more static dimensions of culture: the image of the other, its role in identity definition, and the construction of the text.

WHAT lies between the two uses of the frontispieces to Herodotus? I do not wish to argue that Clio's transfer of affections from politics to culture is complete. Yet there has surely been a great displacement—almost an inversion—of concerns. Once again I must turn to history itself to get a fix on the present ways in which history approaches culture. The central focus here is on the rise and fall of Clio as queen of the disciplines.

The eighteenth century is decisive for the reinvention of cultural history in Europe. Since the Middle Ages, Clio had been the servant of Church and State. Appropriately to the modest function of her discipline in the power structure of academic culture, historians were placed in the faculties of either theology or law.[6] They provided moral example and practical lessons in the support of more august disciplines. In German universities there were no separate chairs in history until the end of the eighteenth century. Clio remained a handmaiden, and her intellectual purposes and even her tools for meaning-making reflected her actual subordination.

In the eighteenth century, theology ceased to be the queen discipline in the European world of learning, and philosophy began to replace it in a secularizing culture. When philosophy began to define in a very general way the goals of society as part of the realization of Reason, history found a new mate—and a new calling. That politics was involved in the bonding of history and philosophy few would deny. The seductive idea of terrestrial progress, replacing the supratemporal teleology of religion, was the brainchild of philosophy and history. Voltaire, and even the skeptical Gibbon, saw themselves as philosophic historians, judging and ordering history not only according to the criteria of Reason but in the light of the progress of Reason. The history of Mind and the history of Society were seen as inextricably linked, and the destiny of humankind as at stake in that union. The Encyclopedists sketched the outlines of an intellectual history centering on the history of science. History as the study of culture—strongly oriented toward a philosophic politics of freedom under law—was born. Kant predicted correctly that historians in the next century—the nineteenth—would devote themselves to constitutional history and international history, the spheres in which humanity would develop its freedom by placing the realm of action under the expanding power of rational law.

I do not wish to maintain that there was general acceptance of the extravagant claims of French *philosophes* and German idealists that history would actualize the potential of Reason for ordering the world of man and nature. But I would argue that, in and out of the academy, even those who resisted such claims found themselves accepting history as the ground on which the problems of man's destiny would have to be debated. History as a mode of thought soon penetrated virtually every branch of European high culture, even as the extravagant hopes and fears attached to it in the French Revolution receded, while the mythic ana-

logues from which it had never been far removed spread through politics
into the populace. As for the academy, chairs of history were established
all over Europe and fields of humanistic learning new and old organized
their teaching on historical premises. Clio, whose whole career had been
lived in dependence on other branches of learning, seemed to win not
just her autonomy, but sovereignty over all. She became queen of the
human sciences. As philosophy had once overmastered theology as the
guide of life and learning, so history now replaced philosophy.

During Clio's short reign as queen of disciplines in the nineteenth
century, political history maintained a clear priority within the field of
history itself, as Kant had prophesied. With it was associated a continuing commitment to a teleological orientation. Though political history
broadened its substance from the rulers to the ruled, from states to nations and peoples, the nonpolitical forms of historiography had difficulty
in asserting themselves, as did other kinds of social analysis, such as sociology, that arose to challenge history's narrative mode of understanding.
It was in this context that cultural history, the other half of Herodotus's
concern, began to emerge from the shadows. The principal pioneers in
this field—Jacob Burckhardt and Fustel de Coulanges, and in some ways
Alexis de Tocqueville—were conservatives who rejected the nineteenth
century's liberal sociopolitical system, its belief in progress, and the political historiography that expressed its aims. Against the prevailing teleological orientation of history, with its diachronic emphasis, they developed a counterproject: history organized in synchronic tableaux, in which
the most diverse, often clashing components of cultural life—institutions, intellectual and artistic production, mores, social relations—could
be displayed in cross section, a horizontal panorama. Burckhardt especially displayed for the first time the colligative power of history, its potential for confronting in coherence the most nonhomogeneous materials
of culture. Time certainly did not stop in the construction of these mas-
ters, but it was, one might say, slowed down. Not the process of transformation, but cultural coherence became the focus of attention. It is worth
observing, for the understanding of the contemporary situation in American historiography, that these authors aroused intellectual excitement
and achieved canonical status among the educated in our country only
after World War II, when the identification of history with progress began to dissolve.

In America, the favored form for history's engagement with culture
was intellectual history. The subject matter here was not culture in the

broad, anthropological sense, but in the narrower sense of history of ideas as generated within the educated class. The term itself, "intellectual history," carries the mark, "made in the U.S.A." It appeared first in close connection with social history. Some of you will remember college history courses entitled "Social and Intellectual History of. . . ." Today this bracketing would be almost unthinkable. These courses carried into education the ideas of the New History of the turn of our century, when a generation of reforming intellectuals that included John Dewey, Charles Beard, and James Harvey Robinson sought to reanimate the Enlightenment tradition and update it for a modern industrial world. Though they did not reject political history, the New Historians fought against its narrow institutional focus by expanding history to include popular social movements and social conditions on the one hand and the ideas that furthered or resisted the reformer-intellectual's democratic project of political empowerment and social justice on the other.

In the manner of the Enlightenment, whose traditions these Americans reanimated, the progress of ideas and the progress of society seemed to advance together and transform each other. The "culture" that such a historical outlook found worthy of note tended to be either religious or political. Its history of ideas was construed in a narrow but dynamic diachronic mode—the opposite of the cultural history of European conservatism à la Burckhardt, with its somewhat static, synchronic comprehensiveness and its abjuration of narrative.

The New History, social *and* intellectual, certainly felt itself, not unlike its European cousin, Marxist history, to be if not queen of the disciplines, then certainly autonomous. It cultivated the social sciences within itself. It patronized and utilized humanistic culture, especially political thought and philosophy, but only to the degree that this culture could be related to its sociopolitical project. The arts were seen not as constituents of history, but as illustrations of social and political processes.

***

HISTORY-as-actuality undermined the American New History's vaulting conception of Clio's nature and function. More: it altered Clio's standing in the belief system of modern society. Two World Wars dealt a series of blows to the confidence that Western liberal culture, especially American culture, had placed in history as the scene of progress, of collective, rational self-realization. With the loss of faith in progress, history was also weakened as a mode of understanding the various domains of human culture, from the arts to the economy. The ties to the past were loosened. Although the complex process of breaking from tradition in the arts and other branches of elite culture reaches back into the nineteenth century, it was accelerated by the crisis of progress.

Somewhere about the 1950s, the break with history acquired the force of a generalized paradigm shift in academic culture. One discipline after the other in the human sciences cut its ties to history, strengthened its autonomy with theory and self-oriented critical analysis, and produced its meanings without that pervasive historical perspective that in the nineteenth century had permeated the self-understanding of almost every branch of learning. While the social sciences turned to behaviorism and natural-scientific models, humanistic disciplines developed self-referential formalistic criticism. Rosalind Krauss, drawing on Clement Greenberg, has well expressed the internalistic orientation of the modernist paradigm shift: "[A] modernist culture's ambition [is] that each of its disciplines be rationalized by being grounded in its unique and separate domain of experience, this to be achieved by using the characteristic methods of that discipline both to narrow and 'to entrench it more firmly in its area of competence.'"[7]

The consequence of this ambition was that the human sciences as a whole became not just specialized but, as a group, polarized. While the social sciences gravitated toward scientific abstraction (mathematical economics, quantification and behaviorism in sociology and politics, and so on), the humanities decontextualized their inquiry and treated their objects wholly internalistically. The social sciences tried to be hard, less humanistic; the humanities abstract and less social.

Where did the paradigm shift, the dehistoricization of academic culture, leave Clio? And what have been its consequences for history in the study of culture?

I can approach an answer to both questions most easily by reminding you once more of that early twentieth-century course entitled "Social and Intellectual History of. . . ." What the old New History had thus joined together around 1900, a variety of New Histories put asunder in the 1960s and 1970s. For within history as a discipline the polarization of the human sciences repeated itself. "Social and intellectual history" came to mean not complementarity but antithesis. Clio, overthrown as queen, was not only no longer courted, but found herself in a bed of Procrustes in her own house, pulled apart between historians who looked for inspiration to the dehistoricized social sciences and historians who looked to the dehistoricized humanities.

Clio now plunged into a real identity crisis that lasted about twenty years. I think she is now emerging from it with a more modest and clearer idea of her powers, and perhaps with a firmer sense of her need for freedom of choice in her relationships.

One can follow well the identity crisis of history in the pages of *History and Theory*, founded in 1961 with the aim of consciousness raising, of bringing history into the age of self-reflection and methodological sophistication. But much of the periodical's effort—and this seems to me the particular characteristic of history's essential nature that surfaced only in the general context of dehistoricization—was devoted to discussion of other disciplines for the light and help and criticism they might offer our very untheoretical field. In the first four years, roughly one-third of the articles were devoted to developing a scientific method for historians. In 1966, quantification emerged as a strong subtheme, with thirteen articles appearing in that area between 1964 and 1983—and a special Beiheft in 1969. The approach to history from anthropology, of all social sciences the one most directly concerned with the mental world of culture, but traditionally the least concerned with temporal transformation, was the subject of eleven articles in roughly the same time period. At the end of the disciplinary spectrum was the domain of high culture from which intellectual history had drawn its subject matter. There the new methods of literary criticism—textual, structural, and linguistic—began to be explored for their applicability to history. Hayden White performed perhaps the boldest act of historical self-criticism when he lifted historiography entirely out of time and specific historical context by analyzing it as a literary genre. Since it appeared in 1975, White's *Metahistory* generated no fewer than fourteen articles in *History and Theory* and a separate Beiheft as well.[8] More importantly, it opened the door to other attempts to redefine intellectual history as a metahistorical field with the armamentarium of intratextual analysis. Until now, that school has devoted its attention mostly to critical reflection on history, and has seldom tried to write history.

Between these two poles, one can also find in *History and Theory* the attempts of Anglo-Saxon analytic school philosophy to clarify historical explanation as well as discussions of hermeneutics. Since 1983, the new topic of representations has inspired eight articles. Meanwhile, psychoanalytical and Marxian approaches to history continue to be explored, and narrative is recuperated as a bottom-line form of historical thought.

The striking feature of the articles in *History and Theory* is the continuously even distribution of the various positions represented in it. It is not what I expected from my personal experience; namely, a strong weighting in the direction of social history and its affiliated social sciences during the sixties, followed by a strong predominance of *discours sur le discours* inspired by literary criticism in the eighties. Not so. The various positions appear quite evenly distributed over the two decades.

In terms of short-term interests, one could—and still can—perceive historians proclaiming the beginnings of a New History based on some new interdisciplinary partnership that gathers followers who productively work the new vein. But each group's militant expectation of prevailing in victory over other modes quickly evaporates.

History and Theory's record speaks the higher truth: that history cannot find a clear identity based on privileging a given discipline outside history as partner. I submit that history has taken into its own body the autonomization of academic disciplines. History is accordingly proliferating a variety of subcultures. Its universalist tradition largely exhausted, it can create no macrocosmic frame or grand periodization. Instead it addresses a vastly expanded subject matter in microcosmic ways. Correspondingly, the need for different extra-historical disciplines, new alliances, is exponentially expanded. Cultural history, both popular and elite, is being transformed by the new modes of analysis that the other disciplines have generated in their posthistorical period. Politics both inside and outside the academy also gives rise to new subdisciplines within history. In a new era of identity politics, groups struggling for social power outside the academy—lower classes, minorities, and women—produce both old-fashioned epic history and a new kind of cultural social history within it.

The history of science can serve us here as model for a principal way in which contemporary intellectual history is addressing its task. The history of science lent itself most readily to a purely internalistic treatment on a progressive premise shared by both the natural scientists and the public. Historians who sought to embed scientific insight in a social matrix were resisted, in part justly, for their inadequate scientific understanding, but also because they tampered with the mythology of the autonomy of science and discovery prevailing in the scientific guild. The main prerequisite to advance in the history of science was mastery of science itself. It required that the historian be formally educated in the subject by professionals in it. To that training the historian of science would add, from history, philosophy, and sociology, such knowledge of context and social-analytic techniques as to construct a convincing relationship between scientific thought and other aspects of the relevant cultural and social space in the past. The history of science still suffers from the division between internalists and contextualists. But the presence of both as participants in the same enterprise raises the standards of performance.

Only recently have historians working in literature and the arts and even psychology imposed similar demands upon themselves. Previously, secure in the centrality of their social or political account, historians simply skimmed the ideological cream from the artistic thought they appropriated. The advent of formal analysis in the arts posed demands for rigor that has undermined such an impressionistic approach. Graduate education reflects the change. I learned about the methods of other disciplines from my colleagues, late and not too rigorously. Students of history today enter seminars in art or literature—or even psychoanalytic training—to acquire the analytic techniques of the subject they wish to explore historically. And in our history seminars appear students from the other disciplines, likewise seeking a more professional way of casting history's light upon their subject. A generation thus educated, as we all know, is just beginning to produce works combining rigorous analysis and well-plaited historical texture.

LOOKING at history today, one may well speak of glasnost. The hierarchical order of disciplines has been thoroughly shaken in our century. For the first time in her long life, Clio is playing the dating game on her own terms. She has lost the illusion of being queen, monarch of all she surveys in the scholarly scene. She is no longer bonded in service to theology or law, nor is she wedded to philosophy in order to realize with her partner liberal bourgeois projects in the world of politics. Now she chooses her own partners freely.

At one level, the new glasnost is exhilarating. We are erupting with new creations at the frontiers of system and convention, just as music is. But let us not be overcome with the euphoria of our pluralistic freedom. There are potential losses too. In relating to other systems of thought, history can forget one of her few fundamental commitments: to chart not only continuity, but change. Anthropology, the discipline that has enriched cultural history more than any other in recent years, has been synchronically oriented, though it too is now developing a more diachronic orientation. It would be a loss if the cross-sectional recuperation of past culture were pursued at the price of the charting of change and the struggles that produce it. Foucault's example, and the linguistic turn that has accompanied it, similarly lead toward a cross-sectional rather than a processual ordering of historical life. Here the model of Herodotus, with his interactive dynamic between culture and politics, and between the diochronic and synchronic dimensions of history, can still serve us well.

NOTES

1. This paper was written for the Scripps conference, where I was one of the few representatives of history as a discipline.
2. Archibald MacLeish, *Poems, 1924–1933* (Boston and New York, 1933), 122–23.
3. For a fuller statement of this position, see Leonard Krieger, "The Horizons of History," *American Historical Review* 63 (1957–1958), 62–74.
4. Arnaldo Momigliano, "The Place of Herodotus in the History of Historiography," *Studies in Historiography* (London, 1966), 141.
5. François Hartog, *Le Miroir d'Hérodote. Essai sur la représentation de l'autre* (Paris, 1980).
6. See the excellent analysis of historiography in terms of the teaching function of historians in Josef Engel, "Die deutschen Universitäten und die Geschichtswissenschaft," in Theodor Schieder, ed., *Hundert Jahre Historische Zeitschrift, 1859–1959* (Munich, 1959), 223–78.
7. See Rosalind E. Krauss, "The Story of the Eye," in Ralph Cohen and Michael S. Roth, eds., *History and . . . Histories within the Human Sciences* (Charlottesville and London, 1995), 74.
8. See Hayden V. White, *Metahistory: The Historical Imagination in Nineteenth-Century Europe* (Baltimore, 1973).

ABOUT THE AUTHOR

Carle E. Schorske is Professor of History Emeritus at Princeton
University. He is the author of *Fin-de-Siècle Vienna: Politics and Culture*
(Knopf) and *German Social Democracy, 1905–1917: The Development of
the Great Schism* (Harvard). He coedited, both with Thomas Bender,
Budapest and New York: Studies in Metropolitan Transformation, 1870–1930
(Russell Sage Foundation) and *American Academic Culture in
Transformation* (Princeton).